THE BEST OF
TOP
SECRET
RECIPES®

FROM THE FILES OF

TODD WILBUR

Illustrated by the Author

A PLUME BOOK

PLUME
Published by the Penguin Group
Penguin Group (USA) Inc., 375 Hudson Street, New York, New York 10014, U.S.A.
Penguin Books Ltd, 80 Strand, London WC2R 0RL, England
Penguin Books Australia Ltd, 250 Camberwell Road, Camberwell, Victoria 3124, Australia
Penguin Books Canada Ltd, 10 Alcorn Avenue, Toronto, Ontario, Canada M4V 3B2
Penguin Books India (P) Ltd, 11 Community Centre, Panchsheel Park, New Delhi –
110 017, India
Penguin Books (N.Z.) Ltd, Cnr Rosedale and Airborne Roads, Albany, Auckland 1310,
New Zealand
Penguin Books (South Africa) (Pty) Ltd, 24 Sturdee Avenue, Rosebank, Johannesburg
2196, South Africa

Penguin Books Ltd, Registered Offices: 80 Strand, London WC2R 0RL, England

First published by Plume, a member of Penguin Group (USA) Inc.

First Printing, July 2003
10 9 8 7 6

Most of the recipes in this edition are selected from *Top Secret Recipes, More Top Secret Recipes, Even More Top Secret Recipes, Top Secret Restaurant Recipes, Low-Fat Top Secret Recipes, Top Secret Recipes Lite!,* and *Top Secret Recipes: Sodas, Smoothies, Spirits, & Shakes,* all published by Plume.

 REGISTERED TRADEMARK—MARCA REGISTRADA

CIP
ISBN: 0-452-28510-0

Printed in the United States of America

Contents

A Little Foreword

In the laboratory (my kitchen), each of these recipes was subjected to a battering array of bakings and mixings, batch after batch, until the closest representation of the actual commercial product was finally achieved. I did not swipe, heist, bribe, or otherwise obtain any formulas through coercion or illegal means. I'd like to think that many of these recipes are the actual formulas for their counterparts, but there's no way of knowing for sure. In such cases of closely guarded secret recipes, the closer one gets to matching a real product's contents, the less likely it is that the protective manufacturer will say so.

The objective here was to match the taste and texture of the products with everyday ingredients. In most cases, obtaining the exact ingredients for these mass-produced food products is nearly impossible. For the sake of security and convenience, many of the companies have contracted confidentially with vendors for the specialized production and packaging of each of their product's ingredients. These prepackaged mixes and ingredients are then sent directly to the company for final preparation.

Debbi Fields of Mrs. Fields Cookies, for example, arranged with several individual companies to custom manufacture many of her cookies' ingredients. Her vanilla alone is specially blended from a variety of beans grown in various places around the world. The other ingredients—the chocolate, the eggs, the sugars, the flour—all get specialized attention specifically for the Mrs. Fields company. The same holds true for McDonald's, Wendy's, KFC, and most of the big-volume companies.

Even if you could bypass all the security measures and somehow get your hands on the secret formulas, you'd have a hard time executing the recipes without locating many ingredients usually impossible to find at the corner market. Therefore, with taste in mind, substitution of ingredients other than those that may be used in the actual products is necessary in many cases to achieve a closely cloned end result.

SOME COOKING TIPS FROM A GUY WHO CARES

Sometimes I can be a real idiot in the kitchen. I've wasted as many as four eggs when separating the whites by accidentally dropping in specks of yolk. I've often burned chocolate when melting it for dipping candy, and I've squandered hours on making dough for a simple recipe just because I forgot to look at the date on the package of yeast.

It was on these days that I determined there is a hard way to pick up little cooking hints, and there's an easy way. The hard way is by doing what I did—screwing up, then having to throw away your mistakes and run to the store in the pouring rain with a fistful of change to buy more ingredients so you can start the whole thing over again.

Then there is the easy way, which is to get cooking tips from somebody who learned the hard way.

Some Words about Chocolate

First off, some words about that delicate substance we call chocolate. Everybody's eaten it, but if you've cooked with it, you know it can be a pain—especially when the recipe requires that you melt it, as some of the recipes in this book do.

There are several different types of chocolate: sweet, semisweet, bittersweet, unsweetened, milk chocolate, and white chocolate (which actually isn't chocolate at all).

You will be using only semisweet and milk chocolate. Both are called for in the form of chocolate chips, which you buy by the bag. The most common are Nestlé and Hershey. Each company makes both milk chocolate and semisweet, and each works equally well.

I have found that the best place to melt chocolate is in the microwave. Semisweet chocolate is much easier to work with than milk chocolate because it contains more chocolate liquor and no milk solids. Semisweet will melt to a much smoother, thinner consistency, and will not scorch as easily. This means that semisweet lends itself much more readily to dipping.

When melting either type of chocolate, use a microwave-safe glass or ceramic bowl that will retain heat. Set your microwave on half power and melt the chips for 1 minute. Stir. Rotate the bowl, and microwave for another minute. Stir again. After 2 minutes, if the chocolate needs to melt more, heat it in 30-second intervals.

With milk chocolate, you have to find a delicate balance between microwaving and stirring. If you heat the chips too much, the chocolate will scorch. If you stir too much, the chocolate won't set up properly when you dip. Perfectly melted milk chocolate should set nearly as firm as it was in its original form at room temperature (68 to 70°F).

If you can't use a microwave to melt your chocolate, use a double boiler. You want to set the heat very low so that the water in the double boiler is only simmering and not boiling. Boiling water will scorch chocolate. Grease the inside of your double boiler lightly before you put the chocolate in, and you'll be able to get practically all of the melted chocolate out of the pan.

For some of the recipes in this book, you may feel like substituting dark, semisweet chocolate instead of milk chocolate or even using white chocolate. It may be worth a try. How about a white chocolate–covered Milky Way? Hmm.

And here's another tip to remember when making anything with chocolate. You can intensify the chocolate flavor by adding some vanilla to the recipe. You'll notice that this is what I've done with the recipes in the book for chocolate icings.

Some Words about Yeast Dough

There are some recipes in this book that call for yeast dough, and I thought it was important to supply you with some pointers that will help you here and in the rest of your dough-making life.

The only yeast you'll need to use with this book is Fleischmann's—the type that comes in the three-envelope packages. That's the only kind I ever use. Always check to be sure the yeast you're using has not expired. Every package of yeast is stamped with an expiration date—usually eight to twelve months from the date you purchased it. Store your unopened yeast packages in the refrigerator.

When kneading dough, use your hands. This is much better than a wooden or plastic spoon because the warmth of your hands will help the yeast start rising (and it brings you back to those carefree Play-Doh days). When the dough pulls away from your hands easily, it has been kneaded enough.

One good way to get the dough rising is to put it in its bowl, uncovered, in the oven (the oven should be off) with a pan of boiling water. The hot water will start the dough rising right away, and the moisture from the water will keep the dough's surface from getting hard and dry.

You can tell when the dough has risen enough by sticking your finger into it up to the first knuckle. If the dough does not bounce back, it's ready. If it giggles, you're in a Pillsbury commercial.

Some Words about Separating Eggs

For the recipes that require egg whites, I've found that one of the easiest ways to separate the white from the yolk is to crack the egg with one hand into the other hand cupped over a small bowl. The egg whites will run out between your fingers, and you will be holding just the yolk in your hand. You can also use a small funnel. Just crack the egg into the funnel, and the egg white will run through, leaving the yolk. Use a container other than the bowl you will be beating the whites in. You don't want to risk ruining all the whites if some yolk should fall through.

If an accident should happen and you do get some yolk into the whites, use one of the egg shells to scoop out the yolk. Strangely, the shells act like a magnet for the specks of stray yolk.

To save your yolks for another recipe, slide them into a small bowl or cup, pour some cold water over them, and store them in the refrigerator. When you want to use the yolks, just pour off the water and slide the yolks into your recipe.

By the way, as a general rule in this book and any other cookbook, when a recipe calls for eggs and does not specify size, always use large eggs. Medium or extra-large eggs could throw off your measurements.

Some Words about Baking

Every once in a while, you should check your oven thermostat with an oven thermometer. I did and found out that my oven was off by twenty-five degrees. That's normal. It can be off by twenty-five degrees in either direction, but if it's any more than that, you should make adjustments when cooking, and get it fixed.

When baking, allow at least fifteen minutes for your oven to preheat. This is especially important if you do not have an indicator light that tells you when your oven is ready.

Several recipes in this book call for baking on cookie sheets. I highly recommend using two cookie sheets and alternating them, putting one sheet in the oven at a time. This will allow you to let one sheet cool before loading it up for the next run. If you don't let the sheet cool, your cooking time may be inaccurate because the dough will start to heat before you put the sheet into the oven.

If you absolutely must bake more than one cookie sheet at a time, you'll have to extend the cooking time. It will take the oven longer to reach the proper temperature with more dough to heat.

If you're baking cookies, you can very easily make them all uniform in size by rolling the dough into a tube with the diameter you need, then slicing it with a very sharp knife.

Keep in mind, especially with cookies, that baked goods will continue to cook for a while even after they've come out of the oven unless you remove them to a rack. The cookie sheet or baking pan will still be hot, and the sugar in the recipe will retain heat. This is why many people tend to overcook their cookies. I know the feeling. When you follow suggested cooking times, it sometimes seems as though the cookies aren't done when they come out of the oven—and they probably aren't. But they'll be fine after sitting for some time on the cookie sheet.

Some Words about Hamburger Patties

Just about every backyard hamburger cookout I've attended included hamburger patties that tipped the scale in size and weight. Most homemade burgers are way too thick to cook properly, and the added thickness doesn't add anything to the taste of the sandwich. In fact, if we cut the amount of beef we use in the hamburger patties, we're cutting out excess fat and calories, decreasing the chance that the burgers may not cook thoroughly, while not compromising anything in overall taste. At the same time, thicker patties tend to shrink up as they cook into unmanageable mutant forms, bulging in the middle, and stacking poorly onto buns and lettuce.

You'll notice that every hamburger recipe in this book requires a very thin patty. This is the way the experts in the business do it—the Dave Thomases, the Carl Karchers, the McDonald brothers—for concerns over cost, taste, and a thorough, bacteria-free cooking process. But just how do we get our patties so thin like the big boys, and still make them easy to cook without breaking? We freeze 'em, folks.

Plan ahead. Hours, even days, before you expect to make your hamburgers, pat the patties out onto waxed paper on a cookie sheet with a diameter slightly larger than the buns you are using, and about ⅛ to ¼ inch thick (with consistent thickness from center to edge). Thickness depends on the burger. If you're making a small hamburger, like the one at McDonald's, which is only about ⅛ ounce before cooking, make the patties ⅛ inch thick.

If you're going for the Quarter Pounder, make your patty ¼ inch thick—never more than that. Lay waxed paper over the top of your patties and put them in the freezer.

When your patties are completely frozen, it's time to cook. You can cook them straight out of the freezer on a hot grill or frying pan for 3 to 7 minutes per side, without worrying about thorough cooking. And the patties will flip easily without falling apart.

Introduction to The
Best of Top Secret Recipes®

Just about every person with taste buds wonders on some occasion after savoring a delicious restaurant dish or an addictive mass-produced convenience food if it's possible to re-create the taste in a home kitchen. I call it "kitchen cloning," and with this book, not only will you see that it is possible, but you'll also find out, first-hand, what a kick it is to duplicate the most famous brand-name foods in your own home using common ingredients.

My mission over the last decade—as I have chosen to accept it—is to develop secret formulas and simple techniques to help you produce home versions of the food on which America most loves to nosh. Throughout the seven previous *Top Secret Recipes* books are hundreds of kitchen clones for famous brand-name foods, often with deep histories and cult followings. These are foods that have made millionaires of their creators, and that trigger a reaction in our salivary glands upon a mere mention. These are foods that have satiated generations before us, and will continue to satisfy long after we are gone.

The mission is not often a simple one, since reverse-engineering foods can be a tedious and time-consuming task. Trial and error is the play of the day, and many of the results take a fateful trip into the garbage disposal or into the super-fat Chow Chow dog, Zebu. But when the finished product hits the mark, all the work is rewarded, and the successful results are passed along to you.

Here, now for the first time, is a collection of my favorite recipes culled from all of my books produced over the last decade, arranged in one easy-to-use volume. These are my all-time favorites—my go-to recipes when I'm cooking from the *Top*

Secret Recipes books, and the recipes I recommend when a friend asks, "What should I make?"

As a cool bonus, I've included 45 brand-new recipes that I've never released in a book before this. These recipes are truly special since they come from hundreds of reader requests, and have been on the *Top Secret* back burner for a long time. I'm talking about recipes such as Skyline Chili, Starbucks Cranberry Bliss Bars, Burger King Onion Rings, Jimmy Dean Sausage, Carnegie Deli Classic New York City Cheesecake, and Popeyes Buttermilk Biscuits. And don't forget to check out the clone for Krispy Kreme Original Glazed Doughnuts! Oh, there go the salivary glands.

So have fun with this unique collection. And beware of other so-called copycat recipes floating around out there. My culinary assignment guarantees these *Top Secret Recipes* to be original creations that are thoroughly tested before I share them with you. That's the only way I can consider this a "mission accomplished."

—Todd Wilbur

Introduction

Within these pages you will find recipes that will help you create home clones of very well-known, well-respected products. But don't mistake these recipes for the actual product formulas. They probably aren't. But they'll just taste like the real thing to you—if all goes well.

It may at first seem silly to spend time making any of these foods that you can simply run out and buy, but there's actually some logic at work here. For instance, there isn't one city in this country where one can buy everything in this book—many of the items are regional. And there are both economic and nutritional concerns that make this book a useful stoveside companion. These recipes will give you a degree of control you didn't have before. You can now determine for yourselves what goes into these world-famous foods and what doesn't. You'll have control over when to make the food. You'll no longer be at the mercy of slow cooks, lines, or closed doors. And you'll have something to do on rainy days when video games start to cross your eyes and blister your firing thumb.

There is a sense of satisfaction that comes from creating something in your own kitchen that tastes just like a product that has tickled the taste buds of millions. Even more exciting are the expressions of amazement from others who taste your creations—"You made this?" Humbly nod and share the recipe.

True, nothing can absolutely replace the authentic creations that have proven themselves to consumers over time. But there are some very concrete and detailed reasons why your next culinary experiment should come from these pages.

Cost

With today's changing economic conditions, Americans are watching their money ever more closely. Now, instead of going out to the store or fast-food restaurant for snacks and meals, a growing number of "frugal gourmets" are staying in the household kitchen, where food can be prepared in a healthier and more cost-effective way.

Availability

In the fall of 1990, I moved from California to the East Coast, leaving behind some of the local goodies I had grown to crave from time to time. The original In-N-Out Double-Double hamburger and Carl's Jr. sandwiches were now all out of reach. But with this book, and some time in the kitchen, clones that quench those cravings are just minutes away.

If you live east of the Mississippi, you've no doubt enjoyed Tastykake products. The brand's popularity in the region attests to that. If you leave the area, though, you're out of luck. Tastykake has a very limited distribution, and the only way you can enjoy a fresh Tastykake treat anywhere else is to have someone send it to you. Unless you've got a recipe.

Or maybe it's raining outside, and you're dying for some Reese's Peanut Butter Cups or a Twinkie. You can get these snacks just about anywhere. But you've got a crackling fire warming the house, a great episode of *Lost in Space* on the tube, and all the ingredients handy in your kitchen. So you tie on the apron and whip up your own. It's easy, it's fresh, and you don't have to comb your hair or put on your shoes.

Ingredients

With this book, not only will you be able to avoid the additives and preservatives that make your food sound like a lab experiment, you will also have the freedom to substitute ingredients to your heart's desire. Now you can replace the ground beef in your favorite hamburgers with ground turkey. You may want to use a low-calorie sweetener in place of the sugar. Or get creative and make your own original peanut-butter-and-jelly-filled Twinkies. The substitutions and variations are only limited by your imagination . . . and your courage.

Curiosity and Creative Fulfillment

Most people never considered it possible to make a Twinkie in the kitchen or taste the twin of a Big Mac they slapped together at home in less than ten minutes. You hold the proof.

As you cook, you will find that most of these recipes taste exactly like, or extremely similar to, their manufactured counterparts. I say most of the recipes, because:

1. Taste is an opinion subject to individual preference, and the memory of a particular taste can vary from person to person. One person might say that a hamburger tastes just like a Big Mac, while another might think it ain't even close. Putting the *Top Secret Recipes* version right next to an original Big Mac, however, should help establish a consensus on the similarity.
2. Although the success of the fast-food concept lies in the security of consistency the customer receives from outlet to outlet, products created at different locations (especially franchises) are not always created equal. I've probably had four different versions of Wendy's chili—some with bigger chunks of meat, some with more onion, some spicier, some runnier.

Developing a reasonable facsimile of a particular food depends on finding a common thread between all versions and replicating it. The recipes in this book are based on random samplings. They do not account for employee miscalculations in cooking or a manufacturer's later change in makeup of the product, nor do they account for variations in cooking time based on gas and electric ranges, or adjustments that need to be made in varying altitudes.

Although ingredient substitutions and experimentation are encouraged, you will create a more accurate clone of the original by using the exact ingredients specified and following the steps carefully.

Some Quick Tips

To help ensure that all goes well, here are some quick words of advice on how to get the best results from your cloning experience:

- Read the entire recipe through before you start cooking. There's been many a time I didn't familiarize myself with a recipe first, only to discover halfway through that I wouldn't be able to finish since I didn't have the right equipment or ingredients. Read ahead and minimize the surprises.
- Read the "Tidbits" section at the end of any recipe that has one. That section may offer some helpful advice or recipe variations you might want to try.
- Know the yield before you start. I've designed several of the recipes, especially sandwiches, to yield only enough for one serving, but those recipes can be easily doubled, tripled, or quadrupled to serve more.
- Refer to the "blueprints." Each of the recipes has been written so that you shouldn't need to refer to a drawing for help. But, you'll find the drawings give you a good idea of what you're shooting for. As they say, a picture is worth a thousand words.

When it comes to kitchen cloning, perhaps it's worth even more than that.

- Identify parts of the recipes that can be used for other dishes. Many of the recipes include dips, dressings, and sauces that are great stand-alone recipes to use in another dish you may create.
- Measure your ingredients very carefully. These recipes copy products that are produced under highly controlled conditions. Although no two of you making these recipes at home will measure the ingredients exactly the same, you should still take the time to make accurate measurements with good measuring tools. Use liquid measuring cups (with the spouts) for the liquids, and dry measuring cups (no spouts) for the dry ingredients. Take time in measuring, never estimate, and resist the urge to make these recipes in a Winnebago kitchen while speeding down a dirt road in Tijuana.
- Don't worry if your clone doesn't look exactly like the real thing. Since many of these products are made by machines in custom molds and may include coloring or thickening additives that we won't use, your clone may look different from the real thing. That's okay. I usually try to include tricks to duplicate a product's appearance whenever possible (such as the foil mold for the Zingers clone, and various food colorings and consumer thickeners in other recipes). But my primary goal is to design a recipe that makes a finished product taste just like the real thing. Taste is job #1.
- Use brand-name ingredients. When I create these recipes I make sure to use popular brands such as Best Foods Mayonnaise (or Hellmann's in the East), and Schilling, McCormick, and Spice Island spices. Generic brands may not be of the same quality and the final taste could be affected. For staple ingredients such as sugar, flour, and milk, you can use any old brand.
- Don't be afraid to experiment. The beauty of making Pay-Day candy bars at home is that we can make them twice as big! The joy of cooking KFC BBQ Baked Beans at home is that we can add more garlic and some kickin' cayenne pepper to our ver-

sion! Tweak your recipes to suit your tastes. Use ground turkey in your hamburgers and top 'em with soy American cheese if you want. That's the best part of home-clone cuisine. If you like to customize your food to create something you can't get in the stores, no one will stop you.

- Have fun, man! Cloning your own brand-name food at home is some of the most fun you'll have in the kitchen. Kids love it, adults dig it. And it's even more of a kick when you genuinely fool somebody with a food that they thought could only be bought in a restaurant or store. That's what makes cleaning up that big mess you just made worth all the trouble!

I hope you enjoy cooking from this book as much as I've enjoyed writing it. If you want more recipes like these, check out the other books in the *Top Secret Recipes* series. You'll also find plenty of recipes and handy cooking tips on the *Top Secret Recipes* Web site at: *www.TopSecretRecipes.com.*

If you have any suggestions for other recipes to clone, I'd love to see your e-mail:

Todd@TopSecretRecipes.com

Enjoy the book, and happy cloning!

AUNTIE ANNE'S PRETZELS

☆   ✌   💣   ✎   ☯   ✂   ☞

The first Auntie Anne's pretzel store opened in 1988 in the heart of pretzel country—a Pennsylvania Amish farmers' market. More than 500 stores later, Auntie Anne's is one of the most requested secret clone recipes around, especially on the Internet. Many of the recipes passed around the Web require bread flour, and some use honey as a sweetener. But by analyzing the Auntie Anne's home pretzel-making kit in the secret underground laboratory, I've discovered a better solution for re-creating the delicious mall treats than any clone recipe out there. For the best-quality dough, you just need all-purpose flour. And powdered sugar works great to perfectly sweeten the dough. Now you just have to decide if you want to make the more traditional salted pretzels, or the sweet cinnamon sugar–coated kind. Decisions, decisions.

1 ¼ cups warm water
1 tablespoon plus ¼ teaspoon
    yeast
3¾ cups all-purpose flour
¾ cup plus 2 tablespoons
    powdered sugar
1 ½ teaspoons salt
2 teaspoons vegetable oil

BATH
4 cups warm water
½ cup baking soda

SALTED
kosher or pretzel salt

CINNAMON TOPPING
½ cup granulated sugar
2 teaspoons cinnamon

¼ cup butter, melted

1. Dissolve the yeast in the warm water in a small bowl or cup. Let it sit for a few minutes.
2. Combine flour, powdered sugar, and salt in a large mixing bowl. Add water with yeast and vegetable oil. Stir with a spoon and then use your hands to form the dough into a ball. Knead the dough for 5 minutes on a lightly floured surface. Dough will be nice and smooth when it's ready. Place the dough into a lightly oiled bowl, cover it, and store it in a warm place for about 45 minutes or until the dough doubles in size.
3. When dough has risen, preheat oven to 425 degrees.
4. Make a bath for the pretzels by combining the baking soda with the warm water, and stir until baking soda is mostly dissolved.
5. Remove the dough from the bowl and divide it into 8 even portions. Roll each portion on a flat non-floured surface until it is about 3 feet long. Pick up both ends of the dough and give it a little spin so the middle of the dough spins around once. Lay the dough down with the loop nearest to you. Fold the ends down toward you and pinch to attach them to the bottom of the loop. The twist should be in the middle.
6. Holding the pinched ends, dip each pretzel into the bath solution. Put each pretzel on a paper towel for a moment to blot the excess liquid. Arrange the pretzels on a baking sheet sprayed with nonstick spray. If you want salt, sprinkle pretzels with kosher salt or pretzel salt. Don't salt any pretzels you plan to coat with cinnamon sugar. You will likely have to use two baking sheets, and be sure to bake them separately. Bake the pretzels for 4 minutes, then spin the pan halfway around and bake for another 4 to 5 minutes or until the pretzels are golden brown.
7. Remove the pretzels from the oven, and let them cool for a couple of minutes. If you want to eat some now, brush 'em with melted butter first, if desired, before serving. If you want the cinnamon sugar coating, make it by combining the $\frac{1}{2}$ cup sugar and 2 teaspoons cinnamon in a small bowl. Brush the unsalted pretzels you plan to coat with a generous amount of melted butter.

Sprinkle a heavy coating of the cinnamon sugar onto the entire surface of the pretzels over a plate. Munch out.

- MAKES 8 PRETZELS.

• • • •

ABOUT 3 FEET LONG

UNBAKED DOUGH

TWISTING THE DOUGH

5½"

SOFT & CHEWY

5½"

ALL BAKED UP

PROJECT: *AUNTIE ANNE'S PRETZELS*

ORIGINATION DATE: *1988*

JOB NO. *AA137556334-P*

BOSTON MARKET
MEATLOAF

☆ ✌ 💣 ✏ ☯ ✂ ☞

In the early 90s Boston Chicken was on a roll. The home meal re-
placement chain's stock was soaring and the lines were filled with
hungry customers waiting to sink their teeth into a serving of the
chain's delicious rotisserie chicken. So successful was the chain
with chicken, that the company quickly decided it was time to introduce other entrée selections, the first of which was a delicious
barbecue sauce–covered ground sirloin meatloaf. But offering
other entrées presented the company with a dilemma: what to
do about the name. The bigwigs decided it was time to change
the name to Boston Market, to reflect a wider menu. That meant
replacing signs on hundreds of units and retooling the marketing
campaigns. That name change, plus rapid expansion of the chain
and growth of other similar home-style meal concepts sent the
company into a tailspin. By 1998, Boston Market's goose was
cooked: the company filed for bankruptcy. Soon McDonald's
stepped in to purchase the company, with the idea of closing
many of the stores for good, and slapping Golden Arches on the
rest. But that plan was scrapped when, after selling off many of the
under-performing Boston Markets, the chain began to fly once
again. Within a year of the acquisition Boston Market was profitable, and those meals with the home-cooked taste are still being
served at over 700 Boston Market restaurants across the country.

1 cup tomato sauce
1 1/2 tablespoons Kraft original
    barbecue sauce
1 tablespoon granulated sugar
1 1/2 pounds ground sirloin
    (10 percent fat)

6 tablespoons all-purpose flour
3/4 teaspoon salt
1/2 teaspoon onion powder
1/2 teaspoon ground black pepper
dash garlic powder

1. Preheat oven to 400 degrees.
2. Combine the tomato sauce, barbecue sauce, and sugar in a small saucepan over medium heat. Heat the mixture until it begins to bubble, stirring often, then remove it from the heat.
3. In a large bowl, add all but 2 tablespoons of the tomato sauce to the meat. Use a large wooden spoon or your hands to work the sauce into the meat until it is very well combined.
4. Combine the remaining ingredients with the ground sirloin— flour, salt, onion powder, ground pepper, and garlic powder. Use the wooden spoon or your hands to work the spices and flour into the meat.
5. Load the meat into a loaf pan (preferably a meatloaf pan with two sections that allows the fat to drain, but if you don't have one of those, a regular loaf pan will work). Wrap foil over the pan and place it into the oven for 30 minutes.
6. After 30 minutes, take the meatloaf from the oven, remove the foil and, if you aren't using a meatloaf pan, drain the fat.
7. Using a knife, slice the meatloaf all the way through into 8 slices while it is still in the pan. This will help to cook the center of the meatloaf. Pour the remaining 2 tablespoons of sauce over the top of the meatloaf, in a stream down the center. Don't spread the sauce.
8. Place the meatloaf back into the oven, uncovered, for 25 to 30 minutes or until it is done. Remove and allow it to cool for a few minutes before serving.

• SERVES 4.

•   •   •   •

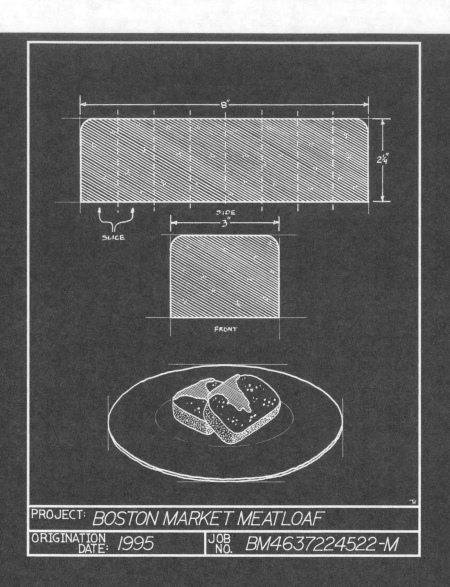

8"

2¼"

SLICE

SIDE
3"

FRONT

PROJECT: *BOSTON MARKET MEATLOAF*

ORIGINATION DATE: *1995*   JOB NO. *BM4637224522-M*

TOP SECRET RECIPES

VERSION OF

BURGER KING ONION RINGS

Since McDonald's doesn't sell onion rings, these crunchy, golden hoops from the world's number two restaurant chain are the most popular onion rings in the world. There's more than 11,400 Burger Kings in 58 countries these days and, after french fries, onion rings are the second-most popular companion to the chain's signature Whopper sandwich. Now check out how simple it is to clone a whopping 4 dozen onion rings from one onion using this triple-breading process. When frying, vegetable shortening makes the best clone here, but you can get by fine using vegetable oil if that's the way you want to go.

6 to 10 cups vegetable shortening
   (or vegetable oil)
1 medium white onion
2 cups milk

2 cups all-purpose flour
2 cups Progresso plain bread
   crumbs
salt

1. In a fryer, heat up 6 to 10 cups of vegetable shortening or oil (use the amount required by your fryer) to 350 degrees.
2. Cut the onion into ¼-inch-thick slices, then separate the slices into rings.
3. Pour the milk into a large shallow bowl, dump flour into another large shallow bowl and pour bread crumbs into a third

large shallow bowl. The large shallow bowls will make bread-ing easier. Easy is good.

4. While the shortening is heating up, bread all of the onion rings: First, dip an onion ring into the milk, then into the flour. Dip it back into the milk, then into the bread crumbs; and once more into the milk and into the bread crumbs. This will give each of the rings a nice, thick breading. Arrange the breaded rings on a plate until all of them are breaded.

5. When the oil is hot, fry the rings, a handful at a time, in the oil for 1½ to 3 minutes or until golden brown. Remove rings from the oil to a rack or paper towels to drain. Lightly salt the onion rings and serve 'em up hot.

• MAKES 5 DOZEN ONION RINGS.

• • • •

TOP SECRET RECIPES

VERSION OF

BURGER KING
ZESTY ONION RING SAUCE

If you're a big fan of onion rings from Burger King, you probably already know about the spicy dipping sauce offered from the world's number two burger chain. It's not necessarily on the menu, and you usually have to request it. The creamy, mayo-based sauce is obviously inspired by the dipping sauce served with Outback's signature Bloomin' Onion appetizer, since both sauces contain similar ingredients, among them horseradish and cayenne pepper. If you're giving the previous clone for Burger King Onion Rings a try, whip up some of this sauce and go for a dip. It's just as good with low-fat mayonnaise if you're into that. And the stuff works really well as a spread for burgers and sandwiches, or for dipping artichokes.

½ cup mayonnaise
1 ½ teaspoons ketchup
1 ½ teaspoons horseradish

½ teaspoon granulated sugar
½ teaspoon lemon juice
¼ teaspoon cayenne pepper

1. Combine all ingredients in a small bowl. Cover and chill for at least an hour before using.

• MAKES ½ CUP.

BURGER KING WHOPPER

In 1954, in Miami, Florida, James McLamore and David Edgerton built the first Burger King Restaurant. By 1991 more than 6,400 Burger King outlets could be found in forty countries and all fifty states. That gives this burger giant more than $6 billion in sales each year, making it the country's second-largest fast-food chain. (McDonald's is the largest.)

For many, the favorite item on the menu is a flame-broiled hamburger conceived by the partners on a business trip from Orlando to Miami in 1957. Dubbed the "Whopper," this sandwich is overwhelmingly popular; figures show that Burger King sells more than 540 million annually, or nearly 2 million each day. And with more than 1,023 different combinations of the eight-or-so ingredients, including a vegetarian version, you really can "have it your way."

1 sesame-seed hamburger bun	3 to 4 onion rings
1/4 pound ground beef	2 tomato slices
dash salt	1/4 cup chopped lettuce
3 dill pickle slices	1 tablespoon mayonnaise
1 teaspoon ketchup	

1. Preheat a barbecue grill on high.
2. Toast both halves of the bun, facedown, in a hot skillet. Set aside.

3. Form the beef into a thin patty slightly larger than the bun.
4. Lightly salt the hamburger patty and cook on the barbecue grill for 2 to 3 minutes per side.
5. Build the burger in the following stacking order from the bottom up:

bottom bun   tomatoes
hamburger patty   lettuce
pickles   mayonnaise
catsup   top bun
onion rings

• MAKES 1 HAMBURGER.

TIDBITS

It's important that your barbecue grill be clean so that the hamburger will not pick up the taste of any food that was previously cooked there. Some foods, such as fish, are especially potent.

Also, be sure your grill is good and hot before cooking.

• • • •

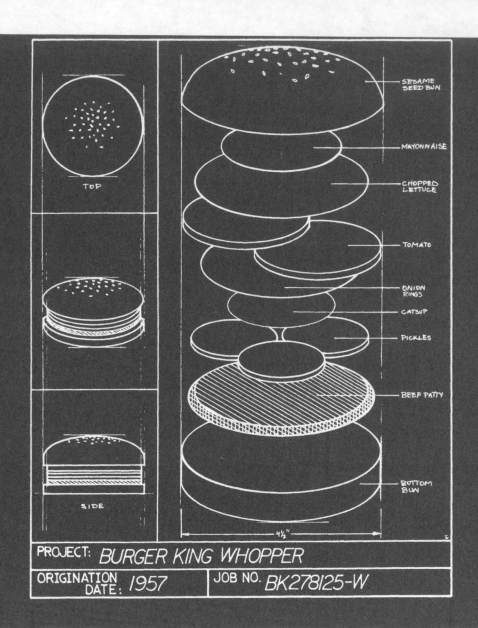

TOP

SIDE

SESAME
SEED BUN

MAYONNAISE

CHOPPED
LETTUCE

TOMATO

ONION
RINGS

CATSUP

PICKLES

BEEF PATTY

BOTTOM
BUN

4½"

PROJECT: BURGER KING WHOPPER

ORIGINATION DATE: 1957

JOB NO. BK278125-W

CARL'S JR.
SANTA FE
CHICKEN

☆　✌　💣　✏　🎱　✂　☞

This has to be one of my favorite fast-food sandwiches of all time. It's only been around since March of 1991, but has become a favorite for those familiar with Carl's Jr. outlets dotting the western United States. Today Carl's Jr. outlets can be found in California, Arizona, Utah, Nevada, Oregon, Mexico, Malaysia, China, Japan, and the Mideast. For all of you who live elsewhere, this is the only way you're going to get to try this fast-food treat. And it is worth trying.

2 whole chicken breasts, skinned,
    boned, and halved
1 cup teriyaki marinade
    (Lawry's is best)
¼ cup mayonnaise
¼ teaspoon paprika
⅛ teaspoon cayenne pepper

¼ teaspoon curry powder
pinch salt
4 whole-wheat hamburger buns
4 lettuce leaves
1 4-ounce can mild green chili
    peppers, well drained
4 slices American cheese

1. Marinate the chicken in the teriyaki marinade in a shallow bowl for 30 minutes.
2. Preheat a clean barbecue to medium grilling heat.
3. Prepare the sauce in a small bowl by mixing the mayonnaise with the paprika, cayenne pepper, curry powder, and salt.
4. Grill the chicken for 5 to 8 minutes per side, or until done.

5. Brown the faces of each bun in a hot frying pan.
6. Spread a tablespoon of sauce on the faces of each bun, top and bottom.
7. On each bottom bun place a lettuce leaf, then a green chili pepper. You want the pepper to be spread over most of the lettuce. To do this, slice the pepper down the middle and spread it open so that it covers more territory. When sliced open like this, some peppers are big enough for 2 sandwiches. Some are much smaller and enough for only one sandwich.
8. Place one chicken breast half on each of the sandwiches, on top of the chili pepper.
9. Place a slice of American cheese on the chicken.
10. Top it all off with the top bun.

• MAKES 4 SANDWICHES.

• • • •

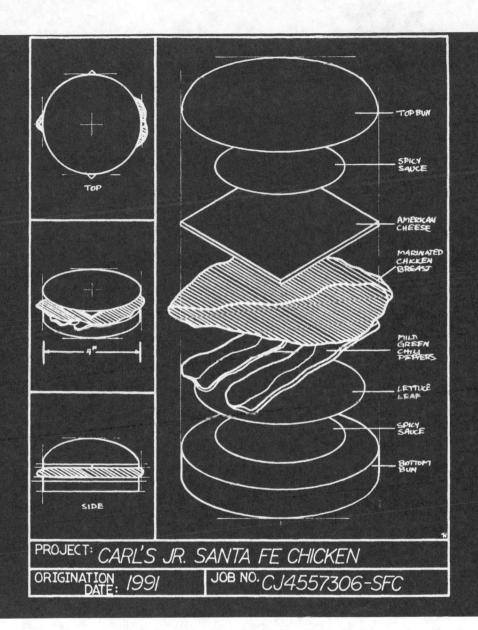

TOP

SIDE

TOP BUN

SPICY SAUCE

AMERICAN CHEESE

MARINATED CHICKEN BREAST

MILD GREEN CHILI PEPPERS

LETTUCE LEAF

SPICY SAUCE

BOTTOM BUN

PROJECT: CARL'S JR. SANTA FE CHICKEN

ORIGINATION DATE: 1991

JOB NO. CJ4557306-SFC

TOP SECRET RECIPES
VERSION OF
CARL'S JR.
THE SIX DOLLAR BURGER

☆　　✌　　💣　　✎　　☯　　✂　　☞

This West Coast chain came up with a great idea: clone the type of burger you'd get at Chili's or T.G.I. Friday's for around six bucks, but sell it for just $3.95. It's ⅓-pound of ground beef stacked on top of plenty of fixings, including red onion and those sweet-tasting bread-and-butter pickle slices. And check this out: cloning your own six-dollar burger at home will cost you less than two bucks. And the product certainly paid off for Carl's Jr., as it quickly became the chain's bestselling new item.

⅓ pound ground beef
salt
pepper
1 large sesame-seed bun
3 teaspoons mayonnaise
1 teaspoon mustard
2 teaspoons ketchup

3 to 4 bread-and-butter pickle
    slices
iceberg lettuce
2 large tomato slices
4 to 5 red onion rings
2 slices American cheese

1. Preheat barbecue or indoor grill to medium heat.
2. Form the ground beef into a patty with a slightly larger di-ameter than the sesame-seed bun.
3. Grill the burger on the grill for 3 to 4 minutes per side or until done. Be sure to generously salt and pepper each side of the patty.

4. While the patty grills, brown the faces of the bun in a hot skillet over medium heat.
5. After the buns have browned, spread about 1 1/2 teaspoons of mayonnaise on the face of the top bun, as well as on the bottom bun.
6. Spread 1 teaspoon of mustard on the face of the top bun, followed by 2 teaspoons of ketchup.
7. Arrange 3 or 4 bread-and-butter pickle slices on the bottom bun.
8. Arrange lettuce on pickles followed by the tomato slices and red onion.
9. When the beef is cooked, arrange two slices of American cheese on the patty, let it melt a bit, then place the top bun on the cheese and scoop up the whole thing with a spatula and place it on the bottom half of the burger. Include a big napkin when serving.

• MAKES 1 HAMBURGER.

• • • •

CARL'S JR. WESTERN BACON CHEESEBURGER

In 1989, Carl's Jr. became the first fast-food chain to allow customers to use their ATM cards to make purchases. Not only can customers buy a Western Bacon Cheeseburger and fries to go without using cash, they can get up to forty bucks out of their account.

The Western Bacon Cheeseburger is definitely up there on my list of favorite burgers. Onion rings, bacon, and cheese combine to make a tasty gut-grinder that can be thoroughly enjoyed when you're taking time off from the saturated-fat watch. The sandwich was introduced in 1983, and has since become so successful that it has spawned variations, from a junior version to the monstrous double, both of which are included here.

2 frozen onion rings
½ pound ground beef
1 sesame-seed hamburger bun
2 slices bacon
salt to taste
1 slice American cheese

2 tablespoons Bull's-Eye Hickory Smoke barbecue sauce (you must use this brand and variety to make it taste just like Carl's; other brands will produce different, but still tasty, results)

1. Preheat a clean barbecue to medium grilling heat.
2. Bake the onion rings in the oven according to the directions on the package.

3. Form the ground beef into a flat burger the same diameter as the bun. It's best to premake your burger and store it in the freezer, then cook it frozen.
4. Grill the faces of the top and bottom bun in a frying pan on the stove over medium heat. Keep the pan hot.
5. Cook the bacon slices in the pan.
6. Grill the burger for 3 to 4 minutes per side, or until done. Salt each side.
7. Spread 1 tablespoon of the barbecue sauce on the faces of each bun, top and bottom.
8. Place both onion rings on the sauce on the bottom bun. Next stack the burger, then the cheese and the 2 bacon slices, crossed over each other.
9. Top off the sandwich with the top bun.

• MAKES 1 SANDWICH.

Carl's Jr. Junior Western Bacon Cheeseburger®

For about a buck, Carl's Jr. sells this smaller version of the preceding sandwich. It's made with a slightly smaller bun, a smaller portion of beef, half the bacon, and half the onion rings.

Here's what you do: Pat out 1/8 pound of ground beef to the same diameter as the bun. Use only one slice of bacon, broken in two, with the pieces crossed over each other. Use only one big onion ring, and build the burger in the same stacking order as the larger, original version.

Carl's Jr. Double Western Bacon Cheeseburger®

For real cholesterol fans, Carl's Jr. has designed a supersize version of this very popular burger. It is essentially the same as the original, with an additional 1/4-pound patty of beef and an additional slice of American cheese stacked on top of the other cheese and beef. Everything else is made the same as in the original. If you try it you'll like it. Just remember to jog an extra mile.

As I was experimenting, I discovered a variation of this sandwich that I think is pretty darn good. I called it a Western Bacon Chicken Sandwich, and it goes something like this:

Prepare your chicken by marinating and cooking it the same way as in the Santa Fe Chicken recipe. Then stack the sandwich as you would for a Western Bacon Cheeseburger, but using the chicken instead. Tastes great, less filling.

Carl, are you paying attention?

• • • •

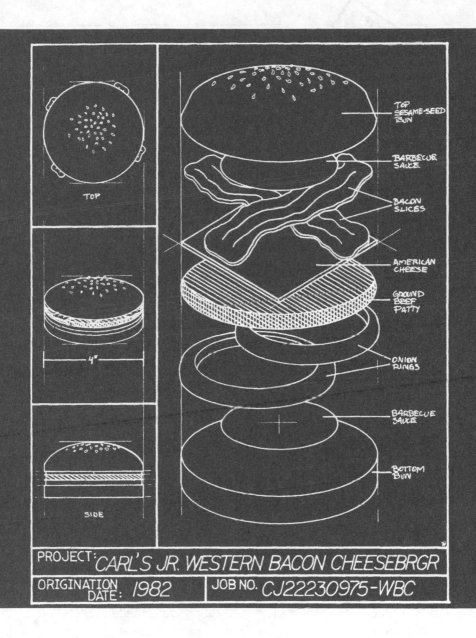

TOP

4"

SIDE

TOP
SESAME-SEED
BUN

BARBECUE
SAUCE

BACON
SLICES

AMERICAN
CHEESE

GROUND
BEEF
PATTY

ONION
RINGS

BARBECUE
SAUCE

BOTTOM
BUN

PROJECT: *CARL'S JR. WESTERN BACON CHEESEBRGR*

ORIGINATION
DATE: *1982*

JOB NO. *CJ22230975-WBC*

CHICK-FIL-A CHICKEN SANDWICH

In 1946 twenty-five-year-old S. Truett Cathy and his younger brother, Ben, opened a restaurant called The Dwarf House in Hapeville, Georgia. In the early sixties Cathy began experimenting with different seasonings and a faster cooking method for his original chicken sandwich. The finished product is the famous pressure-cooked chicken sandwich now served at all 460 Chick-fil-A outlets in thirty-one states.

Annual sales for the chain topped $324 million in 1991. That makes Chick-fil-A the fourth largest fast-food chicken restaurant in the world. And Cathy still adheres to the deeply religious values that were with him in the days of the first Dwarf House. That is why you won't find any Chick-fil-A restaurants open on Sundays.

3 cups peanut oil	2 tablespoons salt
1 egg	2 skinless, boneless chicken
1 cup milk	breasts, halved
1 cup flour	4 plain hamburger buns
2½ tablespoons powdered sugar	2 tablespoons melted butter
½ teaspoon pepper	8 dill pickle slices

1. Heat the peanut oil in a pressure cooker over medium heat to about 400°F.
2. In a small bowl, beat the egg and stir in the milk.

3. In a separate bowl, combine the flour, sugar, pepper, and salt.
4. Dip each piece of chicken in milk until it is fully moistened.
5. Roll the moistened chicken in the flour mixture until completely coated.
6. Drop all four chicken pieces into the hot oil and close the pressure cooker. When steam starts shooting through the pressure release, set the timer for 3½ minutes.
7. While the chicken is cooking, spread a coating of melted butter on the face of each bun.
8. When the chicken is done, remove it from the oil and drain or blot on paper towels. Place two pickles on each bottom bun, add a chicken breast, then the top bun.

• MAKES 4 SANDWICHES.

TIDBITS

Since my recipe was created, most manufacturers of pressure cookers have discouraged frying in their products, and warn that doing so could be hazardous. For that reason you should NEVER use a pressure cooker to fry anything unless the manufacturer has specifically designed the cooker for this use. I understand that there are now only a few cookers available that you can fry in, and finding one may now be difficult. The alternative is to pan fry or deep fry the chicken for roughly double the specified cooking time, until the chicken is golden brown.

It is very important that your oil be hot for this recipe. Test the temperature by dropping some of the flour coating into the oil. If it bubbles rapidly, your oil is probably hot enough. It should take about 20 minutes to heat up.

To make a "deluxe" chicken sandwich, simply add two tomato slices and a leaf of lettuce. Mayonnaise also goes well on this sandwich—it is a side order at the restaurant.

•   •   •   •

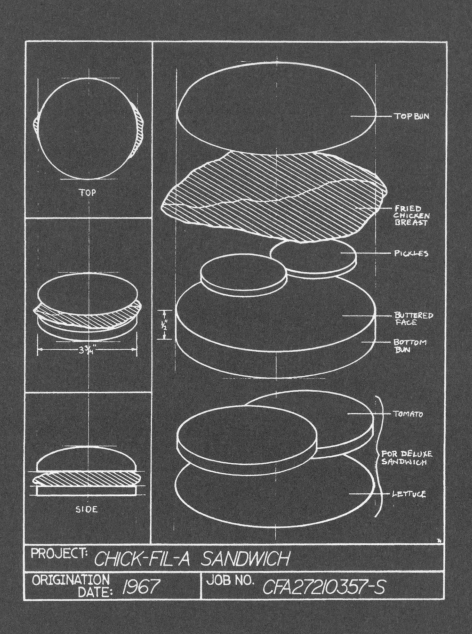

TOP

3¾"

SIDE

TOP BUN

FRIED
CHICKEN
BREAST

PICKLES

½"

BUTTERED
FACE

BOTTOM
BUN

TOMATO

FOR DELUXE
SANDWICH

LETTUCE

PROJECT: *CHICK-FIL-A SANDWICH*

ORIGINATION
DATE: *1967*

JOB NO. *CFA27210357-S*

CINNABON
CINNABONSTIX

☆ ✌ ✴ ✐ ☯ ✂ ☞

Cinnabon product development guys were looking for a new baked cinnamon product that customers could eat on the go while carrying bags and scurrying about. In June of 2000, they found it. Bakers brushed Danish dough with a flavored cinnamon butter, and then rolled the dough in a generous cinnamon sugar coating. These golden brown little sticks of cinnamony delight are sold in bags of five or ten from the company's famous cinnamon roll outlets, most likely found in a mall or airport near you. Now you can create your own version of the tasty pastries at home, and you won't even have to make the dough from scratch. Just grab yourself a tube of Pillsbury crescents and all you have to do is fold and roll up the dough, and then coat it. Run around the house in a hurry while eating these to further re-create the experience.

I tube Pillsbury crescent dinner
   rolls (8)
I stick (1/2 cup) margarine,
   melted
2 teaspoons granulated sugar
1/4 teaspoon cinnamon

1/4 teaspoon vanilla
nonstick cooking spray

COATING
1/2 cup granulated sugar
I tablespoon cinnamon

1. Preheat oven to 400 degrees.
2. Separate the dough into eight portions. Fold over two of the corners of the triangular dough piece so that it forms a rectangle. Roll the dough on a flat surface to make a tube, then

twist the tube a couple of times, and stretch it a little longer.
Repeat for all the dough triangles.

3. Combine the melted margarine, 2 teaspoons sugar, 1/4 teaspoon cinnamon, and 1/4 teaspoon vanilla in a small bowl.

4. Combine 1/2 cup sugar and 1 tablespoon cinnamon for the coating in another small bowl.

5. Brush the melted margarine mixture over the top and bottom of the dough sticks. Toss the dough into the sugar and cinnamon coating mixture. Roll the dough around with your fingers so that it is well coated. Place the coated dough sticks on a cookie sheet that has been sprayed with nonstick cooking spray. Spray the top of the sticks with a light coating of the spray.

6. Bake for 8 minutes or until the sticks are golden brown. Serve the sticks right out of the oven or reheat them in the microwave for just a bit before serving if they have cooled. These puppies are best served hot!

• MAKES 8 STICKS.

•　•　•　•

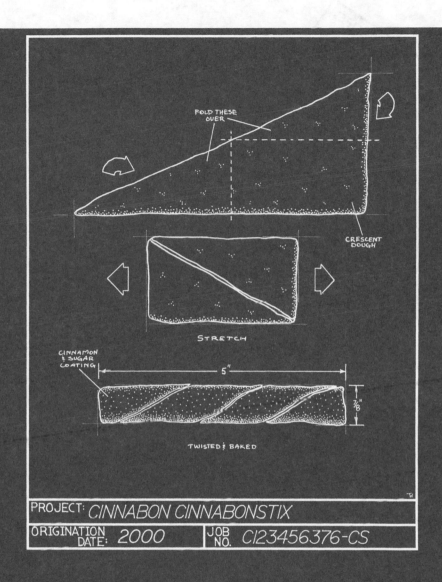

FOLD THESE OVER

CRESCENT DOUGH

STRETCH

CINNAMON & SUGAR COATING

5"

7/8"

TWISTED & BAKED

PROJECT: *CINNABON CINNABONSTIX*

ORIGINATION DATE: *2000*

JOB NO. *CI23456376-CS*

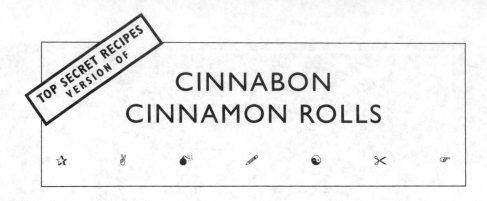

CINNABON
CINNAMON ROLLS

In early 1985, restaurateur Rich Komen decided there was a specialty niche in convenience-food service just waiting to be filled. His idea was to create an efficient outlet that could serve freshly made cinnamon rolls in shopping malls throughout the country. It took nine months for Komen and his staff to develop a cinnamon roll he knew customers would consider the "freshest, gooiest, and most mouthwatering cinnamon roll ever tasted." The concept was tested for the first time in Seattle's Sea-Tac mall later that year, with workers mixing, proofing, rolling, and baking the rolls in full view of the customers. Now, more than 200 outlets later, Cinnabon has become the fastest-growing cinnamon roll bakery in the country.

ROLLS

1 1/4-ounce package active dry
    yeast
1 cup warm milk (105 to 110°F)
1/2 cup granulated sugar
1/3 cup margarine, melted

1 teaspoon salt
2 eggs
4 cups all-purpose flour

FILLING

1 cup packed brown sugar
2 1/2 tablespoons cinnamon

1/3 cup margarine, softened

ICING

8 tablespoons (1 stick) margarine,
softened
1½ cups powdered sugar

¼ cup (2 ounces) cream cheese
½ teaspoon vanilla extract
⅛ teaspoon salt

1. For the rolls, dissolve the yeast in the warm milk in a large bowl.
2. Mix together the sugar, margarine, salt, and eggs. Add flour, and mix well.
3. Knead the dough into a large ball, using your hands dusted lightly with flour. Put in a bowl, cover, and let rise in a warm place about 1 hour, or until the dough has doubled in size.
4. Roll the dough out on a lightly floured surface. Roll the dough flat until it is approximately 21 inches long and 16 inches wide. It should be about ¼ inch thick.
5. Preheat oven to 400°F.
6. For the filling, combine the brown sugar and cinnamon in a bowl. Spread the softened margarine evenly over the surface of the dough, and then sprinkle the cinnamon and sugar evenly over the surface.
7. Working carefully from the top (a 21-inch side), roll the dough down to the bottom edge.
8. Cut the rolled dough into 1¾-inch slices and place 6 at a time, evenly spaced, in a lightly greased baking pan. Let the rolls rise again until double in size (about 30 minutes). Bake for 10 to 15 minutes, or until light brown on top.
9. While the rolls bake, combine the icing ingredients. Beat well with an electric mixer until fluffy.
10. When the rolls come out of the oven, coat each generously with icing.

• MAKES 12 ROLLS.

These rolls can be frozen after baking. Just pop one into the microwave for 20 to 30 seconds to reheat.

• • • •

CREAM CHEESE ICING

CINNAMON &
BROWN SUGAR

BAKED
DOUGH

¼"

DIVIDE AFTER
ROLLING

¼"

1¾"

21"

16"

ROLLED-OUT DOUGH

3½"

2" 2¾"

BAKED CINNAMON ROLL

PROJECT: *CINNABON CINNAMON ROLL*

ORIGINATION
DATE: *1985*

JOB NO. *C5573046-CR*

TOP SECRET RECIPES
VERSION OF
EINSTEIN BROS. BAGELS
SANTA FE
EGGS 4 WAYS SANDWICH

☆　　✌　　💣　　✎　　🎱　　✂　　☞

This way is by far the most creative and tasty of the four ways you can have your bagel breakfast sandwich at Einstein Bagels. The salsa and jalapeño salsa cream cheese make for a slightly spicy affair that anyone who goes for Southwestern-style tastes will thoroughly dig. The sausage used here is a turkey breakfast sausage that you can find in most supermarkets (Wampler makes a good version that comes in a 1-pound tube and is sometimes found in the freezer section). You can also use small uncooked turkey breakfast links. Just squeeze the sausage out of the casing and form your patties, then toss out the casings. In a pinch you can also use good old pork sausage. Either way you go, you're in for a tasty way to rev up your day.

JALAPEÑO SALSA CREAM CHEESE

8 ounces cream cheese
1/4 cup Ortega medium salsa
2 tablespoons minced jalapeño
　　slices (canned)
1/8 teaspoon chili powder

6 ounces turkey breakfast
　　sausage

3 large eggs, beaten
　　(about 2/3 cup)
2 bagels, sliced in half and lightly
　　toasted
2 slices pepper jack Kraft Singles
　　cheese
2 tablespoons Ortega medium
　　salsa

1. First make your jalapeño salsa cream cheese by mixing all ingredients together in a small bowl. Cover and chill cream cheese until it's needed.
2. Make the turkey sausage patties by forming sausage into 2 3-ounce patties that are about 4½ inches in diameter. If you have time, form the patties on wax paper and freeze them to make handling easier. They will shrink when cooking to just the right size.
3. Beat the eggs in a bowl, then measure half (about ⅓ cup) into a bowl with the same approximate diameter as the bagels. Microwave each bowl (separately) for 1 to 1½ minutes on high, or until the egg is completely cooked.
4. Lightly toast all of the bagel halves.
5. Spread about 2 teaspoons of the jalapeño salsa cream cheese on the toasted face of the bottom half of the bagel.
6. When the eggs are cooked, arrange them on the cream cheese on each bagel bottom.
7. Lay a slice of pepper jack cheese on each of the egg layers.
8. Arrange a sausage patty on top of the cheese on each sandwich.
9. Spread about 2 teaspoons of salsa on the toasted face of each of the top bagel halves.
10. Top off the sandwiches with the top bagel halves, slice each sandwich in half, and serve while hot.

- MAKES 2 SANDWICHES.

• • • •

This creamy green sauce is available at the salsa bar at each of the more than 300 El Pollo Loco outlets located throughout the western U.S., and folks are going crazy over it. The problem is, you can only get it at the restaurants in small quantities. So you know what that means: time to put on our crafty kitchen cloning hats. You'll want to use a food processor to mix this one up (everything but the cilantro and onion goes in there). When it's all done, you'll have a delicious, spicy concoction that you can pour over your favorite homemade Mexican-style dishes, from tacos salads to fajitas. A big thanks goes out to Pancho Ochoa, who opened his first roadside chicken stand in Guasave, Mexico, in 1975. Today, Pancho's El Pollo Loco is the number one quick-service, flame-broiled chicken chain in America.

1 ripe avocado
1 jalapeño, stemmed and
   quartered
1 cup water
1 tablespoon white distilled
   vinegar

¾ teaspoon salt
2 tablespoons minced fresh
   cilantro
2 tablespoons diced onion

1. Combine avocado, jalapeño, water, vinegar, and salt in a food processor. Puree the mixture for several seconds on high speed, or until jalapeño is finely minced.
2. Pour mixture into a medium bowl. Stir in cilantro and onion. Cover and chill until ready to serve.

- MAKES 1 ½ CUPS.

• • • •

HONEYBAKED HAM GLAZE

☆ ✌ 💣 ✐ ☯ ✂ ☞

TSR has discovered that the tender hams are delivered to each of the 300 HoneyBaked outlets already smoked, but without the glaze. It is only when the ham gets to your local HoneyBaked store that a special machine thin-slices the tender meat in a spiral fashion around the bone. One at a time, each ham is then coated with the glaze—a blend that is similar to what might be used to make pumpkin pie. This sweet coating is then caramelized with a blowtorch by hand until the glaze bubbles and melts, turning golden brown. If needed, more of the coating is added, and the blowtorch is fired up until the glaze is just right. It's this careful process that turns the same size ham that costs 10 dollars in a supermarket into one that customers gladly shell out 3 to 4 times as much to share during the holiday season.

For this clone recipe, we will re-create the glaze that you can apply to a smoked/cooked bone-in ham of your choice. Look for a ham that's presliced. Otherwise you'll have to slice it yourself with a sharp knife, then the glaze will be applied. To get the coating just right you must use a blowtorch. If you don't have one, you can find a small one in hardware stores for around 10 to 15 bucks. And don't worry—I didn't leave out an ingredient. No honey is necessary to re-create this favorite holiday glaze.

1 fully cooked shank half ham, bone-in (presliced)
1 cup sugar
1/4 teaspoon ground cinnamon
1/4 teaspoon ground nutmeg
1/4 teaspoon ground clove
1/8 teaspoon paprika
dash ground ginger
dash ground allspice

1. If you couldn't find a presliced ham, the first thing you must do is slice it. Use a very sharp knife to cut the ham into very thin slices around the bone. Do not cut all the way down to the bone or the meat may not hold together properly as it is being glazed. You want the slices to be quite thin, but not so thin that they begin to fall apart or off the bone. You may wish to turn the ham onto its flat end and cut around it starting at the bottom. You can then spin the ham as you slice around and work your way up.
2. Mix the remaining ingredients together in a small bowl.
3. Lay down a couple sheets of wax paper onto a flat surface, such as your kitchen counter. Pour the sugar mixture onto the wax paper and spread it around evenly.
4. Pick up the ham and roll it over the sugar mixture so that it is well coated. Do not coat the flat end of the ham, just the outer, presliced surface.
5. Turn the ham onto its flat end on a plate. Use a blowtorch with a medium-size flame to caramelize the sugar. Wave the torch over the sugar with rapid movement, so that the sugar bubbles and browns, but does not burn. Spin the plate so that you can torch the entire surface of the ham. Repeat the coating and caramelizing process until the ham has been well glazed (don't expect to use all of the sugar mixture). Serve the ham cold or reheated, just like the real thing.

• MAKES 1 HOLIDAY HAM.

• • • •

IN-N-OUT
DOUBLE-DOUBLE

☆   ✌   💣   ✏   ☯   ✂   ☞

In 1948 Harry and Esther Snyder opened In-N-Out Burger in Baldwin Park, the first drive-thru restaurant in southern California. When Harry Snyder died in 1976, his son Richard took over the helm of the company, being sure to keep intact the simplicity that was so important to his father. The outlet still has a very small menu—only eight items. The french fries are made from fresh potatoes in each store, all the burgers are made to order, the lettuce is hand-leafed, and the milkshakes are made from fresh ice cream. All of this special treatment means that service is much slower than at most fast-food outlets—an average of twelve minutes per order. The experience is reminiscent of hamburger drive-ins of the fifties.

The company now has more than seventy-one outlets, each of which sells more than 52,000 hamburgers a month. Among these are the increasingly popular Double-Double hamburgers—quite a handful of sandwich.

1 plain hamburger bun
1/3 pound ground beef
dash salt
1 tablespoon Kraft Thousand
   Island dressing
1 large tomato slice
   (or 2 small slices)

1 large lettuce leaf
4 slices American cheese (singles)
   OR 2 slices real American
   cheese
1 onion slice

1. Preheat a frying pan over medium heat.
2. Lightly toast both halves of the hamburger bun, facedown. Set aside.
3. Separate the beef into two even portions, and form each half into a thin patty slightly larger than the bun.
4. Lightly salt each patty and cook for 2 to 3 minutes on the first side.
5. Flip the patties over and place two slices of cheese on top of each one. Cook for 2 to 3 minutes.
6. Build the burger in the following stacking order from the bottom up:

bottom bun   beef patty with cheese
dressing   onion slice
tomato   beef patty with cheese
lettuce   top bun

• MAKES 1 HAMBURGER.

TIDBITS

The recipe requires 4 slices of cheese if you are using the common individually wrapped American cheese slices; also known as "cheese food." However, if you would like to use thicker, real American cheese slices, use only 1 slice on each beef patty.

•   •   •   •

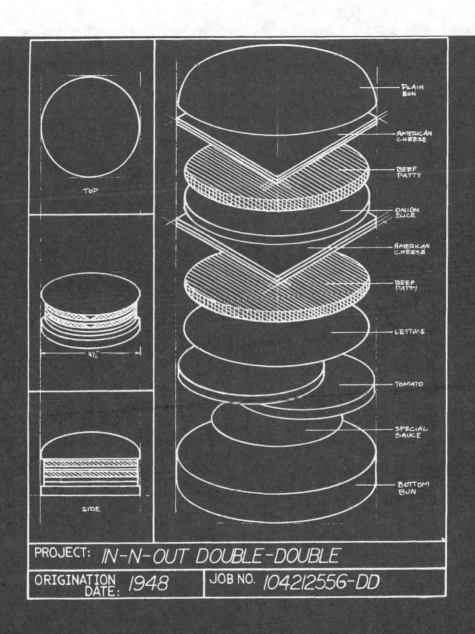

TOP

SIDE

4½"

PLAIN BUN

AMERICAN CHEESE

BEEF PATTY

ONION SLICE

AMERICAN CHEESE

BEEF PATTY

LETTUCE

TOMATO

SPECIAL SAUCE

BOTTOM BUN

PROJECT: IN-N-OUT DOUBLE-DOUBLE

ORIGINATION DATE: 1948

JOB NO. 104212556-DD

KFC
BBQ BAKED BEANS

Here's a clone recipe to add to the table for your next picnic, cookout, or all-purpose pig-out. Just find yourself a couple cans of the small white beans (be sure they're not pinto beans or great northern beans), and the rest is easy. Throw all of the ingredients into a casserole dish and let the sucker bake. While you get on with the party.

2 15-ounce cans small white
    beans (with liquid)
2 tablespoons water
1 tablespoon cornstarch
½ cup ketchup
½ cup dark brown sugar
2 tablespoons white vinegar

4 teaspoons minced fresh onion
2 pieces cooked bacon, crumbled
½ teaspoon dry mustard
¼ teaspoon salt
dash pepper
dash garlic powder

1. Preheat oven to 350°F.
2. Pour entire contents of two 15-ounce cans of beans into a covered casserole dish.
3. Combine the water with the cornstarch in a small bowl until cornstarch dissolves. Stir mixture into the beans.
4. Stir the remaining ingredients into the beans and cover the dish.

5. Bake for 90 minutes or until sauce thickens. Stir every 30 minutes. After removing them from the oven, let the beans sit for 5 to 10 minutes before serving.

- SERVES 4 TO 6.

• • • •

TOP SECRET RECIPES
VERSION OF
KFC
CAJUN HONEY WINGS

☆   ✌   💣   ✎   ☯   ✂   ☞

When the "Limited-time only" signs came down for this one, I just smiled. Because now we've got a clone recipe to last forever that'll closely duplicate the sweet and spicy sauce on these amazing chicken wings. The Colonel's people coat the wings with a KFC-style breading before frying them up and adding the Cajun sauce. But you don't need wings to put this sauce to work. This recipe makes 1 cup of the sauce that you can use to coat beef, pork, or other chicken parts. This recipe requires the meat variety of Paul Prudhomme's Magic Seasoning Blends, but it will also work with other Cajun seasoning blends, which are available in most markets.

SAUCE

¼ cup ketchup

1 cup water

¾ cup white vinegar

1 tablespoon vegetable oil

⅓ cup honey

4 teaspoons Chef Paul
   Prudhomme's Meat Magic

1 tablespoon canned green chilies,
   minced

1¼ teaspoons chili powder

1 teaspoon minced garlic

½ teaspoon liquid smoke (hickory
   flavor)

⅛ teaspoon dried thyme

6 to 12 cups vegetable shortening

1 egg, beaten

1 cup milk

2 cups all-purpose flour

2½ teaspoons salt

¾ teaspoon pepper

¾ teaspoon MSG (such as Accent)

20 chicken wing pieces

1. Combine the sauce ingredients in a small saucepan over medium heat. Stir until ingredients are well combined, and bring to a boil. Then reduce heat and simmer sauce uncovered for 20 to 25 minutes or until it has thickened.
2. As sauce is simmering, heat up 6 to 12 cups of shortening in a deep fryer set to 350 degrees.
3. Combine the beaten egg with the milk in a small bowl.
4. In another small bowl, combine the flour, salt, pepper, and MSG.
5. When shortening is hot, dip each wing first in the flour mixture, then into the milk-and-egg mixture, and back into the flour. Arrange wings on a plate until each one is coated with batter.
6. Fry the wings in the shortening for 9 to 12 minutes or until light golden brown. If you have a small fryer, you may wish to fry 10 of the wings at a time. Drain on paper towels or a rack.
7. When the sauce is done, brush the entire surface of each wing with a coating of sauce. Serve immediately.

• MAKES 2 TO 4 SERVINGS (20 WINGS).

• • • •

KFC
COLE SLAW

In 1935, shortly after the first Kentucky Fried Chicken restaurant had opened, Governor Ruby Laffoon made Harland Sanders a Kentucky colonel in recognition of his contribution to the state's cuisine. In 1952, at the age of sixty-six, Colonel Sanders began to franchise his fried chicken business. Traveling through Ohio, Indiana, and Kentucky, he met with restaurant owners, cooking his chicken for them and their employees. If the restaurant owners liked the chicken, they would agree with a handshake that the Colonel would supply the "secret blend" of spices in exchange for a nickel on each piece of chicken sold. As of 1991 there were more than 8,000 Kentucky Fried Chicken stores worldwide, with sales of more than $5 billion.

The recipe for the Colonel's cole slaw, which is made from scratch in each store, is kept as secret as that for the herbs and spices in the fried chicken. Now taste our "top-secret" version of the Colonel's well-known favorite slaw.

8 cups very finely chopped
   cabbage (1 head)
1/4 cup shredded carrot
   (1 medium carrot)
2 tablespoons minced onions
1/3 cup granulated sugar
1/2 teaspoon salt

1/8 teaspoon pepper
1/4 cup milk
1/2 cup mayonnaise
1/4 cup buttermilk
1 1/2 tablespoons white vinegar
2 1/2 tablespoons lemon juice

1. Be sure that the cabbage, carrots, and onion are chopped up into very fine pieces (about the size of rice kernels).
2. Combine the sugar, salt, pepper, milk, mayonnaise, buttermilk, vinegar, and lemon juice, and beat until smooth.
3. Add the cabbage, carrots, and onions. Mix well.
4. Cover and refrigerate for at least 2 hours before serving.

- SERVES 8.

TIDBITS

The critical part of this cole slaw recipe is the flavor-enhancement period prior to eating. Be absolutely certain the cole slaw sits in the refrigerator for at least a couple of hours prior to serving for a great-tasting slew of slaw.

• • • •

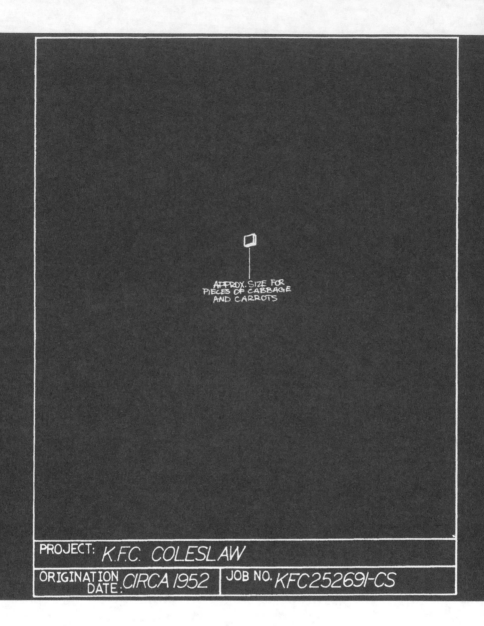

APPROX. SIZE FOR
PIECES OF CABBAGE
AND CARROTS

PROJECT: *K.F.C. COLESLAW*

ORIGINATION
DATE: *CIRCA 1952*   JOB NO. *KFC252691-CS*

KFC
EXTRA CRISPY CHICKEN

☆   ✌   💣   ✏   ☯   ✂   ☞

In 1971, with KFC now out of his control, Colonel Harland Sanders was approached by the company's new owners, the Heublein Company, with a recipe for a crispier version of the famous fried chicken. The marketing department decided they wanted to call the product "Colonel Sanders' New Recipe" but the Colonel would have nothing to do with it. The stern and opinionated founder of the company, who had publicly criticized the changes to his secret formulas (in a newspaper interview he called the revised mashed potatoes "wallpaper paste"), refused to allow the use of his name on the product. Since the Colonel was an important component of the company's marketing plan, KFC appeased him. The new chicken was then appropriately dubbed "Extra Crispy," and sales were finger-licking good. Now you can reproduce the taste and crunchy breaded texture of the real thing with a brining process similar to that used by the fast food chain, followed by a double-dipped coating. Roll the chicken pieces around several times with your fingers as you bread the pieces in the spiced flour to build up that thick, crunchy coating of the real stuff. Unlike the Original Recipe chicken clone, which is pressure-cooked, this version is deep fried.

1 whole frying chicken, cut up	**BRINE SOLUTION**
6 to 12 cups vegetable shortening	4 cups cold water
	2 tablespoons salt
	1/2 teaspoon MSG (see Tidbits)

COATING

2 cups all-purpose flour
1 tablespoon popcorn salt
1 teaspoon MSG (see Tidbits)
½ teaspoon ground black pepper
½ teaspoon paprika

½ teaspoon cayenne pepper
½ teaspoon ground sage
½ teaspoon ground coriander
¼ teaspoon ground thyme
¼ teaspoon garlic powder

1. Trim any excess skin and fat from the chicken pieces. Preheat the shortening in a deep fryer to 350 degrees. Use the amount of shortening recommended by the manufacturer of your fryer.
2. Combine the water, salt, and ½ teaspoon MSG for the brine solution in a large bowl. Stir to dissolve salt. Add the chicken to the bowl and let it sit for 20 minutes.
3. Combine the dry coating ingredients in a large bowl. Mix well.
4. When the chicken has soaked in the brine solution for 20 minutes, coat each piece with the flour mixture and then arrange each piece on a plate or baking sheet. When all the pieces have been coated, drop one at a time back into the water again, then into the flour. This time roll each piece of chicken around with your fingers several times so that the coating builds up. This build-up of coating will make the chicken crispy. Arrange the chicken on the plate again until each piece has been coated. Let the chicken rest for about 5 minutes so that the coating sticks. Preheat oven to 225 degrees.
5. Drop the chicken, one piece at a time, into the hot shortening. Fry 3 to 4 pieces of the chicken at a time for 12 to 15 minutes, or until each one is golden brown. Be sure to turn the chicken halfway through the cooking time so that each piece cooks evenly.
6. Remove the chicken to a rack to drain for about 5 minutes before eating, then put the chicken into the warm oven while the other pieces are frying.

• SERVES 3 TO 4 (8 PIECES OF CHICKEN).

MSG is monosodium glutamate, the solid form of a natural amino acid found in many vegetables. It can be found in stores in the spice sections, and as the brand name Accent Flavor Enhancer. MSG is an important component of many KFC items.

• • • •

MAJORLY CRUNCHY

5¼"

2¼"

CHICKEN LEG
(A.K.A.: DRUMSTICK)

SIDE

2¼"

CHICKEN BONE

CHICKEN MEAT

CRUNCHY COATING

CROSS SECTION

BONE
(DO NOT CONSUME)

CRISPY OUTSIDE

JUICY INSIDE

BACK

PROJECT: *KFC EXTRA CRISPY CHICKEN*

ORIGINATION DATE: *1971*

JOB NO. *KFC4737907-ETCC*

KFC MASHED POTATOES & GRAVY

☆　　✌　　💣　　✏　　☯　　✂　　☞

This gravy recipe should come very close to that tasty tan stuff that's poured over the fluffy mashed potatoes at the Colonel's chain of restaurants. And since the original recipe contains MSG (as does their chicken), this clone was designed with that "secret" ingredient. You may choose to leave out the MSG, which is a natural amino acid found in vegetables and seaweed. But your clone won't taste exactly like the real thing without it.

GRAVY

1 tablespoon vegetable oil
4½ tablespoons all-purpose flour
1 can Campbell's chicken broth
   (plus 1 can water)
   (see Tidbits)
¼ teaspoon salt
⅛ teaspoon MSG or Accent Flavor
   Enhancer
⅛ teaspoon ground black pepper

MASHED POTATOES

1½ cups water
⅓ cup milk
3 tablespoons butter
½ teaspoon salt
1½ cups instant mashed potato
   flakes (Potato Buds)

1. First make a roux by combining the oil with 1½ tablespoons of flour in a medium saucepan over low to medium heat. Heat the mixture for 20 to 30 minutes, stirring often, until it is a chocolate color.

2. Remove the roux from the heat, add the remaining ingredi-ents to the saucepan, and stir.
3. Put the saucepan back over the heat, turn it up to medium, and bring the gravy to a boil. Reduce heat and simmer for 10 to 15 minutes, or until thick.
4. As the gravy is reducing, prepare the potatoes by combining 1½ cups of water, ⅓ cup of milk, butter, and ½ teaspoon of salt in a medium saucepan over medium heat. Bring to a boil, then remove the pan from heat. Add the potato flakes, and whip with a fork until fluffy.
5. Serve the mashed potatoes with gravy poured over the top. As if you didn't know.

- MAKES 3 TO 4 SERVINGS.

TIDBITS

If Campbell's chicken broth is not available you can use 2½ cups of any chicken stock.

• • • •

TOP SECRET RECIPES
VERSION OF
KRISPY KREME
ORIGINAL GLAZED
DOUGHNUTS

☆   ✌   💣   ✏   ◉   ✂   ☞

The specifics of the well-guarded, 65-year-old secret recipe for Krispy Kreme doughnuts may be securely locked away in a safe at the Winston-Salem, North Carolina, headquarters, but discovering the basic ingredients in these puffy, fried cakes of joy was far from impossible. Simply asking to see the ingredients listed on the dry doughnut mix was all it took. Still, knowing the exact ingredients in a Krispy Kreme glazed doughnut is hardly all the information we need to clone one. There's an important cooking technique at work here that's a big part of the secret.

The automated process for creating Krispy Kremes, developed in the 1950s, took the company many years to perfect. When you drive by your local Krispy Kreme store between 5:00 and 11:00 each day (both A.M. and P.M.) and see the "Hot Doughnuts Now" sign lit up, inside the store custom-made stainless steel machines are rolling. Doughnut batter is extruded into little doughnut shapes that ride up and down through a temperature- and humidity-controlled booth to activate the yeast. This creates the perfect amount of air pockets in the dough that will make a fluffy final product. When the doughnuts are swollen with air, they're gently dumped into hot vegetable shortening, where they float on one side until golden brown, then the machine flips them over to cook the other side. As the doughnuts finish frying, they ride up a mesh conveyer belt and through a ribbon of white sugar glaze. If you're lucky enough to taste some of these doughnuts just as they come around the corner from the glazing, you're in for a real treat. The warm circle of glazed goodness practically melts in your mouth. It's this secret process that has helped Krispy Kreme become the fastest-growing doughnut chain in the country.

As for the secret ingredients in a Krispy Kreme, you can probably guess that they are made mostly of basic wheat flour. That part's obvious. But there's also some soy flour in there, plus egg yolk, wheat gluten, non-fat milk, yeast, malted barley flour, modified food starch, ascorbic acid, salt, sugar, corn syrup solids, and natural flavors. For this clone recipe, I decided that some of the ingredients used in the real thing wouldn't be necessary for a home-grown duplicate. After numerous experiments over several weeks, I concluded that we could still create a finished product that's extremely close to the original without some of the harder-to-get ingredients such as soy flour, wheat gluten, malted barley, and modified food starch.

The recipe here requires only commonly found ingredients, since it is truly the process of raising the doughnuts carefully that's going to make them fluffy and tender like the real thing. In this case, the most important step is the one in which you transfer the doughnuts (after they have risen) from the baking sheet into the shortening. You must do this very gently so that the dough does not deflate. The fluffier the doughnuts are when they go into the shortening, the more tender and Krispy Kreme–like they'll be when they come out.

This clone recipe creates doughnuts that are probably very much like the original Krispy Kreme recipe, which founder Vernon Rudolph purchased from a New Orleans chef in 1937. That's long before machines took over the process.

1 pkg. (2¼ teaspoons) yeast
1½ teaspoons granulated sugar
¾ cup warm water (100 degrees
    to 110 degrees)
1¾ cups all-purpose flour

½ teaspoon salt
1 egg yolk
1 tablespoon fat-free milk
¼ teaspoon vanilla extract

GLAZE

1 ¾ cups plus 2 tablespoons
   powdered sugar

¼ cup boiling water

6 to 12 cups vegetable shortening
   (as required by your fryer)

1. Dissolve yeast and sugar in warm water. Let solution stand for 5 minutes or until it becomes foamy on top. Make sure the water isn't too hot, or you may kill the yeast.
2. Combine flour and salt in a large bowl with an electric mixer. Add yeast solution, egg yolk, milk, and vanilla extract and mix well with electric mixer for 30 seconds or just until all ingredients are combined.
3. Form dough into a ball, then let it sit in a bowl, covered, in a warm place for approximately one hour, or until the dough doubles in size.
4. Gently roll out the dough until it's about ½-inch thick on a floured surface. Use a well-floured 3-inch biscuit cutter to cut out circles of dough. Then use a well-floured lid from a plastic soda bottle (about 1⅛-inch diameter) to cut the holes. You can also use a 3-inch doughnut cutter if you have one. Arrange the doughnuts on a couple of lightly floured cookie sheets, cover them with plastic wrap, and let them sit for one hour in a warm place. After about an hour, the doughnuts should have doubled in size.
5. While the doughnuts rest, make the glaze by combining powdered sugar and boiling water. Whisk glaze until smooth, then cover with plastic wrap until you're ready to use it.
6. As doughnuts rise, heat vegetable shortening in fryer to 375 degrees.
7. When doughnuts have doubled in size, carefully transfer 2 to 3 doughnuts at a time to the shortening. You must lift the doughnuts very gently or they will collapse and not turn out as fluffy as the real thing. Fry doughnuts for 1½ to 2 minutes per side, then remove them to a cooling rack.

8. After a minute or so on the cooling rack, spoon glaze generously over the top of each doughnut. You want the entire surface of each doughnut well-coated with glaze. You can also recycle the glaze that falls through the rack by spooning it back into the bowl and stirring it up. Let the doughnuts cool for a few minutes, and they're ready to eat.

- Makes 10 doughnuts.

• • • •

LITTLE CAESAR'S CRAZY BREAD

In 1959, Michael Ilitch and his wife, Marian, opened the first Little Caesar's restaurant in Garden City, Michigan, fifteen miles west of Detroit. Encouraged by their success, the couple opened a second restaurant two years later, and soon Little Caesar's Pizza was a household name in the Detroit area. Biographical material provided by the company claims that Ilitch "thinks pizza," and that when he designed the Little Caesar's conveyor oven, the company was able to serve hot pizza faster than anyone else in the industry.

One of the most popular products available from Little Caesar's is the Crazy Bread, first served in 1982. It's just a pizza crust cut into eight pieces, then coated with garlic salt, butter, and Parmesan cheese.

1 10-ounce tube Pillsbury pizza
   dough
2 tablespoons (¼ stick) butter

1 teaspoon garlic salt
Kraft 100% grated parmesan
   cheese for topping

1. Preheat the oven to 425°F.
2. Unroll the dough on a cutting board. Position it lengthwise (longer from left to right than from top to bottom). With a sharp knife, cut the dough in half down the middle. Then cut each of those halves vertically in half, and then in half once more so that you have 8 even strips of dough.
3. Being careful not to stretch the dough, place each strip on a

lightly greased cookie sheet and bake for 6 to 8 minutes, or until the top just turns golden brown.

4. While the dough bakes, melt the butter (on the stove or in the microwave on high for 15 to 20 seconds), then add the garlic salt and stir until it dissolves.

5. Remove the browned dough from the oven and with a pastry brush or spoon spread a coating of garlic butter over each piece.

6. Sprinkle a generous amount of parmesan cheese on each.

• MAKES 8 PIECES.

•   •   •   •

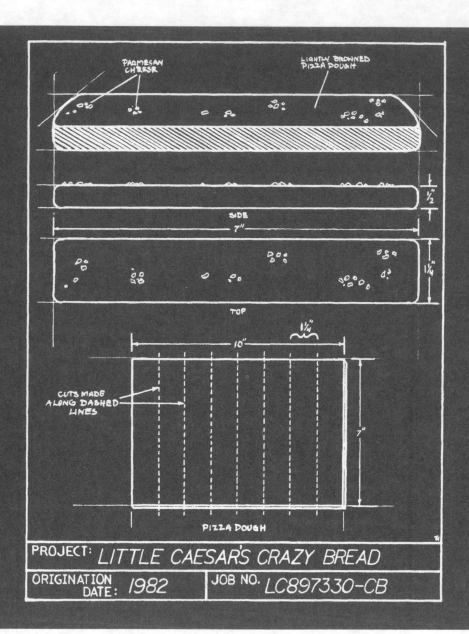

PARMESAN CHEESE

LIGHTLY BROWNED PIZZA DOUGH

SIDE

7"

½"

TOP

1¼"

CUTS MADE ALONG DASHED LINES

10"

1½"

7"

PIZZA DOUGH

PROJECT: *LITTLE CAESAR'S CRAZY BREAD*

ORIGINATION DATE: *1982*

JOB NO. *LC897330-CB*

LITTLE CAESAR'S
CRAZY SAUCE

☆   ✌   💣   ✏   🎱   ✂   ☞

From 1990 to 1993, Little Caesar's sales growth ranked in the top five in the restaurant industry, according to *Nation's Restaurant News* magazine. As of 1993, the company had more than 4,800 outlets raking in $2.3 billion. It's no wonder that founder Michael Ilitch was able to purchase the Detroit Red Wings hockey team in 1982, and then the Detroit Tigers in 1992. Ilitch also owns several arenas and theaters, including the Second City comedy theater in Detroit.

The Crazy Sauce at Little Caesar's is usually served with the Crazy Bread, for dipping. It's a version of pizza sauce, heated in a microwave before you buy it. The sauce can be used with the preceding Crazy Bread recipe, or as a great, fresh sauce for any homemade pizza.

1 15-ounce can tomato puree	1/4 teaspoon dried basil
1/2 teaspoon salt	1/4 teaspoon dried marjoram
1/4 teaspoon pepper	1/4 teaspoon dried oregano
1/4 teaspoon garlic powder	1/4 teaspoon ground thyme

1. Combine all the ingredients in an uncovered saucepan over medium heat.
2. When the sauce begins to bubble, reduce the heat and simmer for 30 minutes, stirring often.
3. Remove the sauce from the heat and let it cool. Store in a tightly sealed container in the refrigerator; it will keep for 3 to 4 weeks. Serve hot.

- MAKES 1 1/2 CUPS.

• • • •

TOP SECRET RECIPES
VERSION OF
MAID-RITE
LOOSE MEAT SANDWICH

☆　　✌　　💥　　✏　　☯　　✂　　☞

It's been an Iowa tradition since 1926, and one of our longtime requested items at TSR. Even ex-comedienne Roseanne and her Iowa native ex-husband Tom Arnold spoke many salivating praises of Maid-Rites when they shared a home together in the state. There are now 83 Maid-Rite stores located throughout Iowa and seven other Midwestern states. Although the sandwich is not much more than a traditional hamburger with the ground beef arranged uncompressed on a white bun, the product has a huge cult following. And since the meat is loose, the sandwich is served with a spoon for scooping up the ground beef that will inevitably fall out.

The nice thing about having a popular Web site (www. TopSecretRecipes.com) is the instant feedback that comes with each posted weekly recipe. This recipe was certainly no exception. In fact, the clone for Maid-Rite elicited more e-mail than any recipe in the site's history. Numerous Midwesterners were keyboard-ready to insist that the clone was far from accurate without inclusion of a few bizarre ingredients, the most common of which was good old Coca-Cola. One letter states: "You evidently have not ever had a Maid-Rite. The secret to the Maid-Rite is coke syrup. Without it, you cannot come close to the taste." Another e-mail reads; "'Having lived in the Midwest all of my life and knowing not only owners of a Maid-Rite restaurant, but also many people who worked there, I can tell you that one of the things you left out of your recipe is Coca-Cola. Not a lot, just enough to keep the meat moist."

Then, on the flip side, I received comments such as this one from a fan who lived in Iowa, the state where Don Taylor's original Maid-Rite franchise was located: "The secret to the best Maid-Rite is the whole beef. Don had a butcher shop in his basement where he cut and ground all his beef. Some people still swear they added seasoning, but that is just not true. Not even pepper. They do add water, which steams the meat."

To create this clone, I did, of course, consume many a Maid-Rite sandwich. Obviously, there's no way I could create a clone recipe for a product I haven't tasted. In fact, I arranged for Maid-Rites to be shipped in dry ice directly from Don Taylor's original store in Marshalltown. As I write this, I still have a few of those puppies in the freezer, and after a couple minutes in the microwave, they're almost as good as fresh.

Upon receiving all the e-mails, I went back to the freezer and back to the drawing board to see if the cloning work on this famous Top Secret Recipe could be bettered. But no matter how hard I examined the meat, I could not detect Coca-Cola in there. There's no sweetness to the meat at all, although the buns themselves seem to include some sugar (when the buns are chewed with the meat, the sandwich does taste mildly sweet). I finally concluded that Coca-Cola is an absolutely unnecessary ingredient for cloning this sandwich. If it's being added to the meat in the Maid-Rite stores, it's an insignificant amount that does not have any noticeable effect on the flavor. Perhaps beef broth is being mistaken as Coca-Cola? Or this could simply be one of those crazy urban food legends that spread so easily on the Web (like chocolate in Skyline Chili? See page 106). So there's still no Coke in the ingredients list, but I've made a few other small changes that improve the recipe.

While my original clone recipe included a dash of black pepper, I have now concluded that there is no such ingredient in the real thing. Black pepper specks would show easily against the white, flour, hamburger bun, and I have not found any after examining several sandwiches. Also, the texture is important, so adding more liquid to the simmering meat is crucial. This revised recipe requires a cup of water in addition to a ¼ cup of beef broth. By simmering the ground beef in this liquid for an hour or so, we can maintain a temperature over 140 degrees that breaks down the collagen in the meat. This makes the final product tender, just like the real thing. The beef broth, plus a little salt, adds all the flavor you'll need. Try it, and you'll see for yourself. And, yes, that's without any Coca-Cola. It also helps to use good quality ground beef. You'll get out of the recipe what you put in.

When building your sandwich, firmly press the beef into a ½-cup measuring cup. Dump the meat onto the bottom of a plain hamburger bun; add your choice of mustard, onions, and pickles; ready a spoon, and dig in. Adding ketchup is up to you, although it's not an ingredient found in Maid-Rite stores. Many say that back in the early days, "hobos" would swipe the ketchup and mix it with water to make tomato soup. Free ketchup was nixed from the restaurants way back then, and the custom has been in place ever since.

1 pound lean ground beef (15% fat is best)	4 plain hamburger buns yellow mustard
1 cup water	minced onion
¼ cup beef broth	dill pickle slices
¼ teaspoon salt	

1. Brown ground beef in a large skillet over medium-low heat. Use a potato masher to help get the ground beef into small pieces. Drain any excess fat. If you use lean meat (15% fat or less) you won't need to drain the fat. As soon as all the pink in the meat is gone, add 1 cup of water and ¼ cup beef broth plus ¼ teaspoon salt. Simmer the meat uncovered for one hour or until all the liquid is gone, stirring every 10 minutes or so.
2. Build each sandwich by pressing the hot ground beef into a ½ cup measuring cup. Dump the meat onto the bottom of a

plain hamburger bun. Add mustard on the top bun, along with pickles and minced onion if desired. Put the sandwich together, and heat it up in your microwave oven for 10 to 15 seconds to warm the buns. Serve with a spoon as they do in the restaurants.

• MAKES 4 SANDWICHES.

•   •   •   •

McDONALD'S FRENCH FRIES

They're the world's most famous french fries, responsible for one-third of all U.S. french fry sales, and many would say they're the best. These fried spud strips are so popular that Burger King even changed its own recipe to better compete with the secret formula from Mickey D's. One quarter of all meals served today in American restaurants come with fries; a fact that thrills restaurateurs since fries are the most profitable menu item in the food industry. Proper preparation steps were developed by McDonald's to minimize in-store preparation time, while producing a fry that is soft on the inside and crispy on the outside. To achieve this same level of texture and taste our clone requires a two-step frying technique: Once before the fries are frozen, and then once afterward before serving. Be sure to use a slicer to cut the fries for a consistent thickness (¼ inch is perfect) and for a cooking result that will make them just like the real thing. McDonald's uses a minuscule amount of beef fat in the blanching stage when preparing the french fries. But we can still get away with a great-tasting clone without having to add lard to our recipe. In the stores the chain uses only vegetable fat for the final frying step.

2 large russet potatoes
One 48-ounce can shortening
salt

RECOMMENDED
Potato slicer

1. Peel the potatoes, dry them, and slice using a mandolin or other slicer with a setting as close to ¼-inch-square strips as you've got. If your fries are a little thicker than ¼ inch the recipe will still work, but you definitely don't want super thick steak fries here.

2. Rinse the fries in a large bowl filled with around 8 cups of cold water. The water should become milky. Dump the water out and add another 8 cups of cold water plus some ice and let the fries sit for an hour.

3. Spoon the shortening into your deep fryer and turn to 375 degrees. On many fryers this is the highest setting.

4. Remove the fries from the water and spread them out on a paper towel to dry for 10 to 15 minutes. Don't let them sit much longer than this or they will begin to turn brown.

5. The shortening should now be hot enough for the blanching stage. Add bunches of the fries to the shortening for 1½ minutes at a time. Watch them carefully to be sure they don't begin to brown. If they start to brown on the edges, take 'em out. Remove the fries to a paper towel or metal rack to drain and cool. When the fries have cooled, put them into a resealable bag or covered container and freeze for 4 to 5 hours or until the potatoes are completely frozen. As the fries freeze you can turn off the fryer, but turn it back on and give it plenty of time to heat up before the final frying stage.

6. Split up the frozen fries and add one half at a time to the hot shortening. Fry for 4½ to 6 minutes or until the fries have become a golden brown color and are crispy on the outside when cool. The second batch may take a tad longer than the first, since the shortening may have cooled. Drain the fries to paper towels or a metal rack and salt generously.

• MAKES 4 SERVINGS.

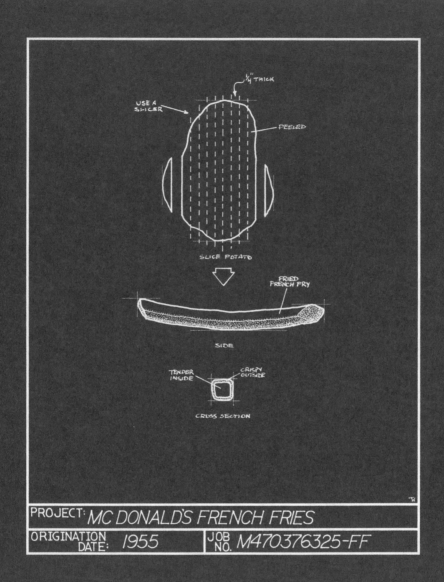

¼" THICK

USE A
SLICER

PEELED

SLICE POTATO

FRIED
FRENCH FRY

SIDE

TENDER
INSIDE

CRISPY
OUTSIDE

CROSS SECTION

PROJECT: *MC DONALD'S FRENCH FRIES*

ORIGINATION DATE: *1955*

JOB NO. *M470376325-FF*

McDONALD'S
BIG MAC

☆   ✌   💣   ✏   ☯   ✂   ☞

Brothers Dick and Mac McDonald opened the first McDonald's drive-in restaurant in 1948, in San Bernardino, California. When the brothers began to order an increasing amount of restaurant equipment for their growing business, they aroused the curiosity of milkshake-machine salesman Ray Kroc. Kroc befriended the brothers and became a franchising agent for the company that same year, opening his first McDonald's in Des Plaines, Illinois. Kroc later founded the hugely successful McDonald's Corporation and perfected the fast-food system that came to be studied and duplicated by other chains over the years.

The first day Kroc's cash register rang up $366.12. Today the company racks up about $50 million a day in sales in more than 12,000 outlets worldwide, and for the past ten years a new store has opened somewhere around the world an average of every fifteen hours.

The double-decker Big Mac was introduced in 1968, the brain-child of a local franchisee. It is now the world's most popular hamburger.

1 sesame-seed hamburger bun
half of an additional hamburger
    bun
¼ pound ground beef
dash salt
1 tablespoon Kraft Thousand
    Island dressing

1 teaspoon finely diced onion
½ cup chopped lettuce
1 slice American cheese
2 to 3 dill pickle slices

1. With a serrated knife, cut the top off the extra bun half, leaving about a ¾-inch-thick slice. This will be the middle bun in your sandwich.
2. Place the three bun halves on a hot pan or griddle, face down, and toast them to a light brown. Set aside, but keep the pan hot.
3. Divide the ground beef in half and press into two thin patties slightly larger than bun.
4. Cook the patties in the hot pan over medium heat for 2 to 3 minutes on each side. Salt lightly.
5. Build the burger in the following stacking order from the bottom up:

bottom bun	remainder of dressing
half of dressing	remainder of onion
half of onion	remainder of lettuce
half of lettuce	pickle slices
American cheese	beef patty
beef patty	top bun
middle bun	

- MAKES 1 HAMBURGER.

TIDBITS

To build a Big Mac Jr.® (it is sold on a "limited time only" basis), follow this stacking order from the bottom up:

bottom bun	½ teaspoon finely diced onion
beef patty	½ tablespoon Kraft
American cheese slice	Thousand Island dressing
2 pickle slices	top bun
¼ cup chopped lettuce	

Using real American cheese slices, not processed cheese food, will yield the best "taste-alike" results. Since the beef patties must be very thin, you may find it easier to cook them slightly frozen (like the real thing).

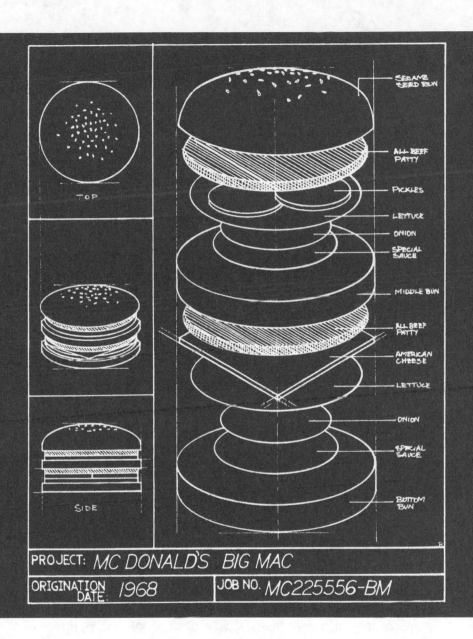

TOP

SIDE

SESAME
SEED BUN

ALL BEEF
PATTY

PICKLES

LETTUCE

ONION

SPECIAL
SAUCE

MIDDLE BUN

ALL BEEF
PATTY

AMERICAN
CHEESE

LETTUCE

ONION

SPECIAL
SAUCE

BOTTOM
BUN

PROJECT: *MC DONALD'S BIG MAC*

ORIGINATION DATE: *1968*   JOB NO. *MC225556-BM*

McDONALD'S BREAKFAST BURRITO

☆　✌　💣　✏　☯　✂　☞

It was in the late seventies, shortly after McDonald's had introduced the Egg McMuffin, that the food giant realized the potential of a quick, drive-thru breakfast. Soon, the company had developed several breakfast selections, including the Big Breakfast with eggs, hash browns, and sausage, and this morning meal in a tortilla, first offered on the menu in 1991.

4 ounces breakfast sausage
1 tablespoon minced white onion
½ tablespoon minced mild green
　chilies (canned)
4 eggs, beaten
salt

pepper
4 8-inch flour tortillas
4 slices American cheese

ON THE SIDE
salsa

1. Preheat a skillet over medium heat. Crumble the sausage into the pan, then add the onion. Sauté the sausage and onion for 3 to 4 minutes or until the sausage is browned.
2. Add the mild green chilies and continue to sauté for 1 minute.
3. Pour the beaten eggs into the pan and scramble the eggs with the sausage and vegetables. Add a dash of salt and pepper.
4. Heat up the tortillas by steaming them in the microwave in moist paper towels or a tortilla steamer for 20 to 30 seconds.
5. Break each slice of cheese in half and position two halves end-to-end in the middle of each tortilla.
6. To make the burrito, spoon ¼ of the egg filling onto the cheese in a tortilla. Fold one side of the tortilla over the filling,

then fold up about 2 inches of one end. Fold over the other side of the tortilla to complete the burrito (one end should remain open). Serve hot with salsa on the side, if desired.

- MAKES 4 BURRITOS.

• • • •

McDONALD'S
EGG McMUFFIN

☆ ✌ 💣 ✐ ☯ ✂ ☞

In March 1988 the first McDonald's in Belgrade, Yugoslavia, set an all-time opening-day record by running 6,000 people under the arches. And in early 1990, when a Moscow McDonald's opened, it became the busiest in the world by serving more than 20,000 people in just the first month of operation. The McDonald's Rome franchise racks up annual sales of more than $11 million. And in August of 1992, the world's largest McDonald's opened in China. The Beijing McDonald's seats 700 people in 28,000 square feet. It has over 1,000 employees, and parking for 200 employee bicycles. McDonald's outlets dot the globe in fifty-two countries today, including Turkey, Thailand, Panama, El Salvador, Indonesia, and Poland. In fact, about 40 percent of the McDonald's that open today stand on foreign soil—that's more than 3,000 outlets.

Back in the United States, McDonald's serves one of every four breakfasts eaten out of the home. The Egg McMuffin sandwich was introduced in 1977 and has become a convenient breakfast-in-a-sandwich for millions. The name for the sandwich was not the brainstorm of a corporate think tank as you would expect, but rather a suggestion from ex-McDonald's chairman and CEO Fred Turner. He says his wife Patty came up with it.

You will need an empty, clean can with the same diameter as an English muffin. (A 6½-ounce tuna can works best.)

1 English muffin
1 slice Canadian bacon

1 egg
1 slice American cheese

1. Split the English muffin and brown each face in a hot pan. Set aside. Keep the pan on medium heat.
2. In a frying pan of boiling water, cook the Canadian bacon for 10 minutes.
3. Grease the inside of the can with shortening or coat with a nonstick spray.
4. Place the greased can in the hot pan over medium heat and crack the egg into the center.
5. Break the yolk. Lightly salt the egg.
6. When the surface of the egg begins to firm, cut around the inside of the can with a butter knife to free the edges.
7. Pull the can off the egg; turn the egg over and cook for 1 minute more.
8. Build the sandwich in the following stacking order from the bottom up:
   bottom English muffin   Canadian bacon
   American cheese   top English muffin
   egg
9. Microwave for 15 to 20 seconds on high for uniform heating, if desired.

• MAKES 1 SANDWICH.

TIDBITS

For a closer clone, use real American cheese slices, not processed cheese food.

• • • •

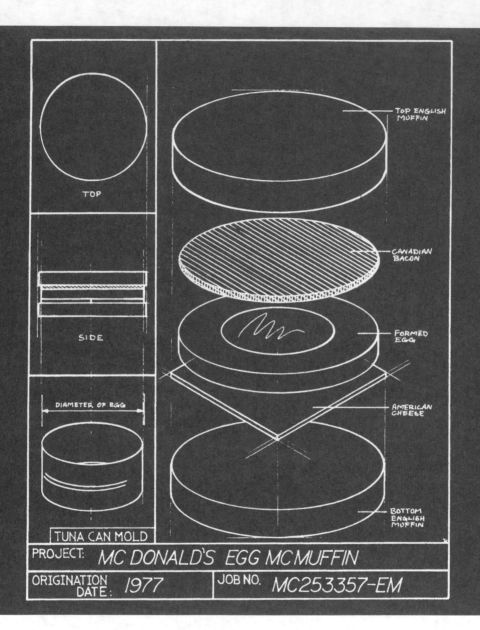

TOP

SIDE

DIAMETER OF EGG

TUNA CAN MOLD

TOP ENGLISH MUFFIN

CANADIAN BACON

FORMED EGG

AMERICAN CHEESE

BOTTOM ENGLISH MUFFIN

PROJECT: MC DONALD'S EGG MC MUFFIN

ORIGINATION DATE: 1977

JOB NO. MC253357-EM

McDONALD'S FILET-O-FISH

☆   ✌   💣   ✏   ☯   ✂   ☞

The year 1963 was a big one in McDonald's history. The 500th McDonald's restaurant opened in Toledo, Ohio, and Hamburger University graduated its 500th student. It was in that same year that McDonald's served its one billionth hamburger in grand fashion on *The Art Linkletter Show*. Ronald McDonald also made his debut that year in Washington, D.C. (one of Willard Scott's earlier jobs—he hasn't changed much). And the Filet-O-Fish sandwich was introduced as the first new menu addition since the restaurant chain opened in 1948.

2 tablespoons mayonnaise
2 teaspoons sweet relish
2 teaspoons minced onion
pinch salt

2 plain hamburger buns
2 Mrs. Paul's breaded fish portions
   (square)
1 slice American cheese

1. In a small bowl, mix together the mayonnaise, relish, minced onion, and salt and set aside. This is your tartar sauce.
2. Lightly grill the faces of the buns.
3. Cook the fish according to the package instructions. You can bake the fish, but your sandwich will taste much more like the original if you fry it in oil.
4. Divide the tartar sauce and spread it evenly on each of the top buns.
5. Slice the cheese in half and place a piece on each of the bottom buns.

6. Place the cooked fish on top of the cheese slice on each sandwich, and top off the sandwiches with the top buns.
7. Microwave each sandwich on high for 10 seconds.

• MAKES 2 SANDWICHES.

TIDBITS

If you can find fish only in wedge shapes, just use two wedges on each sandwich, fitting them together side by side to form a square.

•   •   •   •

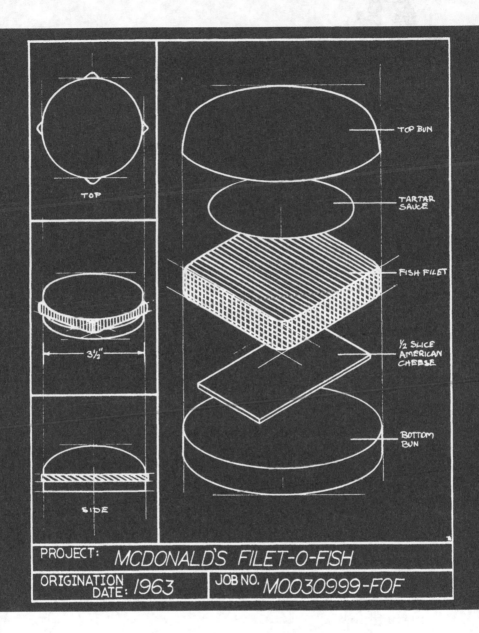

TOP

3½"

SIDE

TOP BUN

TARTAR SAUCE

FISH FILET

½ SLICE AMERICAN CHEESE

BOTTOM BUN

PROJECT: *MCDONALD'S FILET-O-FISH*

ORIGINATION DATE: *1963*

JOB NO. *M0030999-FOF*

TOP SECRET RECIPES
VERSION OF
McDONALD'S
LOBSTER SANDWICH

On an excursion through Maine I practically drove off the road when I first saw a sign advertising a lobster sandwich at the world's most famous hamburger chain. I just had to get a closer look. That's when I discovered that this unique sandwich is served only at select McDonald's locations, mostly in New England, for a limited time only during the summer months. It turns out this is a lobster salad served on a hoagie roll with some lettuce. Simple enough. Since this sandwich is so limited in its availability, it's a perfect candidate for home cloning.

½ cup cooked Maine lobster,
   chilled
½ tablespoon mayonnaise

pinch salt
small hoagie roll
1 lettuce leaf

1. Mix together lobster, mayonnaise, and salt.
2. Slice the hoagie roll lengthwise, and spread the lettuce leaf on the bottom half.
3. Spread lobster over lettuce. Top off sandwich with the top half of the roll.

• MAKES 1 SANDWICH.

TIDBITS

If you don't want to use fresh lobster, you can use canned Maine lobster that can often be found in many supermarkets.

• • • •

PANDA EXPRESS
MANDARIN CHICKEN

☆ ✌ 💣 ✏ ☯ ✄ ☞

Here's a dish from a rapidly growing Chinese food chain that should satisfy anyone who loves the famous marinated bourbon chicken found in food courts across America. The sauce is the whole thing here, and it's quick to make right on your own stovetop. Just fire up the barbecue or indoor grill for the chicken and whip up a little white rice to serve on the side. Panda Express—now 370 restaurants strong—is the fastest-growing Asian food chain in the world. You'll find these tasty little quick-service food outlets in supermarkets, casinos, sports arenas, college campuses, and malls across the country passing out free samples for the asking.

⅔ cup sugar
¼ cup soy sauce
1 tablespoon lemon juice
1 teaspoon vegetable oil
1 teaspoon minced fresh garlic
½ teaspoon minced fresh ginger

¼ cup water
4 teaspoons arrowroot
6 skinless chicken thigh fillets

ON THE SIDE
steamed white rice

1. Combine sugar, soy sauce, lemon juice, oil, garlic, and ginger in a small saucepan. Combine water with arrowroot in a small bowl and stir until arrowroot is dissolved. Add to saucepan and turn heat to high. Stir often while bringing mixture to a boil, then reduce heat and simmer for 4 to 6 minutes or until sauce is thick.
2. Preheat your grill on high for the chicken.

3. When the grill is hot, rub each chicken piece with oil and cook the chicken for 4 to 6 minutes per side or until completely cooked. Chicken should have browned in spots.
4. When chicken is done, chop it into bite-size pieces. Pour the chicken pieces into a large frying pan over medium heat. Heat until chicken sizzles, then reduce heat and cover chicken until ready to serve. Spoon chicken into a medium bowl, then pour all the sauce over the chicken and stir until well coated. Serve with steamed white rice.

- SERVES 4.

• • • •

PANDA EXPRESS ORANGE FLAVORED CHICKEN

As far as Chinese food goes, I think the stuff these guys throw together in sizzling woks is surprisingly tasty for a takeout chain. This dish is something of a twist on the traditional sweet-and-sour chicken commonly found at Chinese restaurants over the years. This popular menu item has a delicious, citrus-laced, tangy-sweet sauce with a spicy nip the regulars find truly addictive. The chain claims to cook all of its food in woks, including the sauces. But this homegrown version will work fine—whether you go for a wok, or not.

SAUCE

1 ½ cups water
2 tablespoons orange juice
1 cup packed dark brown sugar
⅓ cup rice vinegar
2½ tablespoons soy sauce
¼ cup plus 1 teaspoon lemon juice
1 teaspoon minced water chestnuts
½ teaspoon minced fresh ginger
¼ teaspoon minced garlic
1 rounded teaspoon chopped green onion
¼ teaspoon crushed red pepper flakes

5 teaspoons cornstarch
2 teaspoons arrowroot
3 tablespoons water

CHICKEN

4 skinless chicken breast fillets
1 cup ice water
1 egg
¼ teaspoon baking soda
¼ teaspoon salt
1½ cups unsifted cake flour

2 to 4 cups vegetable oil

1. Combine all of the sauce ingredients except the cornstarch, arrowroot, and 3 tablespoons of water in a small saucepan over high heat. Stir often while bringing mixture to a boil. When sauce reaches a boil, remove it from heat and allow it to cool a bit, uncovered.

2. Slice chicken breasts into bite-size chunks. Remove exactly 1 cup of the marinade from the pan and pour it over the chicken in a large resealable plastic bag or another container that allows the chicken to be completely covered with the marinade. The chicken should marinate for at least a couple hours. Cover the remaining sauce and leave it to cool until the chicken is ready.

3. When chicken has marinated, preheat 2 inches of vegetable oil in a wok or skillet to 350 degrees.

4. Combine cornstarch with arrowroot in a small bowl, then add 3 tablespoons of water. Stir until cornstarch and arrowroot have dissolved. Pour this mixture into the sauce and set the pan over high heat. When sauce begins to bubble and thicken, cover and remove it from heat.

5. Beat together the ice water and egg in a medium bowl. Add baking soda and salt.

6. Add ¾ cup of the flour and stir with a fork just until the flour is blended into the mixture. The batter should still be lumpy.

7. Sprinkle another ¼ cup of flour on top of the batter and mix it up with only one or two strokes. Most of the new flour will still be floating on top of the mixture. Put the remaining flour (½ cup) into a separate medium bowl.

8. Dip each piece of chicken first into the flour, then into the batter. Let some of the batter drip off and then slide the chicken into the oil. Fry up to ½ of the chicken pieces at a time for 3 to 4 minutes, or until golden brown. Flip the chicken over halfway through cooking time. Remove the chicken to a rack or paper towels to drain.

9. As the chicken cooks, reheat the sauce left covered on the stove. Stir occasionally.

10. When all of the chicken is done, pour it into a large bowl, and cover with the thickened sauce. Stir gently until all of the pieces are well coated.

• SERVES 4.

• • • •

TOP SECRET RECIPES
VERSION OF
POPEYES
BUTTERMILK BISCUITS

☆ ✌ 💣 ✏ 🎱 ✂ ☞

In 2001, the number one Cajun-style restaurant celebrated its 30th birthday with 1,620 stores worldwide. But Popeyes didn't start out with the name that most people associate with a certain spinach-eating cartoon character. When Al Copeland opened his first Southern-fried-chicken stand in New Orleans in 1972, it was called Chicken on the Run. The name was later changed to "Popeyes" after Gene Hackman's character in the movie "The French Connection." In addition to great, spicy fried chicken, Popeyes serves up wonderful biscuits that we can now easily duplicate at home. The secret is to cut cold butter into the mix with a pastry knife so that the biscuits turn out flaky and tender like the real deal.

2 cups all-purpose flour
1 tablespoon sugar
1 ½ teaspoons salt
1 ½ teaspoons baking powder
½ teaspoon baking soda
½ cup butter, cold (1 stick)

½ cup buttermilk
¼ cup milk

TO BRUSH ON TOP
2 tablespoons butter, melted

1. Preheat oven to 400°F.
2. Mix together flour, sugar, salt, baking powder, and baking soda in a medium bowl.
3. Slice cold butter into cubes and use a pastry knife or potato masher to cut butter into dry mixture until no large chunks of butter remain.
4. Add buttermilk and milk and stir with a spoon until dough forms. Roll out to ½-inch thick on a floured surface.
5. Cut biscuits with a 3-inch biscuit cutter and arrange on a lightly greased or parchment paper–lined baking sheet. Bake for 22 to 24 minutes or until tops begin to turn light brown. Remove biscuits from the oven and cool for a couple of minutes, then brush each biscuit top with melted butter.

• MAKES 10 BISCUITS.

• • • •

TOP SECRET RECIPES
VERSION OF
POPEYES
CAJUN GRAVY

Chicken gizzard. It took more than ten years to get around to cloning a recipe that absolutely requires chicken gizzard. I've seen the official ingredients list for the Cajun gravy from Popeyes, and if we're gonna do this one right there's just got to be some gizzard in there. Pour this delicious creamy stuff over the Popeyes Buttermilk Biscuits clone that precedes this one, or onto whatever begs to be swimming in pure flavor. Cajun or not, get ready for some of the best gravy that's ever come off your stovetop.

1 tablespoon vegetable oil	2 teaspoons milk
1 chicken gizzard	2 teaspoons distilled white vinegar
2½ ounces ground beef (¼ cup)	1 teaspoon sugar
2½ ounces ground pork (¼ cup)	1 teaspoon salt
2 tablespoons minced green bell pepper	½ teaspoon coarse ground black pepper
2 cups water	¼ teaspoon cayenne pepper
14-ounce can Swanson beef broth	⅛ teaspoon garlic powder
2 tablespoons corn starch	⅛ teaspoon onion powder
1 tablespoon flour	dash dried parsley flakes

1. Heat 1 tablespoon vegetable oil in a large saucepan over medium heat. Sauté chicken gizzard in the oil for 4 to 5 minutes until cooked. Remove gizzard from the pan and let it cool so that you can handle it. Finely mince the chicken gizzard.

2. Combine ground beef and ground pork in a small bowl. Smash the meat together with your hands until it's well-mixed. Add bell pepper to the saucepan and sauté it for 1 minute. Add ground beef and pork to the pan and cook it until it's brown. Use a potato masher to smash meat into tiny rice-size pieces as it browns.
3. Add water and beef broth to the pan. Immediately whisk in cornstarch and flour.
4. Add remaining ingredients and bring the mixture to a boil. Reduce heat and simmer gravy for 30 to 35 minutes or until thick.

• MAKES 3 CUPS.

• • • •

POPEYES
FAMOUS
FRIED CHICKEN

☆   ✌   💣   ✏   ☯   ✂   ☞

Popeyes Famous Fried Chicken & Biscuits has become the third largest quick-service chicken chain in the world in the twenty-two years since its first store opened in New Orleans in 1972. (KFC has the number-one slot, followed by Church's Chicken.) Since then, the chain has grown to 813 units, with many of them overseas in Germany, Japan, Jamaica, Honduras, Guam, and Korea.

I picked this recipe because the chicken has a unique Cajun-style spiciness. See what you think.

6 cups vegetable oil
⅔ cup all-purpose flour
1 tablespoon salt
2 tablespoons white pepper

1 teaspoon cayenne pepper
2 teaspoons paprika
3 eggs
1 frying chicken with skin, cut up

1. Heat the oil over medium heat in a deep frying or in a wide, deep pan on the stove.
2. In a large, shallow bowl, combine the flour, salt, peppers, and paprika.
3. Break the eggs into a separate shallow bowl and beat until blended.
4. Check the oil by dropping in a pinch of the flour mixture. If the oil bubbles rapidly around the flour, it is ready.

5. Dip each piece of chicken into the eggs, then coat generously with the flour mixture. Drop each piece into the hot oil and fry for 15 to 25 minutes, or until it is a dark golden brown.
6. Remove the chicken to paper towels or a rack to drain.

• MAKES 8 PIECES.

• • • •

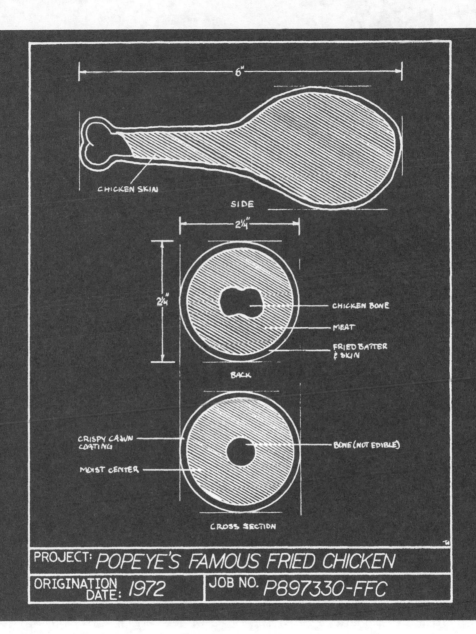

CHICKEN SKIN

6"

SIDE

2¼"

2¼"

CHICKEN BONE

MEAT

FRIED BATTER & SKIN

BACK

CRISPY CAJUN COATING

BONE (NOT EDIBLE)

MOIST CENTER

CROSS SECTION

PROJECT: *POPEYE'S FAMOUS FRIED CHICKEN*

ORIGINATION DATE: *1972*

JOB NO. *P897330-FFC*

TOP SECRET RECIPES
VERSION OF
POPEYES
RED BEANS & RICE
(IMPROVED)

☆   ✌   💣   ✏   ☯   ✂   ☞

I created the clone for this recipe back in 1994 for the second TSR book, *More Top Secret Recipes,* but I've never been absolutely pleased with the end result, and vowed to one day rework it. After recently convincing a Popeyes manager to show me the ingredients written on the box of red bean mixture, I determined that the best way to clone this one accurately is to include an important ingredient omitted from the first version: pork fat. Emeril screams "pork fat rules" on his cooking show all the time, and now we get to play with the stuff here at TSR. After some work, I found a good way to get the best flavor from the right type of fat is to render it from smoked ham hocks. Ham hocks, which are pretty cheap at most markets, are placed in the oven for several hours so that the fat drains out. There's your rendering. If you don't feel like waiting around for four or five hours while ham hocks render, you can also use ¼ cup of the bacon grease that's left over from breakfast. As for the beans, find red beans (they're smaller than kidney beans) in two 15-ounce cans. If you're having trouble tracking down red beans, red kidney beans will substitute splendidly.

BEANS

2 pounds smoked ham hocks
2 15-ounce cans red beans
½ cup water
½ teaspoon brown sugar
⅛ teaspoon salt
dash garlic powder
dash onion powder

RICE

2¼ cups water
¼ cup butter
¼ teaspoon salt
1 cup converted rice

1. First you must render the fat from the smoked ham hocks. Preheat oven to 375 degrees and place the ham hocks in a deep pan. Cover pan with foil and bake for 4 to 5 hours or until ¼ cup of fat has rendered from the hocks (you may substitute with ¼ cup of bacon grease).

2. Combine ¼ cup pork fat with one 15-ounce can red beans plus liquid in a medium saucepan. Add ½ cup water, brown sugar, ⅛ teaspoon salt, garlic powder, and onion powder. Bring mixture to a boil, then reduce heat and simmer for 20 minutes. Use a potato masher to smash beans into a pastelike consistency. Add entire contents of remaining can of beans to the mixture and cook for an additional 10 minutes or until thick.

3. Prepare rice for 4 servings. For Uncle Ben's converted rice you bring 2¼ cups water to a boil. Add ¼ cup butter and ¼ teaspoon salt. Add 1 cup of rice, reduce heat to low, and simmer rice for 20 minutes or until tender.

4. To prepare each serving, scoop ½ cup of beans into a bowl. Add ½ cup of rice on top of the beans and serve.

• MAKES 4 REGULAR-SIZE SERVINGS.

• • • •

TOP SECRET RECIPES
VERSION OF
SKYLINE
CHILI

Nope, there's no chocolate in it. Or coffee. Or Coca-Cola. The ingredient rumors for Skyline Chili are plentiful on the Internet, but anyone can purchase cans of Skyline chili from the company and find the ingredients listed right on the label: beef, water, tomato paste, dried torula yeast, salt, spices, corn starch, and natural flavors. You can trust that if chocolate were included in the secret recipe, the label would reflect it—that's something that comes in handy for those with a chocolate allergy. So go ahead and eat your chocolate bar then wash it down with Coca-Cola, since all it takes to re-create the unique flavor of Skyline is a special blend of easy-to-find spices plus some beef broth. Let the chili simmer for an hour or so, then serve it up on its own or in one of the traditional Cincinnati-style serving suggestions (the "ways" they call 'em) with the chili poured over cooked spaghetti noodles, topped with grated cheddar cheese and other good stuff:

3-Way: Pour chili over cooked spaghetti noodles and top with grated cheddar cheese.

4-Way: Add a couple teaspoons of grated onion before adding the cheese.

5-Way: Add cooked red beans over the onions before adding the cheese.

1 pound ground beef
2 14.5-ounce cans Swanson beef
   broth
½ cup water
6-ounce can tomato paste
2 tablespoons cornstarch
4 teaspoons chili powder
1 tablespoon white distilled
   vinegar

1¼ teaspoons salt
1 teaspoon cardamom
1 teaspoon nutmeg
¼ teaspoon allspice
¼ teaspoon cayenne pepper
¼ teaspoon coriander
¼ teaspoon garlic powder
⅛ teaspoon ground black pepper
⅛ teaspoon ground cinnamon

1. Brown ground beef in a large saucepan over medium heat. Do not drain. Use a potato masher to mash the ground beef into very small pieces that are about the size of uncooked rice.
2. Turn off the heat, then add the rest of the ingredients to the pan. Whisk the ingredients so that the tomato paste and cornstarch is mixed in. Crank heat back up to medium and bring mixture to a boil. Reduce heat and simmer for 60 to 75 minutes or until thick.

• MAKES 5 CUPS.

• • • •

TOP SECRET RECIPES
VERSION OF
"THE SOUP NAZI"'S CRAB BISQUE

☆   ✌   💣   ✎   ☯   ✂   ☞

New Yorkers have lined up around the block for years now to get a hot cup of Al Yeganeh's delicious soup at Soup Kitchen International. Many are familiar with the demands: "Pick the soup you want!", "Have your money ready!", and "Move to the *extreme* left after ordering!" Customers know if they don't stick to the rules, they'll be quickly scolded and may not get served; even after waiting for as long as two hours to get to the front of the line. This is precisely how the nonsmiling Yeganeh was portrayed by actor Larry Thomas in *Seinfeld* episode number 115, when he forever became known as "The Soup Nazi."

4 pounds snow crab clusters (legs)
4 quarts water (16 cups)
1 small onion, chopped
1½ stalks celery, chopped
2 cloves garlic, quartered
2 potatoes, peeled and chopped
¼ cup fresh chopped Italian
    parsley
2 teaspoons mustard seed
1 tablespoon chopped pimento

½ teaspoon coarse ground
    pepper
2 bay leaves
⅓ cup tomato sauce
2 tablespoons half-and-half
¼ cup unsalted butter
¼ teaspoon thyme
⅛ teaspoon basil
⅛ teaspoon marjoram

1. Remove all the crab meat from the shells and set it aside.
2. Put half the shells into a large pot with 4 quarts of water over high heat. Add onion, 1 stalk of chopped celery, and garlic, then bring mixture to a boil. Continue to boil for 1 hour, stirring occasionally (the white part of the shells will start to become transparent), then strain stock. Discard the shells, onion, celery, and garlic, keeping only the stock.
3. Measure 3 quarts (12 cups) of the stock into a large saucepan or cooking pot. If you don't have enough stock, add enough water to make 3 quarts.
4. Add potatoes, bring mixture to a boil, then add ½ of the crab and the remaining ingredients to the pot and bring it back to boiling. Reduce heat and simmer for 4 hours, uncovered, until it reduces by about half and starts to thicken. Add the remaining crab and simmer for another hour until the soup is very thick.

• MAKES 4–6 SERVINGS.

•   •   •   •

TOP SECRET RECIPES
VERSION OF
"THE SOUP NAZI"'S CREAM OF SWEET POTATO SOUP

☆   ✌   💣   ✏   ☯   ✂   ☞

Posted above the counter of the take-out-only Soup Kitchen International in New York City is a sign laying out the important three steps to properly buying soup: "Pick the soup you want!", "Have your money ready!", and "Move to the *extreme* left after ordering!" Knowing that to violate the rules is to risk being refused service, I decided to ask owner Al Yeganeh a few questions about the November 1995 *Seinfeld* episode that made him famous. Needless to say, the interview was very brief:

> TW: How do you feel about all the publicity that followed the *Seinfeld* episode?
> AY: I didn't need it. I was known well enough before that. I don't need it.

> TW: But it must have been good for business, right?
> AY: He [Seinfeld] used me. He used me. I didn't use him, he used me.

> TW: How many people do you serve in a day?
> AY: I cannot talk to you. If I talk, I cannot work.

> TW: How many different soups do you serve?
> AY: (getting very upset) I cannot talk (pointing to sign). Move to the left. Next!

I felt truly honored to have been yelled at by the Soup Nazi himself. Here now is a clone of one of Al's popular selections, Cream of Sweet Potato Soup.

4 sweet potatoes
   (about 1 pound each)
8 cups water
1/3 cup butter
1/2 cup tomato sauce

2 tablespoons half-and-half
2 teaspoons salt
1/8 teaspoon pepper
dash thyme
1 cup cashews (split in half)

1. Preheat oven to 400°F. Bake the sweet potatoes for 45 minutes or until they are soft. Cool the potatoes until they can be handled.
2. Peel away the skin, then put the potatoes into a large bowl. Mash the potatoes for 15–20 seconds, but you don't need to mash them until they are entirely smooth.
3. Spoon the mashed sweet potato into a large saucepan over medium/high heat, add the remaining ingredients and stir to combine.
4. When the soup begins to boil, reduce the heat and simmer for 50–60 minutes. Cashews should be soft. Serve hot with attitude.

• MAKES 6–8 SERVINGS.

• • • •

TOP SECRET RECIPES

VERSION OF

"THE SOUP NAZI"'S INDIAN MULLIGATAWNY

☆　✌　💣　✏　☯　✂　☞

Elaine: "Do you need anything?"

Kramer: "Oh, a hot bowl of Mulligatawny would hit the spot."

Elaine: "Mulligatawny?"

Kramer: "Yeah, it's an Indian soup. Simmered to perfection by one of the great soup artisans in the modern era."

Elaine: "Oh. Who, the Soup Nazi?"

Kramer: "He's not a Nazi. He just happens to be a little eccentric. You know, most geniuses are."

Kramer was right. Al Yeganeh—otherwise known as the Soup Nazi from the *Seinfeld* episode that aired in 1995—is a master at the soup kettle. His popular soup creations have inspired many inferior copycats in the Big Apple, including The Soup Nutsy, only 10 blocks away. Yeganeh's mastery shows when he combines sometimes unusual ingredients to create unique and delicious flavors in his much-raved-about soups. In this one, you may be surprised when you discover pistachios and cashews among the many vegetables. But it's a combination that works.

A few years back, I took a trip to New York and tasted around a dozen of the Soup Nazi's creations. The Mulligatawny was among my faves. After each daily trip to Soup Nazi headquarters, I immediately headed back to the hotel and poured samples of the soups into labeled, sealed containers that were then chilled for the trip back home. There, in the "lab," portions of the soup were rinsed through a sieve and ingredients were identified. After that, it was a matter of trial and error figuring out the measurements for those ingredients. The result was a successful clone that I can now share with you. Just be sure when you make this soup that you simmer it for at least four hours or until the soup reduces by more than half. The soup will darken as the flavors intensify, the potatoes will begin to fall apart, and the nuts will soften. If you follow these directions, you should end up with a clone that would fool even Cosmo himself

4 quarts water (16 cups)
6 cups chicken stock
2 potatoes, peeled and sliced
2 carrots, peeled and sliced
2 stalks celery, with tops
2 cups peeled and diced eggplant
    (about ½ of an eggplant)
1 medium onion, chopped
1 cup frozen yellow corn
⅔ cup canned roasted red
    pepper, diced
½ cup tomato sauce
½ cup shelled pistachios

½ cup roasted cashews
½ cup chopped fresh Italian
    parsley
¼ cup lemon juice
¼ cup butter
3 tablespoons sugar
½ teaspoon curry powder
½ teaspoon pepper
¼ teaspoon thyme
1 bay leaf
dash marjoram
dash nutmeg

1. Combine all ingredients in a large pot over high heat.
2. Bring to a boil, then reduce heat and simmer for 4–5 hours or until soup has reduced by more than half, and is thick and brownish in color. It should have the consistency of chili. Stir occasionally for the first few hours, but stir often in the last hour. The edges of the potatoes should become more rounded, and the nuts will soften. Serve hot.

- MAKES 4–6 SERVINGS.

Because of the extreme reduction, I found that the salt in the chicken stock was enough for the recipe. However, if you use a stock that isn't so salty, you may find you need to add extra salt to the soup.

•　•　•　•

TOP SECRET RECIPES
VERSION OF
"THE SOUP NAZI"'S
MEXICAN CHICKEN CHILI

☆ ✌ 💣 ✐ ☯ ✂ ☞

In Zagat's New York City Restaurant Survey, Le Cirque 2000, one of the city's most upscale restaurants, received a 25 rating out of a possible 30. In the same guide, Al "The Soup Nazi" Yeganeh's International Soup Kitchen scored a whopping 27. That puts the Soup Nazi's eatery in 14th place among the city's best restaurants!

It's common to see lines stretching around the corner and down the block as hungry patrons wait for their cup of one of five daily hot-soup selections. Most of the selections change every day, but of the three days that I was there doing research, the Mexican Chicken Chili was always on the menu. The first two days it was sold out before I got to the front of the line. But on the last day, I got lucky, "One extra-large Mexican Chicken Chili, please." Hand over money, move to the extreme left.

So here now is a clone for what has apparently become one of the Soup Nazi's most popular culinary masterpieces. The secret to this soup, as with many of his creations, seems to be the long simmering time. If you like, you can substitute turkey breast for the chicken to make turkey chili, which was the soup George Costanza ordered on the show.

1 pound chicken breast fillets (4 fillets)	10 cups water
1 tablespoon olive oil	2 cups chicken stock
	½ cup tomato sauce

1 potato, peeled and chopped
1 small onion, diced
1 cup frozen yellow corn
½ carrot, sliced
1 celery stalk, diced
1 cup canned diced tomatoes
1 15-ounce can red kidney beans,
    plus liquid
¼ cup diced canned pimento
1 jalapeño, diced
¼ cup chopped Italian parsley

1 clove garlic, minced
1½ teaspoons chili powder
1 teaspoon cumin
¼ teaspoon salt
dash cayenne pepper
dash basil
dash oregano

ON THE SIDE
sour cream
pinch chopped Italian parsley

1. Sauté the chicken breasts in the olive oil in a large pot over medium/high heat. Cook the chicken on both sides until done—about 7–10 minutes per side. Cool the chicken until it can be handled. Do not rinse the pot.
2. Shred the chicken by hand into bite-size pieces and place the pieces back into the pot.
3. Add the remaining ingredients to the pot and turn heat to high. Bring mixture to a boil, then reduce heat and simmer for 4–5 hours. Stir mixture often so that many of the chicken pieces shred into much smaller bits. Chili should reduce substantially to thicken and darken (less orange, more brown) when done.
4. Combine some chopped Italian parsley with sour cream and serve it on the side for topping the chili, if desired.

• MAKES 4–6 SERVINGS.

•   •   •   •

TOP SECRET RECIPES
VERSION OF
STARBUCKS
CLASSIC COFFEE CAKE

☆　✌　💣　🖊　☯　✂　☞

A good coffee house will have good coffee cake, and Starbucks is no exception. The world's biggest coffee house chain offers cake that is tasty and moist, with a perfect cinnamon streusel crumb topping that goes great with a hot cup of joe. Since Starbucks works with local bakeries, you may find slight variations of the cake at different Starbucks locations. Sometimes there is a ribbon of cinnamon running through the middle of the cake, and sometimes the cake is dusted with a bit of powdered sugar. You'll also find some versions with a few chopped pecans in the topping; and that's the version cloned here. You can certainly leave the pecans out if you like yours a bit less nutty.

TOPPING

1 cup all-purpose flour
1 cup light brown sugar, packed
1/2 cup butter, softened
1 teaspoon cinnamon
1/2 cup chopped pecans

1 cup butter, softened
3/4 cup light brown sugar, packed

1/2 cup granulated sugar
2 eggs
1 1/2 teaspoons vanilla
2 cups all-purpose flour
1 teaspoon baking powder
1/4 teaspoon salt
1/3 cup milk

1. Preheat oven to 325°F.
2. Make topping by combining 1 cup flour with brown sugar, a stick of softened butter, and 1 teaspoon cinnamon in a medium bowl. Mixture should have the consistency of moist sand. Add ½ cup chopped pecans.
3. In a large bowl, cream together 1 cup butter, ¾ cup light brown sugar, and ½ cup granulated sugar with an electric mixer until smooth and fluffy. Add eggs and vanilla and mix well.
4. In a separate bowl, combine flour, baking powder, and salt. Add this dry mixture to the moist ingredients a little bit at a time. Add milk and mix well.
5. Spoon the batter into a 9 x 13–inch baking pan that has been buttered and dusted with a light coating of flour.
6. Sprinkle the crumb topping over the batter. Be sure the topping completely covers the batter.
7. Bake cake for 50 minutes, or until the edges just begin to turn light brown. Cool and slice into 8 pieces.

- SERVES 8.

• • • •

TOP SECRET RECIPES
VERSION OF
STARBUCKS
CRANBERRY BLISS BAR

☆ ✌ 💣 ✏ ☯ ✂ ☞

Each holiday season Starbucks brings out one of its most beloved dessert recipes: a soft triangle of white chocolate and cranberry cake, covered with delicious creamy lemon frosting and dried cranberries. But, when the holidays leave us, so do the Cranberry Bliss Bars, and that's when the dozens of requests to clone the dessert start rolling in here at TSR. Each of the more than 3,500 Starbucks stores contracts with local bakeries so that the Bliss Bars are fresh for customers each day. The end result may vary slightly from city to city, but the basic recipe is the same, and it rules. Now you can get your Bliss Bar fix anytime of the year, at a fraction of the cost of the real thing, with a little sneaky kitchen cloning.

CAKE
1 cup (2 sticks) butter, softened
1 1/4 cups light brown sugar, packed
3 eggs
1 1/2 teaspoons vanilla
1 teaspoon ginger
1/4 teaspoon salt
1 1/2 cups all-purpose flour
3/4 cup dried cranberries, diced

6 ounces white chocolate, cut into
 chunks

FROSTING
4 ounces cream cheese, softened
3 cups powdered sugar
4 teaspoons lemon juice
1/2 teaspoon vanilla extract

TOPPING

¼ cup dried cranberries, diced

DRIZZLED ICING

½ cup powdered sugar
1 tablespoon milk
2 teaspoons vegetable shortening

1. Preheat oven to 350°F.
2. Make cake by beating butter and brown sugar together with an electric mixer until smooth. Add eggs, vanilla, ginger, and salt and beat well. Mix in flour until smooth. Mix ¾ cup diced dried cranberries and white chocolate into the batter by hand. Pour batter into a greased 9 x 13–inch baking pan. Use a spatula to spread the batter evenly across the pan. Bake for 35 to 40 minutes or until cake is light brown on the edges. Allow the cake to cool.
3. Make frosting by combining softened cream cheese, 3 cups powdered sugar, lemon juice, and vanilla extract in a medium bowl with an electric mixer until smooth. When the cake has cooled, use a spatula to spread frosting over the top of the cake.
4. Sprinkle ¼ cup of diced cranberries over the frosting on the cake.
5. Whisk together ½ cup powdered sugar, 1 tablespoon milk, and shortening until smooth. Drizzle icing over the cranber-ries in a sweeping motion or use a pastry bag with a fine tip to drizzle frosting across the top of the cake.
6. Allow cake to sit for several hours, then slice the cake length-wise (the long way) once through the middle. Slice the cake across the width three times, making a total of 8 rectangular slices. Slice each of those 8 slices once diagonally, creating 16 triangular slices.

- MAKES 16 BARS.

• • • •

TOP SECRET RECIPES
VERSION OF
SUBWAY
SWEET ONION SAUCE

☆   ✌   💣   ✏   ☯   ✂   ☞

The Sweet Onion Chicken Teriyaki Sandwich is one of Subway's biggest new product rollouts. The sandwich is made with common ingredients: Teriyaki glazed chicken-breast strips, onions, lettuce, tomatoes, green peppers, and olives. But what sets it apart from all other teriyaki chicken sandwiches is Subway's delicious Sweet Onion Sauce. You can ask for as much of the scrumptious sauce as you want on your custom-made sub at the huge sandwich chain, but you won't get any extra to take home, even if you offer to pay. Now, with this recipe, you can add a clone version of the sauce to your home-built sandwich masterpieces whenever you want.

½ cup light corn syrup
1 tablespoon minced white onion
1 tablespoon red wine vinegar
2 teaspoons white distilled vinegar
1 teaspoon balsamic vinegar
1 teaspoon brown sugar

1 teaspoon buttermilk powder
¼ teaspoon lemon juice
⅛ teaspoon poppy seeds
⅛ teaspoon salt
pinch cracked black pepper
pinch garlic powder

1. Combine all ingredients in a small microwave-safe bowl.
2. Heat mixture uncovered in the microwave for 1 to 1 ½ minutes on high until mixture boils rapidly.
3. Whisk well, cover, and cool.

• MAKES ABOUT ⅔ CUP.

• • • •

TOP SECRET RECIPES
VERSION OF
TACO BELL
BAJA SAUCE

This is the spicy sauce that you can order on your Gordita or Chalupa at Taco Bell, but you won't get much extra sauce—even if you order it on the side—to use later at home. That's too bad since this stuff is good enough to use on all sorts of homemade Mexican masterpieces, from tacos to fajitas to breakfast burritos. Now, with this original TSR clone of the creamy sauce, you'll have enough to hold you over for a while. You need a food processor to puree the vegetables, but don't expect to use all the puree. I've made the measurements for the puree larger than required so that your food processor will have something to grab on to. And, by the way, this is a mayo-based sauce, so if you want to knock down the fat grams, use light mayonnaise in the recipe. You won't even be able to tell the difference.

1/4 of a red bell pepper, seeded
   and coarsely chopped
1 large jalapeño, chopped in half
2 tablespoons diced Spanish onion
1 cup mayonnaise

1 tablespoon vinegar
1/4 teaspoon cracked black pepper
dash garlic powder
dash cumin

1. Using a food processor, puree peppers and onion.
2. Mix 1 cup mayonnaise and 4 teaspoons of the vegetable puree in a medium bowl. Add remaining ingredients and mix well. Chill for several hours to let flavors develop.

• MAKES 1 CUP.

•   •   •   •

TOP SECRET RECIPES

VERSION OF

TACO BELL
MILD BORDER SAUCE

☆   ✌   💣   ✏   ☯   ✂   ☞

If you like the flavor of Taco Bell's sauce, but don't like the burn, this is the sauce for you to clone. It used to be that you could only get this sauce in the little blister packs from Taco Bell restaurants, but now the chain has partnered with Kraft Foods to sell the stuff in 7.5-ounce bottles in most supermarkets. For the record, those bottles of hot sauce will set you back around $1.59 at the store, while the 6-ounce can of tomato paste required for this recipe is only 59 cents—and you end up with more than three times the amount of sauce!

3 cups water
2 teaspoons cornstarch
1 6-ounce can tomato paste
3 tablespoons white distilled
    vinegar

4 teaspoons chili powder
2 teaspoons salt
1 teaspoon cayenne pepper

1. Dissolve cornstarch in water in a medium saucepan.
2. Add remaining ingredients and stir well. Bring mixture to a boil over medium heat, then reduce heat and simmer for 5 minutes. Turn off heat and cover until cool. Keep in a covered container in the refrigerator to store.

• MAKES 3 CUPS (24 OUNCES).

• • • •

TOP SECRET RECIPES
VERSION OF
TACO BELL
CHICKEN QUESADILLA

☆　✌　💥　✏　☯　✂　☞

Taco Bell takes the fast-food quesadilla into new territory with three different cheeses and a creamy jalapeño sauce, all of which you can now cheerfully re-create in the comfort of your warm kitchen. Gather up the crew, since this recipe will make four of the tasty tortilla treats.

CREAMY JALAPEÑO SAUCE

¼ cup mayonnaise
2 teaspoons minced jalapeño
　　slices (nacho slices)
2 teaspoons juice from jalapeño
　　slices (nacho slices)
¾ teaspoon sugar
½ teaspoon paprika
½ teaspoon cumin
⅛ teaspoon cayenne pepper
⅛ teaspoon garlic powder
dash salt

4 chicken breast tenderloins
vegetable oil
salt
pepper
4 large flour tortillas (10-inch)
1 cup shredded cheddar cheese
1 cup shredded monterey jack
　　cheese

2 slices American cheese

1. Prepare creamy jalapeño sauce by combining all ingredients in a small bowl. Cover and chill so that flavors develop. Stir occasionally.
2. Preheat your barbecue grill to medium heat.
3. Rub chicken tenderloins with vegetable oil. Salt and pepper each side of each tenderloin. Grill for 3 to 5 minutes per side. When chicken is done, slice it very thin.
4. When you are ready to build your quesadillas, preheat a 12-inch skillet over medium-low heat.
5. When the pan is hot, lay one tortilla in the pan. Arrange about ¼ cup of shredded cheddar cheese and ¼ cup of shredded jack cheese on half of the tortilla. Tear up half a slice of American cheese and arrange the pieces on the other cheeses.
6. Arrange about ¼ cup of sliced chicken over the cheese.
7. Spread about 1 tablespoon of jalapeño sauce over the tortilla on the half with no ingredients on it.
8. Fold the sauced-covered half of the tortilla over onto the ingredients on the other half, and press down with a spatula. Cook for about 1 minute, then turn the quesadilla over and cook for a couple more minutes or until the cheese inside is melted. Slice into four pieces and serve hot. Repeat with the remaining ingredients.

- MAKES 4 QUESADILLAS.

• • • •

TACO BELL
MEXICAN PIZZA

Hope you're hungry, 'cause this recipe makes four of the Mexican Pizzas like those served at the Bell. Prepare to blow your diners away with this one if they're at all familiar with the real thing.

½ pound ground beef
2 tablespoons all-purpose flour
1 ½ teaspoons chili powder
   (Spanish blend is best)
¾ teaspoon salt
¼ teaspoon dried minced onion
¼ teaspoon paprika
dash garlic powder
dash onion powder
2 tablespoons water

1 cup Crisco shortening
8 small (6-inch diameter) flour
   tortillas
1 16-ounce can refried beans
⅔ cup mild Picante salsa
½ cup shredded cheddar cheese
½ cup shredded Monterey Jack
   cheese
⅓ cup diced tomato
¼ cup chopped green onion

1. In a medium bowl, combine the ground beef with the flour, chili powder, salt, dried onion, paprika, garlic powder, and onion powder. Use your hands to thoroughly incorporate everything into the ground beef.
2. Preheat a skillet over medium heat and add the ground beef mixture to the pan along with the water. Brown the beef mixture for 5 to 6 minutes, using a wooden spoon or spatula to break up the meat as it cooks.
3. Heat shortening in a frying pan over medium heat. When shortening is hot, fry each tortilla for about 30 to 45 seconds

per side and set aside on paper towels. When frying each tortilla, be sure to pop any bubbles that form so that tortilla lies flat in the shortening. Tortillas should become golden brown.

4. Heat up refried beans in a small pan over the stove or in the microwave. Preheat oven to 400°F.

5. When meat and tortillas are done, stack each pizza by first spreading about ⅓ cup refried beans on the face of one tortilla. Next spread ¼ to ⅓ cup of meat, then another tortilla. Coat your pizzas with 2 tablespoons of salsa on each, then combine the cheeses and sprinkle the blend evenly over the top of each pizza. Split up the diced tomato and arrange it evenly over the cheese on each pizza, followed by the green onion.

6. Place pizzas in your hot oven for 8 to 12 minutes or until the cheese on top is melted. Cut each pizza into four slices, and serve.

• MAKES 4 PIZZAS.

• • • •

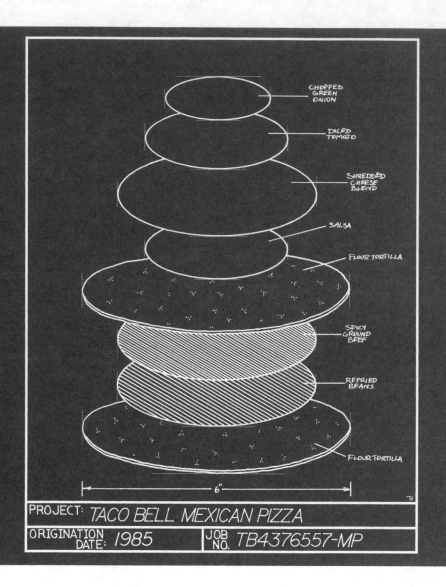

CHOPPED GREEN ONION

DICED TOMATO

SHREDDED CHEESE BLEND

SALSA

FLOUR TORTILLA

SPICY GROUND BEEF

REFRIED BEANS

FLOUR TORTILLA

6"

PROJECT: *TACO BELL MEXICAN PIZZA*

ORIGINATION DATE: *1985*

JOB NO. *TB4376557-MP*

TACO BELL
SOFT TACO

☆   ✌   💣   ✏   🎱   ✂   ☞

If you don't think those packets of Taco Bell spices you buy in the grocery stores make spiced ground meat that tastes like the stuff they use at the giant Mexican food chain, you'd be correct. If you want the taco meat to taste like the chain's then you're going to have to whip it up from scratch using this original TSR recipe. Once you've prepped your meat, the steps below will help you build your tacos the Taco Bell way, hopefully without any pesky talking Chihuahuas running through the kitchen. If you want crispy tacos, just replace the flour tortillas with crunchy corn shells.

I pound lean ground beef
¼ cup all-purpose flour
I tablespoon chili powder
I teaspoon salt
½ teaspoon dried minced onion
½ teaspoon paprika
¼ teaspoon onion powder

dash garlic powder
½ cup water
12 soft taco flour tortillas (6-inch
   tortillas)
2 cups shredded lettuce
I cup shredded cheddar cheese

1. In a medium bowl, combine the ground beef with the flour, chili powder, salt, minced onion, paprika, onion powder, and garlic powder. Use your hands to thoroughly mix the ingredients into the ground beef.
2. Add the seasoned beef mixture to the water in a skillet over medium heat. Mix well with a wooden spoon or spatula, and break up the meat as it cooks. Heat for 5 to 6 minutes, or

until browned. The finished product should be very smooth, somewhat pasty, with no large chunks of beef remaining.

3. Heat up the flour tortillas in your microwave for 20 to 30 seconds, or until warm.

4. Build each taco by spooning 2 to 3 tablespoons of the meat into a warm tortilla. Spread some of the shredded lettuce over the meat and then sprinkle some cheese over the top. Repeat with the remaining ingredients and serve immediately.

• MAKES 12 SOFT TACOS.

• • • •

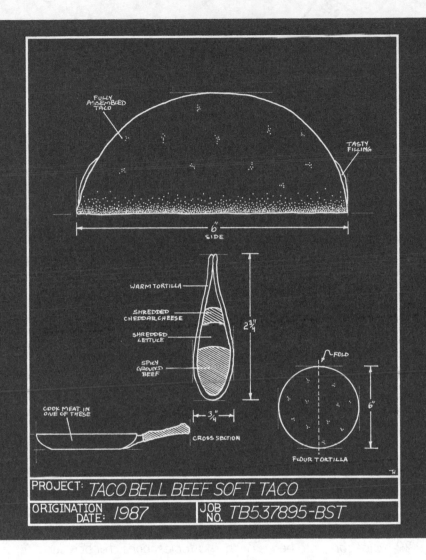

FULLY ASSEMBLED TACO

TASTY FILLING

6" SIDE

WARM TORTILLA

SHREDDED CHEDDAR CHEESE

SHREDDED LETTUCE

SPICY GROUND BEEF

2¾"

FOLD

6"

COOK MEAT IN ONE OF THESE

¾"

CROSS SECTION

FLOUR TORTILLA

PROJECT: TACO BELL BEEF SOFT TACO

ORIGINATION DATE: 1987

JOB NO. TB537895-BST

WENDY'S CHILI

☆ ✌ 💣 ✏ ☯ ✂ ☞

In 1969, at the ripe old age of thirty-seven, R. David Thomas left a job at Arthur Treacher's Fish & Chips to open the first Wendy's at 257 E. Broad Street in downtown Columbus, Ohio. Only three years later Thomas began franchising the Wendy's concept, and by the end of its first nine years, Wendy's International had dotted the country with more than 1,000 units.

Thomas served this chili since day one. The recipe has changed a bit over the years, but the chili you'll taste here is a clone of Wendy's current recipe. Try topping it with freshly grated cheese and chopped onion, extras that you can request at the restaurant.

2 pounds ground beef
1 29-ounce can tomato sauce
1 29-ounce can kidney beans
   (with liquid)
1 29-ounce can pinto beans (with
   liquid)
1 cup diced onion (1 medium
   onion)

½ cup diced green chili (2 chilies)
¼ cup diced celery (1 stalk)
3 medium tomatoes, chopped
2 teaspoons cumin powder
3 tablespoons chili powder
1 ½ teaspoons black pepper
2 teaspoons salt
2 cups water

1. Brown the ground beef in a skillet over medium heat; drain off the fat.
2. Using a fork, crumble the cooked beef into pea-size pieces.
3. In a large pot, combine the beef plus all the remaining ingredi-

ents, and bring to a simmer over low heat. Cook, stirring every 15 minutes, for 2 to 3 hours.

- MAKES ABOUT 12 SERVINGS.

VARIATIONS

For spicier chili, add ½ teaspoon more black pepper.

For much spicier chili, add 1 teaspoon black pepper and 1 tablespoon cayenne pepper.

And for a real stomach stinger, add 5 or 6 sliced jalapeño peppers to the pot.

Leftovers can be frozen for several months.

• • • •

WENDY'S FROSTY

The founder of Wendy's International, R. David Thomas, named the restaurant he established in 1969 after his eight-year-old daughter, Melinda Lou, who was nicknamed Wendy by her brother and sisters. Wendy says, "Dad wanted a name that was easy to remember and that was an all-American mug." Wendy is grown up now, but Wendy's still uses her eight-year-old freckle-faced likeness on the restaurant signs. Thomas commented that his daughter was very embarrassed by the exposure. He told *People* magazine, "I'm not sure I would do it again."

Wendy's International now operates some 3,800 restaurants in 49 states and 24 countries overseas, racking up sales of more than $3 billion a year. Wendy's restaurants have served the now-famous Frosty since 1969. In 1991 an astounding 17.5 million gallons of the frozen confection were served worldwide.

¾ cup milk
¼ cup chocolate-drink powder
   (Nestlé Quik is best)

4 cups vanilla ice cream

1. Combine all of the ingredients in a blender. Blend on medium speed until creamy. Stir if necessary.
2. If too thin, freeze the mixture in the blender or in cups until thicker.

• MAKES 2 DRINKS.

• • • •

TOP SECRET RECIPES
VERSION OF
WENDY'S
GARDEN SENSATIONS
MANDARIN CHICKEN
SALAD

☆   ✌   💣   ✏   ☯   ✂   ☞

Of the four salads on Wendy's new "Garden Sensations" menu, this is the one that draws all the cloning requests. It's the sesame dressing that everyone's nuts about. The clone below gives you a nice 1½ cups of the tasty stuff, so it'll fit perfectly into a standard dressing cruet. Once you've got your dressing made, building the rest of the salad is a breeze.

SESAME DRESSING

½ cup corn syrup
3 tablespoons white distilled
    vinegar
2 tablespoons pineapple juice
4 teaspoons granulated sugar
1 tablespoon light brown sugar
1 tablespoon rice wine vinegar
1 tablespoon soy sauce
1 teaspoon sesame oil
¼ teaspoon ground mustard
¼ teaspoon ground ginger
⅛ teaspoon salt
⅛ teaspoon paprika

dash garlic powder
dash ground black pepper
½ cup vegetable oil
½ teaspoon sesame seeds

4 chicken breast fillets
1 large head iceberg lettuce,
    chopped
4 cups red leaf lettuce, chopped
1⅓ cups canned mandarin
    orange wedges
1 cup rice noodles
1 cup roasted sliced almonds

1. Prepare dressing by combining all dressing ingredients except vegetable oil and sesame seeds in a blender on high speed. Slowly add oil to mixture (to create an emulsion). Add sesame seeds and blend for just a couple seconds. Pour dressing into a covered container (such as a dressing cruet) and chill until needed.
2. Rub each chicken breast fillet with oil, then lightly salt and pepper each piece. Grill on medium-high heat until done. Chill chicken breasts in refrigerator until cold.
3. When chicken is cold, build each salad by first arranging about 4 cups of iceberg lettuce in the bottom of a large salad bowl or on a plate.
4. Arrange a cup of red leaf lettuce on the iceberg lettuce.
5. Dice each chicken breast into bite-size pieces and sprinkle the pieces from each one over each salad.
6. Arrange about ⅓ cup of mandarin orange wedges on each salad.
7. Next, sprinkle about ¼ cup of rice noodles and ¼ cup of roasted sliced almonds on top of each salad.
8. Add desired amount of sesame dressing and serve.

- MAKES 4 LARGE SALADS.

• • • •

WENDY'S SPICY CHICKEN FILLET SANDWICH

☆　　✌　　💣　　✎　　☯　　✂　　☞

There once was a time when Wendy's offered this sandwich for a "limited time only." Apparently the tasty zing from this breaded chicken sandwich won it many loyal customers and a permanent place on the fast food chain's menu. Now you can re-create the spicy kick of the original with a secret blend of spices in the chicken's crispy coating. Follow the same stacking order as the original, and you've just made four sandwich clones at a fraction of the cost of the real thing.

6 to 8 cups vegetable oil
⅓ cup Frank's Original Red Hot Pepper Sauce
⅔ cup water
1 cup all-purpose flour
2½ teaspoons salt
4 teaspoons cayenne pepper
1 teaspoon coarse ground black pepper

1 teaspoon onion powder
½ teaspoon paprika
⅛ teaspoon garlic powder
4 skinless chicken breast fillets
4 plain hamburger buns
8 teaspoons mayonnaise
4 lettuce leaves
4 tomato slices

1. Preheat 6 to 8 cups of oil in a deep fryer to 350°F.
2. Combine the pepper sauce and water in a small bowl.

3. Combine the flour, salt, cayenne pepper, black pepper, onion powder, paprika, and garlic powder in another shallow bowl.
4. Pound each of the chicken pieces with a mallet until about ⅜-inch thick. Trim each breast fillet if necessary to help it fit on the bun.
5. Working with one fillet at a time, coat each piece with the flour, then dredge it in the diluted pepper sauce. Coat the chicken once again in the flour mixture and set it aside until the rest of the chicken is coated.
6. Fry the chicken fillets for 8 to 12 minutes or until they are light brown and crispy. Remove the chicken to a rack or to paper towels to drain.
7. As chicken is frying, prepare each sandwich by grilling the face of the hamburger buns on a hot skillet over medium heat. Spread about 2 teaspoons of mayonnaise on the face of each of the inverted top buns.
8. Place a tomato slice onto the mayonnaise, then stack a leaf of lettuce on top of the tomato.
9. On each of the bottom buns, stack one piece of chicken.
10. Flip the top half of each sandwich onto the bottom half and serve hot.

- MAKES 4 SANDWICHES.

• • • •

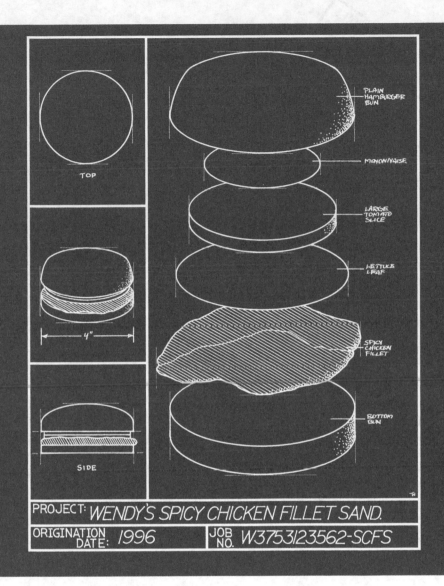

TOP

SIDE

4"

PLAIN
HAMBURGER
BUN

MAYONNAISE

LARGE
TOMATO
SLICE

LETTUCE
LEAF

SPICY
CHICKEN
FILLET

BOTTOM
BUN

PROJECT: WENDY'S SPICY CHICKEN FILLET SAND.

ORIGINATION DATE: 1996

JOB NO. W3753123562-SCFS

135

WHITE CASTLE BURGERS

Nicknamed "Sliders" and "Gut Bombers," these famous tiny burgers were one of the earliest fast-food creations. It all started in 1921 when E. W. Ingram borrowed $700 to open a hamburger stand in Wichita, Kansas. He was able to pay the loan back within ninety days. Ingram chose the name White Castle because "white" signified purity and cleanliness, while "castle" represented strength, permanence, and stability. White Castle lived up to its name, maintaining permanence and stability by growing steadily over the years to a total of 275 restaurants.

Ingram's inspiration was the development of steam-grilling, a unique process that helps the burgers retain moisture. The secret is simply to grill the meat over a small pile of onions. Five holes in each burger help to ensure thorough cooking without having to flip the patties.

Today customers can still buy these burgers "by the sack" at the outlets, or pick them up in the freezer section of most grocery stores.

1 pound ground beef
8 hot-dog buns or 16 hamburger
    buns
½ medium onion

salt to taste
pepper to taste
American cheese (optional)
pickle slices (optional)

1. Prepare the beef ahead of time by separating into 16 1-ounce portions and flattening each on waxed paper into very thin square patties, about 2½ inches on a side. Using a small circular object like the tip of a pen cap, make five small, evenly spaced holes in each patty. Freeze the patties (still on the waxed paper) completely, and you're ready to cook.
2. If you're using hot-dog buns, cut off the ends and then cut each bun in half to make 2 buns from each. If you're using hamburger buns, cut each down to about a 2½-inch square.
3. Slice the onion into match-size pieces.
4. Grill the faces of the buns in a large pan over medium heat.
5. In the hot pan, spread out tablespoon-size piles of onions 3 inches apart. Salt and pepper each pile of onions.
6. On each pile of onions place a frozen beef patty. You may have to spread the onions out some so that the hamburger lies flat. Salt each patty as it cooks.
7. Cook each burger for 4 to 5 minutes on the onions. If you made the burgers thin enough, the holes will ensure that each patty is cooked thoroughly without flipping them over. Covering the frying pan will help to ensure that the patties cook through.
8. Assemble by sandwiching the patty and onions between each grilled bun.

• MAKES 16 BURGERS.

TIDBITS

If you want to add pickle slices to your burger, as you can at White Castle outlets, stack them on top of the grilled onions.

For a cheeseburger, you'll have to cut a slice of American cheese to the same size as your burger, and then it goes on top of the onions, under the pickles, if you use pickles. Got it?

•　•　•　•

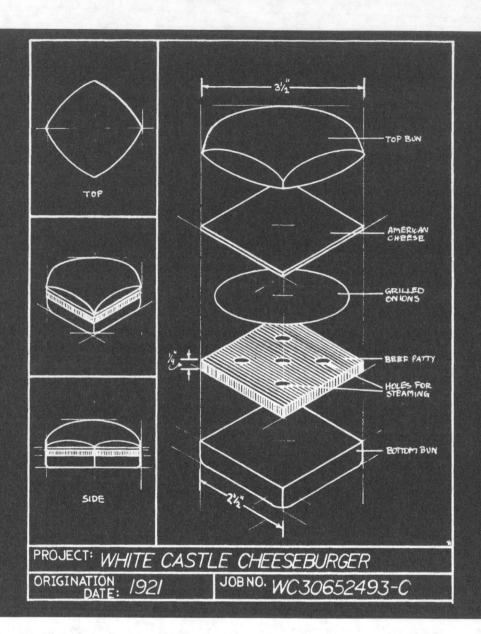

TOP

SIDE

3½"

TOP BUN

AMERICAN CHEESE

GRILLED ONIONS

BEEF PATTY

HOLES FOR STEAMING

BOTTOM BUN

¼"

2½"

PROJECT: WHITE CASTLE CHEESEBURGER

ORIGINATION DATE: 1921

JOB NO. WC30652493-C

138

TOP SECRET RECIPES
VERSION OF
BISQUICK
BAKING MIX

So you've got a hankerin' for pancakes, but you're all out of Bisquick. Not to worry, home cloners. Now you can easily whip up your own version of the popular baking mix with just four simple ingredients. Since the real thing includes shortening, salt, flour, and leavening, that's exactly what we'll use here to duplicate it. This recipe makes about 6 cups of the stuff, which, just like the original, you can keep sealed up in a container in your pantry until it's flapjack time. Then you simply add milk and eggs for pancakes or waffles, or just milk if it's biscuits you want. You'll find the specifics on those recipes in the Tidbits section.

4 cups all-purpose flour
2 tablespoons baking powder

1 ½ teaspoons salt
1 cup shortening

1. Combine all dry ingredients in a large bowl.
2. Add shortening and mix with an electric mixer on medium speed until all shortening is blended with the flour.
3. Use the mix as you would the real thing. Check out the Tidbits below.

• MAKES 6 CUPS.

Follow these recipes to use the baking mix you just cloned like a champ:

Pancakes: Stir 2 cups baking mix with 1 cup milk and 2 eggs in a bowl until blended. Pour ¼ cup portions onto a hot griddle. Cook until edges are dry. Turn; cook until golden. Makes 14 pancakes.

Waffles: Stir 2 cups baking mix with 1⅓ cups milk, 1 egg, and 2 tablespoons vegetable oil in a bowl until blended. Pour onto a hot waffle iron. Bake until the steaming stops. Makes 12 4-inch waffles.

Biscuits: Preheat oven to 450°F. Stir 2¼ cups baking mix with ⅔ cup milk. When the dough forms, turn it out onto a surface sprinkle with extra mix. Knead 10 times. Roll dough ½-inch thick. Cut with 2½–inch cutter. Place on an ungreased cookie sheet. Bake for 8 to 10 minutes or until golden brown.

• MAKES 9 BISCUITS.

• • • •

BORDEN
CRACKER JACK

☆   ✂   💣   ✏   🎱   ✂   ☞

In 1871 a German immigrant named F. W. Reuckheim came to Chicago with $200 in his pocket. He used all of his money to open a small popcorn shop in the city and started selling a sweet caramel- and molasses–coated popcorn confection. Rueckheim's big break came in 1893, when the treat was served at Chicago's first world's fair. From then on the popcorn's popularity grew enormously. In 1896 a salesman tasting the treat for the first time said, "That's a cracker jack," and the name stuck. Shortly after Cracker Jack's debut another customer commented, "The more you eat, the more you want," and that's still the slogan today.

In 1912 the Cracker Jack Company started adding toy surprises, ranging from small books to miniature metal toy trains. To date they have given away more than 17 billion toy surprises. In 1964 Borden, Inc. bought the Cracker Jack Company, and today the Cracker Jack division is the largest user of popcorn in the world, popping more than twenty tons of corn a day.

4 quarts popped popcorn (or 1⅓ bags microwave popcorn)	1 cup brown sugar
	½ cup light corn syrup
1 cup Spanish peanuts	2 tablespoons molasses
4 tablespoons (½ stick) butter	¼ teaspoon salt

1. Preheat the oven to 250°F.
2. Combine the popcorn and peanuts in a metal bowl or on a cookie sheet and place in the preheated oven.
3. Combine all of the remaining ingredients in a saucepan.
4. Stirring over medium heat, bring the mixture to a boil.
5. Using a cooking thermometer, bring the mixture to the hard-crack stage (290°F, or the point at which the syrup, when dripped into cold water, forms a hard but pliable ball). This will take about 20 to 25 minutes (or until you notice the mixture turning a slightly darker brown).
6. Remove the popcorn and peanuts from the oven and, working quickly, pour the caramel mixture in a fine stream over them. Then place them back in the oven for 10 minutes.
7. Mix well every five minutes, so that all of the popcorn is coated.
8. Cool and store in a covered container to preserve freshness.

• MAKES 4 QUARTS.

• • • •

BROWN &
HALEY
ALMOND ROCA

☆　✌　💣　✏　☯　✂　☞

Founded in 1914 by Harry Brown and J. C. Haley in Tacoma, Washington, the Brown & Haley Candy Company is one of the oldest confectioners in the country. In 1923 the company hit the jackpot when Harry Brown and the former cook from what would eventually become M&M/Mars, created a chocolate-coated butter candy, sprinkled with California almonds. They took the sweet to Tacoma's head librarian, and she named it Almond Roca—roca means "rock" in Spanish. In 1927 the two men decided to wrap the little candies in imported gold foil and pack them into the now-familiar pink cans to extend their shelf life threefold. In fact, because of the way the candy was packaged, it was carried by troops in World War II, the Korean War, the Vietnam War, and the Gulf War.

The Brown & Haley candy company is still housed in the former shoe factory that it has occupied since 1919. Almond Roca is so popular today that it can be found in sixty-four countries and is a market leader in Hong Kong, Singapore, Korea, Taiwan, the Philippines, and Japan. The company sells more than 5 million pounds of Almond Roca each year and is the United States's leading exporter of packaged confections.

1 cup (2 sticks) butter
1 cup granulated sugar
3 tablespoons water
1 teaspoon light corn syrup

1 cup finely chopped toasted
   almonds
1 cup milk-chocolate chips

1. Melt the butter in a saucepan.
2. Add the sugar, water, and corn syrup.
3. Cook the mixture over medium heat, stirring.
4. When the sugar dissolves and the mixture begins to boil, raise the heat and bring the mixture to 290°F on a cooking thermometer. (This is called the *soft-crack stage.*) It will be light brown in color, and syrup will separate into threads that are not brittle when dribbled into cold water.
5. Quickly stir in ½ cup chopped almonds.
6. Immediately pour the mixture onto an ungreased baking sheet.
7. Wait 2 or 3 minutes for the candy surface to firm, then sprinkle on the chocolate chips.
8. In a few minutes, when the chips have softened, spread the chocolate evenly over the surface.
9. Sprinkle the remaining almonds over the melted chocolate.
10. When the chocolate hardens, crack the candy into pieces. Store covered.

- MAKES 1½ POUNDS.

Heath Bar or Hershey's® Skor®

These two candy bars are very similar, and both are composed of ingredients similar to those in Almond Roca. One obvious difference is that there are no almonds on top of these bars. To make these candy bars, simply follow the same directions for Almond Roca, omitting step 9.

These recipes taste very much like the candies they clone, but you may notice right away that the finished products don't look like their corporate counterparts. This is largely due to the fact that the chocolate is only a top coating, surrounding the almond candy centers. This was done in the interest of simplicity—to make the recipes easier on the chef (that's you, right?). You could make your almond candy center first, then crack it into smaller pieces and dip those into chocolate. But is it really worth the trouble?

• • • •

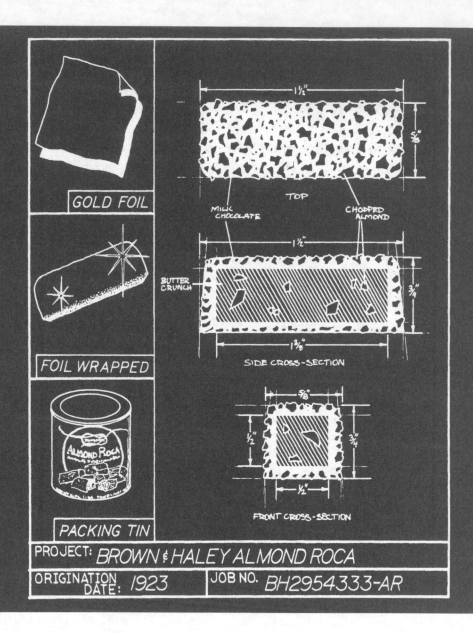

GOLD FOIL

FOIL WRAPPED

PACKING TIN

1½"

⅝"

TOP

MILK CHOCOLATE

CHOPPED ALMOND

1½"

BUTTER CRUNCH

¾"

1⅜"

SIDE CROSS-SECTION

⅝"

½"

¾"

½"

FRONT CROSS-SECTION

PROJECT: BROWN & HALEY ALMOND ROCA

ORIGINATION DATE: 1923

JOB NO. BH2954333-AR

TOP SECRET RECIPES
VERSION OF
CRUNCH 'N MUNCH
BUTTERY TOFFEE
POPCORN WITH PEANUTS

☆　✌　💣　✏　☯　✂　☞

Just look at what F. W. Ruckheim started. He was the guy who, back in the late 1800s made candy-coated popcorn a national treasure with the invention of Cracker Jack. Now we've got Fiddle-Faddle, Screaming Yellow Zonkers, Crunch 'n Munch and several brands of candy-coated microwave popcorn, to name just a few. Sure, these other varieties don't have the traditional prize inside the box, but let's face it, those prizes are pretty weak compared to what used to be found at the bottom of a box of Cracker Jack when I was a kid. And the old-fashioned molasses formula used on Cracker Jack just doesn't have the pizzazz as some of the other tantalizing flavors coating popcorn today. The butter-toffee coating is a good example, so that's what I've reverse-engineered for you here. It's a simple recipe that makes a finished product so addictive you'll have to beg someone to take it away from you before you finish the whole bowl by yourself. All you need is a candy thermometer, some microwave popcorn, a few other basic ingredients, and you're about 15 minutes away from candy-coated heaven.

8 cups popped microwave
　　popcorn (natural flavor)
¼ cup Spanish peanuts

½ cup butter (1 stick)
½ cup sugar
¼ cup light corn syrup

1. Spread popcorn and peanuts on a baking sheet and keep warm in your oven set to 300°F while you prepare the butter toffee. You don't need to preheat the oven.
2. Melt the butter in a medium saucepan over medium-low heat.
3. Add sugar and corn syrup and simmer, stirring occasionally. Pop a candy thermometer into the mixture and watch it closely.
4. When the thermometer reaches 300°F pour the candy over the warm popcorn and peanuts. Stir well so that the candy coats the popcorn. Put the popcorn back into the oven for 5 minutes, then take it out and stir it all around again to coat the popcorn even more. Repeat if necessary to thoroughly coat all of the popcorn.
5. Pour coated popcorn and peanuts onto wax paper. When cool, break up the chunks into bite-size pieces and store it all in a covered container.

• MAKES 8 CUPS.

•　•　•　•

DOLLY MADISON ZINGERS (DEVIL'S FOOD)

☆ ✌ 💣 ✎ ☯ ✂ ☞

Former U.S. president James Madison's wife did not create this baking company, despite the fact that her name is on every carrot cake, crumb cake, and Zinger that comes off the production line. It was instead company founder Roy Nafziger's brainstorm to use the former first lady's name, since she was notorious for throwing huge shindigs featuring a fine selection of desserts and baked goods. Nafziger said his company would create cakes "fine enough to serve at the White House." While I don't expect you'll be treated to a tray of Zingers on your next stay in the Lincoln Bedroom, I will agree that these little snack cakes are a tasty way to appease a sweet tooth.

The cake batter is easy, since you just use any instant devil's food cake mix. I like Duncan Hines. As for the frosting, it may not come out as dark brown as the original since the recipe here doesn't include brown food coloring (caramel coloring). But the taste will be right on. And I think former president Clinton would agree that as long as the sweet little treats taste good, appearance is secondary.

CAKE

Duncan Hines devil's food cake mix

1 1/3 cups water

1/2 cup oil

3 large eggs

FILLING

2 teaspoons hot water

¼ teaspoon salt

2 cups marshmallow creme (one
    7-ounce jar)

½ cup shortening

⅓ cup powdered sugar

½ teaspoon vanilla

FROSTING

1 cup powdered sugar

¼ cup Hershey's chocolate syrup

2 tablespoons shortening

½ teaspoon vanilla

dash salt

1. Prepare the cake batter following the directions on the box. If you use Duncan Hines brand, you will need 1⅓ cups of water, ½ cup of oil, and 3 eggs. Preheat oven to 350 degrees.

2. To prepare the cake pans that will make cakes the size of Zingers, tear off 20 pieces of aluminum foil that are each about 8 inches wide. Fold the foil in half and then in half once more so that you have a rectangular piece of foil. Wrap this piece of foil around a small prescription medicine bottle. Tuck in the ends and take the bottle out, leaving the foil open at the top. This will form a little pan. Flatten the bottom so that the mini pan stands up straight. Place this into a baking pan and repeat with the remaining pieces of foil. When you have arranged all of the foil pans in a baking pan, spray the inside of all the pans with nonstick cooking spray. Fill each little pan about halfway with cake batter. Bake cakes for 15 to 17 minutes or until a toothpick stuck in the center comes out clean. Remove the cakes from the oven and allow them to cool completely.

3. To make the filling, combine the hot water with the salt in a small bowl and stir until the salt is dissolved. Let this mixture cool.

4. Combine the marshmallow creme, shortening, powdered sugar, and vanilla in a medium bowl and mix well with an electric mixer on high speed until fluffy. Add the salt mixture to the bowl and mix.

5. To make the chocolate frosting, combine all the frosting in-

gredients in a medium bowl and mix well with an electric mixer until smooth.

6. To assemble your snack cakes first poke three holes with a toothpick or skewer in the top of a cake and swirl around inside the holes, making little caverns for your filling.

7. Use a pastry bag with a small tip to squeeze some filling into each hole. Careful not to overfill, or your cake will burst open. Sure, it looks cool when they explode, but this mess won't make for a very good clone.

8. Once the cake is filled, use a butter knife to spread frosting on top of the cake over the holes, concealing your secret injection work. Drag a fork lengthwise over the frosting, making grooves just like the real thing.

• MAKES 20 SNACK CAKES.

• • • •

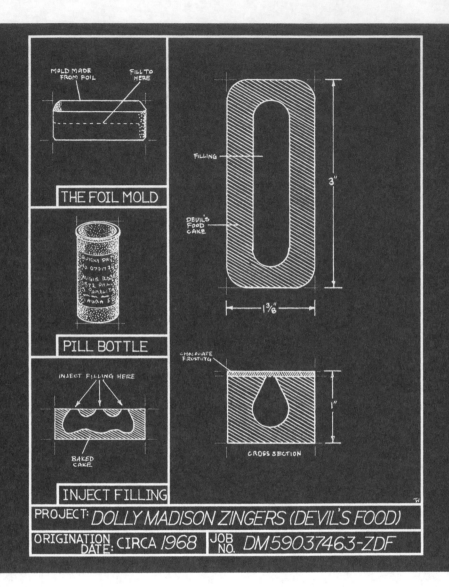

THE FOIL MOLD

MOLD MADE FROM FOIL

FILL TO HERE

PILL BOTTLE

QUICKY DRY
NO 070147 3 5
AUGIE ROGE
1572 DAILY
CARMLITA
LAURA SO

INJECT FILLING

INJECT FILLING HERE

BAKED CAKE

FILLING

DEVIL'S FOOD CAKE

3"

1 3/8"

CHOCOLATE FROSTING

1"

CROSS SECTION

PROJECT: *DOLLY MADISON ZINGERS (DEVIL'S FOOD)*

ORIGINATION DATE: CIRCA *1968*   JOB NO. *DM59037463-ZDF*

152

DOUBLETREE
CHOCOLATE CHIP COOKIES

☆   ✌   💣   ✏   ☯   ✂   ☞

When you check in at one of 240 hotels run by this U.S. chain, you are handed a bag from a warming oven that contains two soft and delicious chocolate chip cookies. This is a tradition that began in the early 90s using a recipe from a small bakery in Atlanta. All of the cookies—which weigh in at an impressive two ounces each—are baked fresh every day on the hotel premises. Raves for the cookies from customers convinced the hotel chain to start selling the chocolatey munchables by the half-dozen. But if you've got an insatiable chocolate chip cookie urge that can't wait for a package to be delivered in the mail, you'll want to try this cloned version fresh out of your home oven.

½ cup rolled oats
2¼ cups all-purpose flour
1½ teaspoons baking soda
1 teaspoon salt
¼ teaspoon cinnamon
1 cup (2 sticks) butter, softened
¾ cup brown sugar, packed

¾ cup granulated sugar
1½ teaspoons vanilla
½ teaspoon lemon juice
2 eggs
3 cups semisweet chocolate chips
1½ cups chopped walnuts

1. Preheat oven to 350°F.
2. Grind oats in a food processor or blender until fine. Combine the ground oats with the flour, baking soda, salt, and cinnamon in a medium bowl.

3. Cream together the butter, sugars, vanilla, and lemon juice in another medium bowl with an electric mixer. Add the eggs and mix until smooth.
4. Stir the dry mixture into the wet mixture and blend well. Add the chocolate chips and nuts to the dough and mix by hand until ingredients are well incorporated.
5. Spoon rounded 1/4-cup portions onto an ungreased cookie sheet. Place the scoops about 2 inches apart. You don't need to press the dough flat. Bake for 16 to 18 minutes or until cookies are light brown and soft in the middle. Store in a sealed container when cool to keep soft.

• MAKES 20 COOKIES.

• • • •

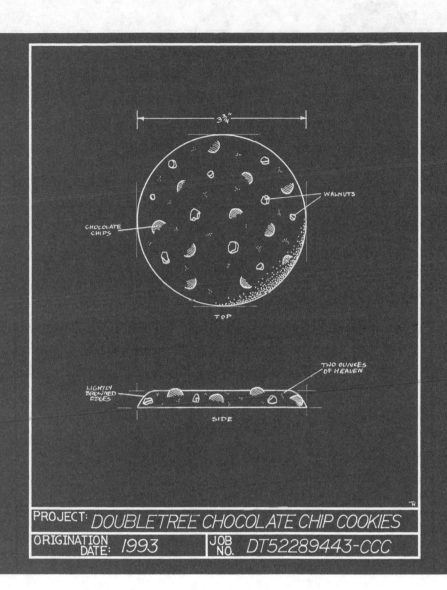

$3\frac{3}{4}$"

WALNUTS

CHOCOLATE
CHIPS

TOP

TWO OUNCES
OF HEAVEN

LIGHTLY
BROWNED
EDGES

SIDE

PROJECT: *DOUBLETREE CHOCOLATE CHIP COOKIES*

ORIGINATION DATE: *1993*   JOB NO. *DT52289443-CCC*

TOP SECRET RECIPES
VERSION OF
FRITOS
HOT BEAN DIP

Re-create the popular bean dip at home in just minutes with a food processor—simply pour all the ingredients in and fire it up. The best part about this recipe is that we can duplicate the taste of the popular dip without any added fat. If you check out the label of the real thing, you'll see that there's hydrogenated oil in there. We can avoid this saturated fat without sacrificing flavor in our home clone, which is a perfectly satisfying and healthy choice for dipping. Now bring on the greasy chips!

1 15-ounce can pinto beans, drained
4 bottled jalapeño slices (nacho slices)
1 tablespoon juice from bottled jalapeño slices

½ teaspoon salt
½ teaspoon sugar
¼ teaspoon onion powder
¼ teaspoon paprika
⅛ teaspoon garlic powder
⅛ teaspoon cayenne pepper

1. Combine drained pinto beans with the other ingredients in a food processor. Puree ingredients on high speed until smooth. Cover and chill for at least an hour before serving.

• MAKES 1¼ CUPS.

• • • •

GIRL SCOUT COOKIES
THIN MINTS

☆   ✌   💣   ✏   ☯   ✂   ☞

If those cute little cookie peddlers aren't posted outside the market, it may be tough to get your hands on these—the most popular cookies sold by the Girl Scouts each year. One out of every four boxes of cookies sold by the girls is Thin Mints. This recipe uses an improved version of the chocolate wafers created for the Oreo cookie clone in the second TSR book, *More Top Secret Recipes*. That recipe creates 108 cookie wafers, so when you're done dipping, you'll have the equivalent of three boxes of the Girl Scout Cookies favorite. (See? That's why you bought those extra cookie sheets.) You could, of course, reduce the recipe by baking only ⅓ of the cookie dough for the wafers and then reducing the coating ingredients by ⅓, giving you a total of 36 cookies.

CHOCOLATE COOKIE WAFERS

1 18.25-ounce package Betty Crocker chocolate fudge cake mix
3 tablespoons shortening, melted
½ cup cake flour, measured then sifted
1 egg
3 tablespoons water
nonstick cooking spray

COATING

3 12-ounce bags semisweet chocolate chips
¾ teaspoon peppermint extract
6 tablespoons shortening

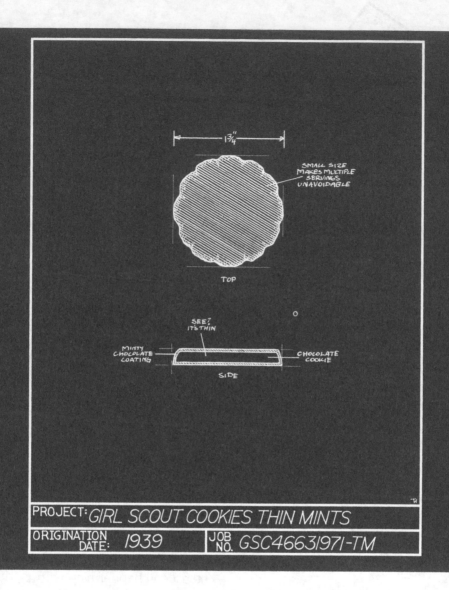

1 3/4"

SMALL SIZE
MAKES MULTIPLE
SERVINGS
UNAVOIDABLE

TOP

SEE?
ITS THIN

MINTY
CHOCOLATE
COATING

CHOCOLATE
COOKIE

SIDE

PROJECT: GIRL SCOUT COOKIES THIN MINTS

ORIGINATION DATE: 1939

JOB NO. GSC4663I971-TM

1. Combine the cookie ingredients in a large bowl, adding the water a little bit at a time until the dough forms. Cover and chill for 2 hours.
2. Preheat oven to 350°F.
3. On a lightly floured surface roll out a portion of the dough to just under 1/16 of an inch thick. To cut, use a lid from a spice container with a 1 1/2–inch diameter (Schilling brand is good). Arrange the cut dough rounds on a cookie sheet that is sprayed with a light coating of nonstick spray. Bake for 10 minutes. Remove wafers from the oven and cool completely.
4. Combine chocolate chips with peppermint extract and shortening in a large microwave-safe glass or ceramic bowl. Heat on 50 percent power for 2 minutes, stir gently, then heat for an additional minute. Stir once again, and if chocolate is not a smooth consistency, continue to zap in microwave in 30-second intervals until smooth.
5. Use a fork to dip each wafer in the chocolate, tap the fork on the edge of the bowl so that the excess chocolate runs off, and then place the cookies side-by-side on a wax paper–lined baking sheet. Refrigerate until firm.

- MAKES 108 COOKIES.

• • • •

HERSHEY'S PAYDAY CANDY BAR

In December of 1996, Hershey Foods snagged the U.S. operations of Leaf Brands for a pretty penny. This added several well-known candies to Hershey's already impressive roster, including Good & Plenty, Jolly Rancher, Milk Duds, Whoppers, Heath, and this delicious peanut roll, which we can now clone at home. The center is sort of a white fudge that we can make by combining a few ingredients on the stove, then getting the mixture up to just the right temperature using a candy thermometer (you've got one, right?). Once cool, this candy center is coated with a thin layer of caramel, then quickly pressed onto roasted peanuts. Looks just like the real thing! This recipe will make 8 candy bars. But it's up to you to make the dental appointment.

CENTERS

¼ cup whole milk	¼ teaspoon salt
5 unwrapped caramels	1¼ cups powdered sugar
1 tablespoon light corn syrup	20 unwrapped caramels
1 teaspoon smooth peanut butter	1½ teaspoons water
¼ teaspoon vanilla	2 cups dry roasted peanuts

1. Combine all ingredients for the centers, except the powdered sugar, in a small saucepan over low heat. Stir often as the caramel slowly melts. When the mixture is smooth, add ¾ cup of powdered sugar. Stir. Save the remaining ½ cup of powdered sugar for later.

2. Use a candy thermometer to bring the mixture to exactly 230°F, stirring often, then turn off the heat.

3. When the temperature of the candy begins to drop, add the remaining ½ cup powdered sugar to the pan, then use a hand mixer on high speed to combine. Keep mixing until the candy cools and thickens and can no longer be mixed. That should take a minute or two.

4. Let the candy cool in the pan for 10 to 15 minutes, or until it can be touched. Don't let it sit too long—you want the candy to still be warm and pliable when you shape it. Take a tablespoon-size portion and roll it between your palms or on a countertop until it forms a roll the width of your index finger and measures about 4½ inches long. Repeat with the remaining center candy mixture and place the rolls on wax paper. You should have 8 rolls. Let the center rolls sit out for an hour or two to firm up.

5. Combine the 20 caramels with the 1½ teaspoons of water in a small saucepan over low heat. Stir often until the caramels melt completely, then turn off the heat. If you work fast this caramel will stay warm while you make the candy bars.

6. Pour the peanuts onto a baking sheet or other flat surface. Using a basting brush and working quickly, "paint" a coating of caramel onto one side of a center roll. Quickly turn the center over, caramel-side-down, onto the peanuts and press gently so that the peanuts stick to the surface of the candy. Paint more caramel onto the other side of the roll and press it down onto the peanuts. The candy should have a solid layer of peanuts covering all sides. If needed, brush additional caramel onto the roll, then turn it onto the peanuts to coat the roll completely. Place the candy bar onto wax paper, and repeat with the remaining ingredients. Eat when completely cool.

• MAKES 8 CANDY BARS.

•   •   •   •

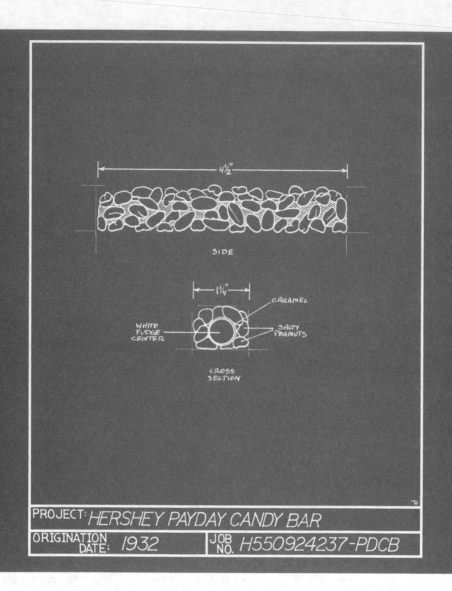

4½"

SIDE

1¼"

CARAMEL

WHITE
FUDGE
CENTER

SALTY
PEANUTS

CROSS
SECTION

PROJECT: *HERSHEY PAYDAY CANDY BAR*

ORIGINATION
DATE: *1932*

JOB
NO. *H550924237-PDCB*

TOP SECRET RECIPES

VERSION OF

HIDDEN VALLEY
ORIGINAL RANCH
DRESSING

☆   ✌   💣   ✎   ☯   ✂   ☞

Ranch dressing was indeed invented at a place called Hidden Valley Ranch near Santa Barbara, California, by a real salad-wranglin' rancher. In the '50s and '60s, Steve Henson and his wife, Gayle, shared their 120-acre dude ranch with University of California at Santa Barbara students and other festive partiers for rousing weekend shindigs. The dozens of guests were served meals of steaks and salads topped with Steve's special blend of herbs, spices, mayonnaise, and buttermilk. As word got out about the fabulous dressing, more guests were showing up at the ranch and walking home with complimentary take-home jars filled with the stuff. Eventually, Steve figured he could make a little cash on the side by packaging the dressing as a dry mix and selling it through the mail. At first he was filling envelopes himself, but within a few months Steve had to hire 12 more people to help with the packaging. Soon, Steve had a multimillion-dollar business on his hands, from a product that for 10 years he had been giving away for free.

½ cup mayonnaise
½ cup buttermilk
½ teaspoon dried parsley flakes
¼ teaspoon ground black pepper
¼ teaspoon MSG (such as Accent)

¼ teaspoon salt
⅛ teaspoon garlic powder
⅛ teaspoon onion powder
pinch dried thyme

1. Combine all ingredients in a medium bowl and whisk until smooth. Cover and chill for several hours before using.

• MAKES 1 CUP.

• • • •

TOP SECRET RECIPES
VERSION OF
HOSTESS
TWINKIE

The Twinkie was invented in 1930 by the late James A. Dewar, then the Chicago-area regional manager of Continental Baking Company, the parent corporation behind the Hostess trademark. At the time, Continental made "Little Short Cake Fingers" only during the six-week strawberry season, and Dewar realized that the aluminum pans in which the cakes were baked sat idle the rest of the year. He came up with the idea of injecting the little cakes with a creamy filling to make them a year-round product and decided to charge a nickel for a package of two.

But Dewar couldn't come up with a catchy name for the treat—that is, until he set out on a business trip to St. Louis. Along the road he saw a sign for TWINKLE TOE SHOES, and the name TWINKIES evolved. Sales took off, and Dewar reportedly ate two Twinkies every day for much of his life. He died in 1985.

The spongy treat has evolved into an American phenomenon, from which nearly everyone has slurped the creamy center. Today the Twinkie is Continental's top Hostess-line seller, with the injection machines filling as many as 52,000 every hour.

You will need a spice bottle (approximately the size of a Twinkie), ten 12 × 14–inch pieces of aluminum foil, a cake decorator or pastry bag, and a toothpick.

CAKE
nonstick spray
4 egg whites

1 16-ounce box golden pound cake mix
⅔ cup water

FILLING
2 teaspoons very hot water
rounded 1/4 teaspoon salt
2 cups marshmallow creme (one
    7-ounce jar)

1/2 cup shortening
1/3 cup powdered sugar
1/2 teaspoon vanilla

1. Preheat the oven to 325°F.
2. Fold each piece of aluminum foil in half twice. Wrap the folded foil around the spice bottle to create a mold. Leave the top of the mold open for pouring in the batter. Make 10 of these molds and arrange them on a cookie sheet or in a shallow pan. Grease the inside of each mold with a light coating of nonstick spray.
3. Disregard the directions on the box of cake mix. Instead, beat the egg whites until stiff. In a separate bowl combine cake mix with water, and beat until thoroughly blended (about 2 minutes). Fold egg whites into cake batter, and slowly combine until completely mixed.
4. Pour the batter into the molds, filling each one about 3/4 inch. Bake in the preheated oven for 30 minutes, or until the cake is golden brown and a toothpick stuck in the center comes out clean.
5. For the filling, combine the salt with the hot water in a small bowl and stir until salt is dissolved. Let this mixture cool.
6. Combine the marshmallow creme, shortening, powdered sugar, and vanilla in a medium bowl and mix well with an electric mixer on high speed until fluffy.
7. Add the salt solution to the filling mixture and combine.
8. When the cakes are done and cooled, use a toothpick to make three small holes in the bottom of each one. Move the toothpick around the inside of each cake to create space for the filling,
9. Using a cake decorator or pastry bag, inject each cake with filling through all three holes.

• MAKES 10.

• • • •

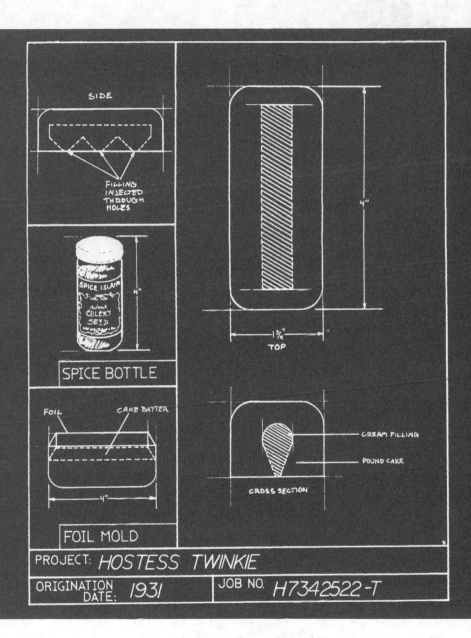

SIDE

FILLING
INJECTED
THROUGH
HOLES

SPICE ISLAND

CELERY
SEED

4"

SPICE BOTTLE

FOIL   CAKE BATTER

4"

FOIL MOLD

4"

1 3/4"

TOP

CREAM FILLING

POUND CAKE

CROSS SECTION

PROJECT: *HOSTESS TWINKIE*

ORIGINATION
DATE: *1931*

JOB NO.   *H7342522-T*

TOP SECRET RECIPES
VERSION OF
JIMMY DEAN
BREAKFAST SAUSAGE

Before he became America's sausage king, Jimmy Dean was known for crooning the country hit "Big Bad John." That song came out in 1962 and sold over 8 million copies. His singing success launched a television career on ABC with *The Jimmy Dean Show,* on which Roy Clark, Patsy Cline, and Roger Miller got their big breaks. The TV exposure led to acting roles for Jimmy as a regular on *Daniel Boone* and in feature films, including his debut in the James Bond flick *Diamonds Are Forever.* Knowing that a show business career is an unpredictable one, Jimmy socked his money away in hog-farming investments. In 1968, the Jimmy Dean Meat Company developed a special recipe to transform those piggies into the sausage that has now become a household name. Today, the company is part of the Sara Lee Corporation, but Jimmy is still chairman of the board of his division, and he still appears on TV in commercials for the brand, even at the age of 71.

This clone recipe re-creates three varieties of the famous roll sausage that you form into patties and cook in a skillet. Use ground pork found at the supermarket (make it lean pork, if you like), or grind some up yourself if you have a meat grinder lying around, for some good old-fashioned fun.

SAGE

16 ounces ground pork
1 teaspoon salt
½ teaspoon dried parsley
¼ teaspoon rubbed sage
¼ teaspoon ground black pepper

¼ teaspoon dried thyme
¼ teaspoon crushed red
   pepper
¼ teaspoon coriander
¼ teaspoon MSG (such as Accent)

HOT

16 ounces ground pork
1 teaspoon salt
½ teaspoon cayenne pepper
¼ teaspoon rubbed sage
¼ teaspoon ground black pepper
¼ teaspoon crushed red pepper
¼ teaspoon coriander
¼ teaspoon MSG
   (such as Accent)

MAPLE

16 ounces ground pork
3 tablespoons maple-flavored
   syrup
1 teaspoon salt
½ teaspoon MSG
   (such as Accent)
¼ teaspoon coriander

1. Combine all ingredients for the flavor of your choice in a medium bowl. Form the sausage into patties and cook in a skillet over medium heat until brown.

- MAKES 1 POUND OF SAUSAGE.

•   •   •   •

KEEBLER PECAN SANDIES

This company was founded as the United Biscuit Company of America back in 1927. It was made up of sixteen bakeries from Philadelphia to Salt Lake City, marketing cookies and crackers under a variety of brand names. That system lasted for twenty-two years, and eventually the name Keebler was adopted for the entire conglomerate. Keebler was linked with the United Biscuit name once again after it was bought in 1974 by a British company of that name.

Today the company makes 50 billion cookies and crackers each year; among them are the popular Pecan Sandies, first sold in 1955. The Toffee variety came thirty-eight years later.

1 ½ cups vegetable shortening
¾ cup granulated sugar
1 ½ teaspoons salt
2 eggs

4 cups all-purpose flour
¼ teaspoon baking soda
2 tablespoons water
1 cup shelled pecans

1. Preheat the oven to 325°F.
2. In a large bowl, cream together the shortening, sugar, and salt with an electric mixer on medium speed.
3. Add the eggs and beat well.
4. While mixing, slowly add the flour, baking soda, and add extra water as necessary to make the dough stick together.
5. Chop the pecans into very small bits using a food processor or blender on low speed. Be careful not to overchop; you

don't want to make pecan dust. The pieces should be about the size of rice grains.

6. Add the pecans to the dough and knead with your hands until the pecans are well blended into the mixture.

7. Roll the dough into 1-inch balls and press flat with your hands onto ungreased baking sheets. The cookies should be about 2 inches in diameter and ½ inch thick.

8. Bake for 25 to 30 minutes, or until the edges of the cookies are golden brown.

- MAKES 4 DOZEN COOKIES.

Keebler® Toffee Sandies®
Follow the Pecan Sandies recipe, above, replacing the chopped pecans with one 6-ounce package of Heath® Bits 'o Brickle®.

• • • •

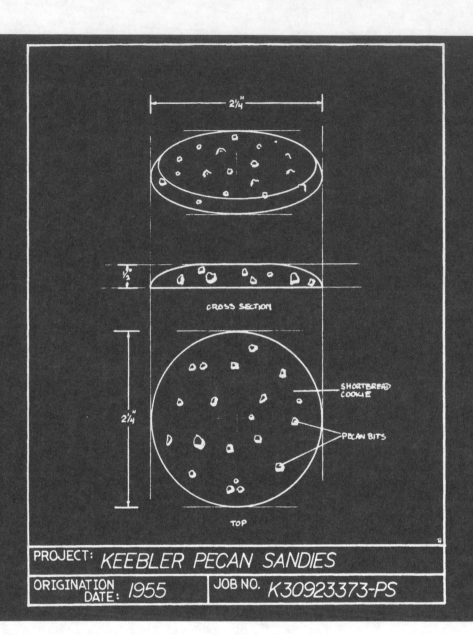

2¼"

½

CROSS SECTION

SHORTBREAD
COOKIE

2¼"

PECAN BITS

TOP

PROJECT: KEEBLER PECAN SANDIES

ORIGINATION DATE: 1955

JOB NO. K30923373-PS

M&M/MARS
SNICKERS BAR

☆ ✌ 💣 ✏ ☯ ✂ ☞

In 1992 *Fortune* magazine estimated the Mars family's personal worth at somewhere around $12.5 billion—quite a fistful of peanuts. This solid foundation of wealth, built on the country's undying passion for chocolate and other sweets, has made this clan the richest family in America—and the most reclusive. A family rule prohibits photographs to be taken of the Mars family and corporate executives. According to *Fortune,* a photographer who once tried to get a shot of Forrest Mars, Sr., found himself enveloped in a cloth that was thrown as he was about to snap the picture.

The empire started in 1902, when nineteen-year-old Franklin C. Mars began selling homemade candy. In 1910 he started a wholesale candy business in Tacoma, Washington. Ten years later Frank moved to Minneapolis, where he used the family kitchen to make buttercreams, which were personally delivered to retailers in the city by his wife, Ethel. Business grew steadily, and in 1940 Frank's son Forrest established M&M Limited in Newark, New Jersey.

By 1967 the family's confectionery business in the United States had been consolidated into M&M/Mars. The fortune grew steadily larger as the corporation routinely kept four brands in the top-ten-selling chocolates in the country: Milky Way, M&M's Plain and Peanut, and, in the number-one spot, Snickers.

1 tablespoon plus 2 tablespoons
  water
¼ cup light corn syrup
2 tablespoons butter
1 teaspoon vanilla extract
2 tablespoons peanut butter
dash salt

3 cups powdered sugar
35 unwrapped Kraft caramels
1 cup (or 2 3.5-ounce
  packages) dry-roasted
  unsalted peanuts
2 12-ounce bags milk-chocolate
  chips

1. With the mixer on high speed, combine 1 tablespoon water, corn syrup, butter, vanilla, peanut butter, and salt until creamy. Slowly add the powdered sugar.
2. When the mixture has the consistency of dough, remove it from the bowl with your hands and press it into a lightly greased 9 x 9–inch pan. Set in the refrigerator.
3. Melt the caramels in a small pan with 2 tablespoons water over low heat.
4. When the caramel is soft, mix in the peanuts. Pour the mixture over the refrigerated nougat in the pan. Let this cool in the refrigerator.
5. When the refrigerated mixture is firm, melt the chocolate over low heat in a double boiler or in a microwave oven set on high for 2 minutes. Stir halfway through cooking time.
6. When the mixture in the pan has hardened, cut it into 4 x 1–inch sections.
7. Set each chunk onto a fork and dip into the melted chocolate. Tap the fork against the side of the bowl or pan to knock off any excess chocolate. Then place the chunks on waxed paper to cool at room temperature (less than 70°F). This could take several hours, but the bars will set best this way. You can speed up the process by placing the bars in the refrigerator for 30 minutes.

• MAKES ABOUT 2 DOZEN BARS.

• • • •

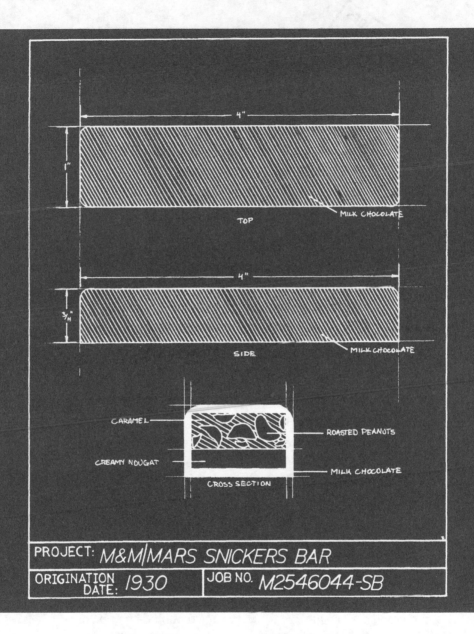

4"

1"

MILK CHOCOLATE

TOP

4"

3/4"

MILK CHOCOLATE

SIDE

CARAMEL

ROASTED PEANUTS

CREAMY NOUGAT

MILK CHOCOLATE

CROSS SECTION

PROJECT: M&M/MARS SNICKERS BAR

ORIGINATION DATE: 1930

JOB NO. M2546044-SB

MRS. FIELDS
CHOCOLATE CHIP
COOKIES

In 1975 eighteen-year-old Debbi Sivyer perfected the chocolate chip cookies she had been making since the age of twelve. Little did she know then that her delicious cookies would soon launch her into a successful career with her own multimillion-dollar business. It happened two years later, when her new husband, financial consultant Randy Fields, noticed that his clients couldn't resist the batches of cookies that Debbi sent to work with him. With the help of Randy and a banker who lent her $50,000 because he loved her chocolate chip cookies so much, she opened her first cookie store in Palo Alto, California, in 1977. The second store opened two years later in San Francisco.

Without spending a dollar on advertising, the Mrs. Fields Company is now listed on the London Stock Exchange, claims more than 600 stores worldwide, and has purchased the 113-unit bakery chain, La Petite Boulangerie, from PepsiCo.

1 cup (2 sticks) softened butter
1/2 cup granulated sugar
1 1/2 cups packed brown sugar
2 eggs
2 1/2 teaspoons vanilla extract
2 1/2 cups all-purpose flour

3/4 teaspoon salt
1 teaspoon baking powder
1 teaspoon baking soda
1 1/2 twelve-ounce bags semisweet
    chocolate chips

1. Preheat the oven to 350°F.
2. In a large mixing bowl, cream the butter, sugars, eggs, and vanilla.
3. Mix together the flour, salt, baking powder, and baking soda.
4. Combine the wet and dry ingredients.
5. Stir in the chocolate chips.
6. With your fingers, place golf-ball-size dough portions 2 inches apart on an ungreased cookie sheet.
7. Bake for 9 minutes, or until edges are light brown.

• MAKES 30 COOKIES.

TIDBITS

It's very important that you not exceed the cooking time given above, even if the cookies appear to be underbaked. When the cookies are removed from the oven, the sugar in them will stay hot and continue the cooking process. The finished product should be soft in the middle and crunchy around the edges.

For variations of this cookie, substitute milk chocolate for the semisweet chocolate and/or add 1½ cups of chopped walnuts or macadamia nuts to the recipe before baking. Although you can substitute margarine for butter in this recipe, you will have the best results from butter. The cookie will have a richer taste and will be crispier around the edges like the original.

• • • •

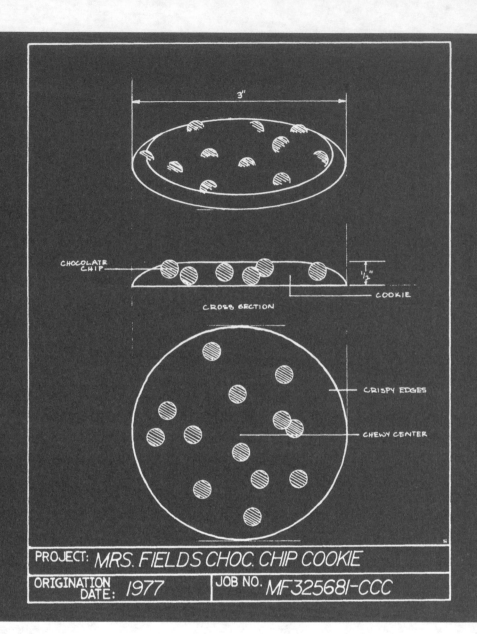

3"

CHOCOLATE
CHIP

½"

COOKIE

CROSS SECTION

CRISPY EDGES

CHEWY CENTER

PROJECT: MRS. FIELDS CHOC. CHIP COOKIE

ORIGINATION DATE: 1977

JOB NO. MF325681-CCC

MRS. FIELDS
PEANUT BUTTER
DREAM BARS

☆   ✌   💣   ✎   🎱   ✂   ☞

In 1987 the Mrs. Fields Corporation devised a rather clever treat called the Peanut Butter Dream Bar—a delicious combination of peanut butter, chocolate, and a cookie-crumb crust. It was not only a tasty product but an economical one. Mrs. Fields has always had the policy of removing cookies that are more than two hours old from outlet display cases. Now, instead of being thrown away, the cookies are crumbled up and mixed with melted butter to form the Dream Bar Crust.

8 Mrs. Fields Chocolate Chip
    Cookies (see previous recipe)
5 tablespoons melted butter
¾ cup peanut butter

1½ cups powdered sugar
1 12-ounce bag milk-chocolate
    chips

1. Preheat the oven to 350°F.
2. Crumble the cookies into a medium mixing bowl.
3. Add the melted butter; stir until the mixture darkens and the butter is evenly mixed in.
4. Pour the mixture into an ungreased 9 x 9–inch baking pan.
5. Press the dough down solidly into the pan and bake for 10 minutes, or until firm around edges. When done, cool in the refrigerator.

6. Mix the peanut butter and sugar until blended. The mixture should have a doughy texture that allows you to knead it with your hands.
7. Melt the chocolate chips in a double boiler over low heat, stirring often. You may also melt them in a microwave oven set on high for 2 minutes, stirring halfway through the heating time.
8. When the dough is cool, spread half of the melted chocolate over the surface.
9. Cool in the refrigerator for 20 to 30 minutes, or until hardened.
10. Spread the peanut butter mixture evenly over the surface of the chocolate.
11. Spread the remaining chocolate over the peanut butter, covering to the edges of the pan.
12. Cool the finished product in the refrigerator or let it sit at room temperature until hardened.
13. Slice into five even rows and then once down the middle.

• MAKES 10 BARS.

•　•　•　•

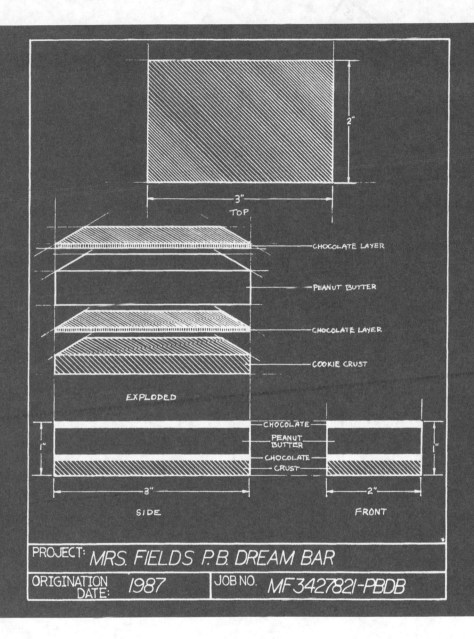

2"

3"

TOP

CHOCOLATE LAYER

PEANUT BUTTER

CHOCOLATE LAYER

COOKIE CRUST

EXPLODED

CHOCOLATE
PEANUT BUTTER
CHOCOLATE
CRUST

1"

3"

SIDE

1"

2"

FRONT

PROJECT: MRS. FIELDS P.B. DREAM BAR

ORIGINATION DATE: 1987

JOB NO. MF342782I-PBDB

181

NABISCO
NUTTER BUTTER

Formerly called the National Biscuit Company, Nabisco was formed in the late 1800s by several bakeries that joined together to meet a growing demand. In the 1870s Nabisco's forefathers had introduced the first individually packaged baked goods. Before this, cookies and crackers had been sold from open barrels or biscuit boxes. The company has become the world's largest manufacturer of cookies and crackers, selling some 42 million packages of Nabisco products each day to retail outlets on every continent.

Nutter Butter Cookies were introduced in 1969 and have quickly taken their place alongside Nabisco's most popular products, including Oreos, Chips Ahoy!, and Fig Newtons.

COOKIES
½ cup vegetable shortening
⅔ cup granulated sugar
1 egg
½ teaspoon salt

3 tablespoons peanut butter
½ cup old-fashioned Quaker oats
1 cup all-purpose flour

FILLING
½ cup peanut butter
¾ cup powdered sugar

1 tablespoon fine graham cracker
    crumbs

1. Preheat the oven to 325°F.
2. In a large bowl, cream together the shortening and sugar with an electric mixer.
3. Add the egg, salt, and peanut butter and beat until well blended.
4. Put the oats in a blender and blend on medium speed until they are almost as finely ground as flour.
5. Add the oats and flour to the mixture and blend well.
6. Pinch out small portions of dough and roll into 1-inch balls in the palm of your hand. Press these flat on ungreased cookie sheets so that they form 2-inch circles. If you're a stickler for a cookie that looks just like the original, you can form the dough into flat peanut shapes similar to those illustrated.
7. Bake for 8 to 10 minutes, or until light brown around the edges.
8. While the cookies bake, combine the filling ingredients in a small bowl.
9. When the cookies are cool, use a butter knife to spread a thin layer of filling on the flat side of a cookie, and press another on top. Repeat.

• MAKES 2 DOZEN COOKIES.

•   •   •   •

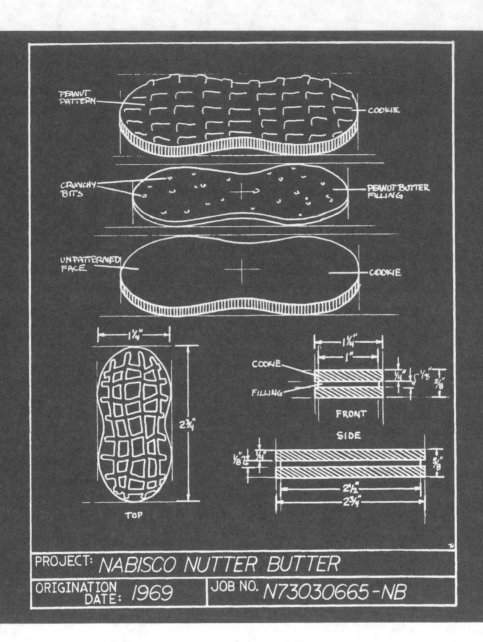

PEANUT PATTERN

COOKIE

CRUNCHY BITS

PEANUT BUTTER FILLING

UNPATTERNED FACE

COOKIE

1¼"

2¾"

TOP

COOKIE

FILLING

1¼"

1"

¼"

⅛"

⅝"

FRONT

SIDE

⅛"

¼"

⅝"

2½"

2¾"

PROJECT: *NABISCO NUTTER BUTTER*

ORIGINATION DATE: *1969*

JOB NO. *N73030665-NB*

NABISCO
OREO COOKIE

☆　　　✌　　　💣　　　✏　　　👁　　　✂　　　☞

At one time Nabisco actually conducted a study that determined that 50 percent of Oreo consumers twist the cookie apart before eating it. I guess this is important information, since it concerns the world's top-selling cookie. Historians at Nabisco aren't sure who came up with the idea for this sandwich cookie back in 1912, but they do know that it was introduced along with two other cookie creations that have long since died. The name may have come from the Greek word for mountain, *oreo*, which would once have made sense because the first test version was hill-shaped. When the Oreo was first sold to the public, it was much larger than today's cookie, but it kept shrinking over the years until Nabisco realized it had become much too small and had to en-large it again to today's current 1¾–inch diameter.

In 1975, Nabisco figured we couldn't have too much of a good thing, so the company gave us Double Stuf Oreos, with twice the filling. A smart move. Today Double Stuf holds its own rank as the fifth most popular cookie in America.

COOKIE

1 18.25-ounce package Betty
　Crocker chocolate fudge cake
　mix
3 tablespoons shortening, melted
½ cup cake flour, measured then
　sifted

1 egg
3 tablespoons water
2 tablespoons brown paste food
　coloring (optional)

FILLING

3¾ cups powdered sugar
½ cup shortening
½ tablespoon granulated sugar

2 tablespoons hot water
½ teaspoon vanilla extract

1. Combine the cookie ingredients in a large bowl. Add the water a little bit at a time until the dough forms. Cover and chill for 2 hours.

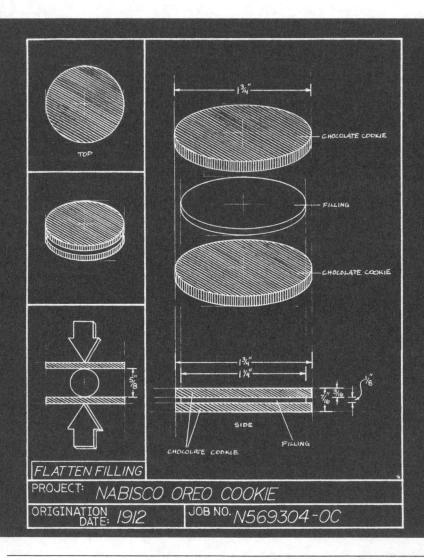

TOP

CHOCOLATE COOKIE

FILLING

CHOCOLATE COOKIE

SIDE

CHOCOLATE COOKIE

FILLING

FLATTEN FILLING

PROJECT: NABISCO OREO COOKIE

ORIGINATION DATE: 1912

JOB NO. N569304-OC

2. Preheat oven to 350°F.
3. On a lightly floured surface, roll out a portion of the dough to just under 1/16 inch thick. To cut, use a lid from a spice container with a 1½–inch diameter (Schilling brand is good). Arrange the cut dough rounds on a cookie sheet that is sprayed with a light coating of nonstick spray. Bake for 10 minutes. Remove wafers from the oven and cool completely.
4. As the cookies cool, combine the filling ingredients well with an electric mixer.
5. With your hands, form the filling into balls about ½ to ¾ inch in diameter.
6. Place a filling ball in the center of the flat side of a cooled cookie and press with another cookie, flat side down, until the filling spreads to the edge.

• MAKES 60 COOKIES.

TIDBITS

If the cookie dough seems too tacky, you can work in as much as ¼ cup of flour as you pat out and roll the dough. Use just enough flour to make the dough workable but not tough.

This may be obvious to you, but you can expand your own homemade line of Oreos by creating your own versions of Double Stuf® or the giant Oreos called Oreo Big Stuf®. Just add twice the filling for Double Stuf, or make the cookie twice the size for Big Stuf. Go crazy. Try Triple Stuf or Quadruple Stuf or Quintuple Stuf . . . somebody stop me.

The brown paste food coloring gives the cookies the dark brown, almost black color of the originals. If you do not use the paste food coloring be sure to change the amount of water added to the wafer cookies from 3 tablespoons to ¼ cup. The coloring can be found with cake decorating supplies at art supply and craft stores.

• • • •

NESTLÉ
100 GRAND BAR

☆　　　✌　　　💣　　　✏　　　☯　　　✂　　　☞

Nestlé is the world's largest packaged food manufacturer, coffee roaster, and chocolate maker. It is the largest single company in Switzerland today, but Nestlé derives only 2 percent of its revenue from its home country.

The company is quite diverse. Nestlé's product lines include beverages and drinks, chocolate and candy, dairy products, and frozen foods. The company also operates more than thirty Stouffer Hotels and owns 25 percent of the French cosmetics giant L'Oréal. In the United States, where the company is called Nestlé USA, it ranks third behind Mars, Inc., and Hershey USA in chocolate sales.

This candy bar was introduced in 1966 as the $100,000 Bar, then its name was changed to 100 Grand Bar in 1985.

30 unwrapped Kraft caramels, at   *¾ cup Rice Krispies*
   room temperature
1 12-ounce bag milk chocolate
   chips

1. With your fingers, flatten each caramel into a rectangle about ¼ inch thick.
2. Melt the chocolate chips in a microwave-safe bowl in a microwave set on half power for 2 minutes. Stir halfway through the heating time. Melt thoroughly, but do not overheat.
3. Add the Rice Krispies and stir just until blended.

4. Dip each caramel into the chocolate to coat completely and then place on waxed paper. Cool until firm at room temperature, 1 to 2 hours.

- MAKES 30 CANDY BARS.

• • • •

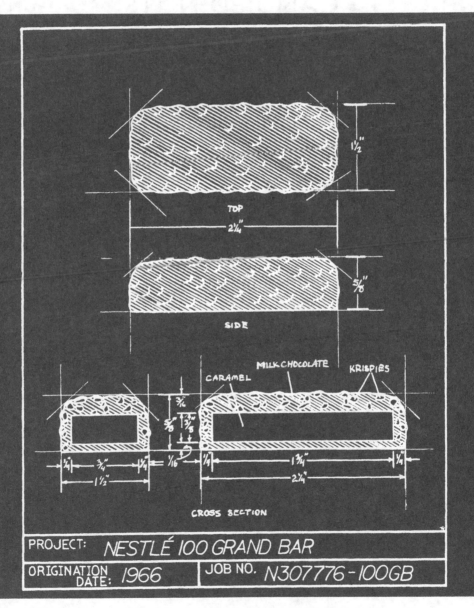

TOP SECRET RECIPES
VERSION OF
NUTS 4 NUTS
CANDIED NUTS

☆   ✌   💥   ✎   ◉   ✂   ☞

The streets of New York City are peppered with Nuts 4 Nuts vendors selling freshly candied nuts that you can smell a block away. For a buck or two you get your choice of warm, sugar-coated peanuts, cashews, or almonds wrapped up in a little paper bag with the corners twisted closed. The nuts are candied right there on the carts in a large, metal bowl over a heating element. Sugar and water is added to the nuts, which are stirred often as the water evaporates so they develop a nice, even coating without burning. They're easy to make on the street, which means they're even easier to clone at home. All you need for your own quick version of this addictive street snack is 1¼ cups of your favorite nuts, some sugar, a little water, a hot pan and you're about 5 minutes away from an authentic New York City treat. Give this recipe a try with pecans or walnuts, and then use them on a spinach salad, along with a little goat cheese, and some diced apples or pears for a real gourmet touch.

2 tablespoons water
¼ cup sugar

1¼ cups nuts (almonds, peanuts,
or cashews)

1. Bring 2 tablespoons water and ¼ cup sugar to a boil in a medium saucepan over medium heat.

2. Add the nuts and stir often until water evaporates. Continue stirring until the sugar begins to harden on the nuts. When the sugar on the nuts begins to turn light brown, pour them onto a plate to cool. Be careful not to cook the nuts too long, or the sugar will burn.

- MAKES 1 ¼ CUPS.

TOP SECRET RECIPES
VERSION OF

OLD BAY
SEASONING

With spice grinder in hand, Gustav Brunn traveled to America from Germany, and settled down in Baltimore on the Chesapeake Bay. There on the bay, steamed crabs are a staple. So Gustav started grinding. In 1939, Gustav found just the right mix for his top-secret blend of spices that for generations would be the most used seasoning on steamed crabs, shrimp, lobster, and other tasty seafood dishes. But the celery salt–based blend is not just for seafood, according to McCormick & Co., which purchased Old Bay in 1990. You can also use the blend on chicken, french fries, popcorn, baked potatoes, deviled eggs, hamburgers, and even pizza. If you've got a recipe that requires Old Bay, but don't have any in the cupboard, head to the spice cabinet and throw these ingredients together to make the perfect clone.

1 tablespoon celery salt
1/4 teaspoon paprika
1/8 teaspoon black pepper
1/8 teaspoon cayenne pepper
pinch ground dry mustard
pinch mace

pinch cinnamon
pinch cardamom
pinch allspice
pinch ground clove
pinch ginger

1. Combine all ingredients in a small bowl. Store in a sealed container.

- MAKES 4 TEASPOONS.

• • • •

PETER PAUL MOUNDS AND ALMOND JOY

At the train station in Naugatuck, Connecticut, candy and ice-cream shop owner Peter Paul Halajian used to meet the commuter trains carrying baskets full of fresh hand-made chocolates. The most popular of his candies was a blend of coconut, fruits, nuts, and chocolate that he called *Konabar.*

In 1919, when demand for his confections grew, Halajian and five associates, all of Armenian heritage, opened a business in New Haven to produce and sell his chocolates on a larger scale. Because there were no refrigerators, they made the chocolate by hand at night, when the air was the coolest, and sold the candy during the day. In 1920 the first Mounds bar was introduced.

Peter Paul merged with Cadbury U.S.A. in 1978, and in 1986 Cadbury U.S.A. merged with the Hershey Foods Corporation, now the world's largest candy conglomerate.

Today the recipes for Mounds and Almond Joy are the same as they were in the roaring twenties.

5 ounces *Eagle* sweetened
    condensed milk
1 teaspoon vanilla extract
2 cups powdered sugar

14 ounces premium shredded or
    flaked coconut
1 24-ounce package semisweet
    chocolate chips

1. Blend the condensed milk and vanilla.
2. Add the powdered sugar to the above mixture a little bit at a time, stirring until smooth.
3. Stir in the coconut. The mixture should be firm.
4. Pat the mixture firmly into a greased 9 x 13 x 2-inch pan. Chill in the refrigerator until firm.
5. In a double boiler over hot (not boiling) water, melt the chocolate, stirring often. You may also use a microwave oven. Place the chips in a bowl and heat for 1 minute on high; stir, then heat for 1 minute more.
6. Remove the coconut mixture from the refrigerator and cut it into 1 x 2-inch bars.
7. Set each coconut bar onto a fork and dip into the chocolate. Tap the fork against the side of the pan or bowl to remove any excess chocolate.
8. Air-dry at room temperature on waxed paper. This could take several hours, but chocolate sets best at cool room temperature (below 70°F). You may speed up the process by placing the bars in the refrigerator for about 30 minutes.

- MAKES ABOUT 3 DOZEN BARS.

Peter Paul Almond Joy
And if you feel like a nut, follow the above recipe with these changes:

1. Add 1 cup dry-roasted almonds to the list of ingredients.
2. Substitute milk-chocolate chips for semisweet chocolate.
3. In step 7, place two almonds atop each bar before dipping.

• • • •

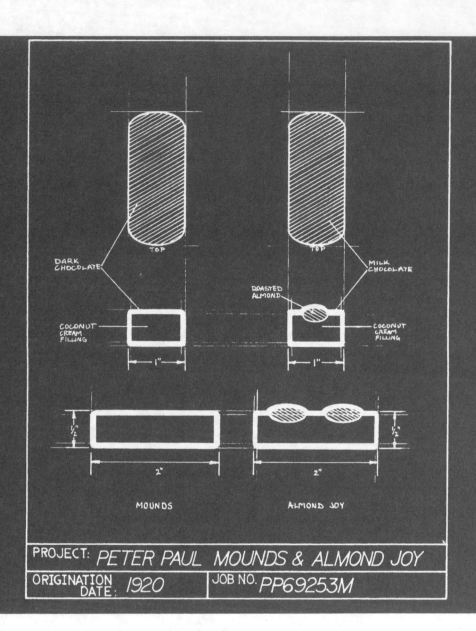

DARK CHOCOLATE

TOP

COCONUT CREAM FILLING

1"

1/2"

2"

MOUNDS

ROASTED ALMOND

MILK CHOCOLATE

TOP

COCONUT CREAM FILLING

1"

1/2"

2"

ALMOND JOY

PROJECT: *PETER PAUL MOUNDS & ALMOND JOY*

ORIGINATION DATE: *1920*

JOB NO. *PP69253M*

TOP SECRET RECIPES
VERSION OF
RAGU
PASTA SAUCE

It's America's most popular pasta sauce and now you can whip up clones of two varieties at home at a fraction of the cost. Just snag yourself a large can of tomato sauce and a few other common ingredients and get simmering. These recipes duplicate the traditional "Meat" variety of the sauce and the newer "Chunky Garden Style" version with tomato, basil, and Italian cheese. Feel free to doctor these sauces up with your own creative additions just as many do to perk up real Ragu.

MEAT

2 ounces ground beef
29-ounce can tomato sauce
5 teaspoons granulated sugar
4 teaspoons olive oil
1 1/2 teaspoons minced dried
  onions

1 1/2 teaspoons shredded Romano
  cheese
1/8 teaspoon ground black pepper
1 bay leaf

1. Brown ground beef in a medium saucepan over medium heat. Add remaining ingredients, bring to a boil, then reduce heat and simmer for 15 to 20 minutes, stirring often.

• MAKES 2 1/2 CUPS.

TOMATO, BASIL, AND ITALIAN CHEESE

29-ounce can tomato sauce
½ cup canned diced tomatoes
5 teaspoons granulated sugar
1 tablespoon olive oil
1 tablespoon shredded Romano
    cheese
1 teaspoon shredded parmesan
    cheese

1 teaspoon dried basil
½ teaspoon dried parsley
¼ teaspoon garlic powder
⅛ teaspoon black pepper
1 bay leaf

1. Combine all ingredients in a medium saucepan over medium heat. Bring to a boil then reduce heat and simmer for 15 to 20 minutes, stirring often.

• MAKES 3 CUPS.

• • • •

REESE'S
PEANUT BUTTER
CUPS

☆   ✌   💣   ✏   ☯   ✂   ☞

In south central Pennsylvania, in 1917, a thirty-eight-year-old man named H. B. Reese moved to Hershey, Pennsylvania, to operate one of Milton Hershey's dairy farms. Inspired by Hershey's success, and possibly urged on by his growing family (he was to have six sons and seven daughters), Reese soon left the dairy to make his living in the candy business. Then in 1923, after achieving a small success with a few products, Reese produced a candy consisting of specially processed peanut butter covered with Hershey's milk chocolate. It changed a struggling candy plant into a solid business concern. During World War II conditions prompted Reese to discontinue his other products and focus on the peanut butter cup. He thereby developed something unique in America's food industry—a major company built and thriving on one product.

In 1963 the names Hershey and Reese were linked once again when the Hershey Foods Corporation purchased the successful H. B. Reese Candy Company. Today the Reese's Peanut Butter Cup often tops the list of America's best-selling candies.

You will need a muffin tin with shallow cups.

1 cup peanut butter
1/4 teaspoon salt
1/2 cup powdered sugar

1 12-ounce package Hershey's
   milk-chocolate chips

1. In a small bowl, mix the peanut butter, salt, and powdered sugar until firm.
2. Slowly melt the chocolate chips in a double boiler over hot, not boiling, water. You may also melt them in a microwave oven set on high for 2 minutes, stirring halfway through the heating time.
3. Grease the muffin-tin cups and spoon some chocolate into each cup, filling halfway.
4. With a spoon, draw the chocolate up the edges of each cup until all sides are coated. Cool in the refrigerator until firm.
5. Spread about a teaspoon of peanut butter onto the chocolate in each cup, leaving room for the final chocolate layer.
6. Pour some chocolate onto the top of each candy and spread it to the edges.
7. Let sit at room temperature, or covered in the refrigerator. Turn out of the pan when firm.

- MAKES 12 PIECES.

TIDBITS

It is best to use a shallow muffin tin or candy tin for this recipe. But if you only have the larger, more common, muffin tin, it will work just fine—simply fill each tin only halfway with the chocolate and peanut butter. Unless, that is, you want to make giant-size, mutant peanut butter cups. In that case, fill those cups up all the way!

For even better clones, make your Peanut Butter Cups inside paper baking cups. Cut each baking cup in half horizontally to make it shallower, and "paint" your first layer of chocolate onto the inside of each cup with a spoon. Put the cups into a muffin tin so that they hold their shape, and then put the tin into the refrigerator to set. Add your peanut butter and the top layer of chocolate according to the instructions in the recipe.

• • • •

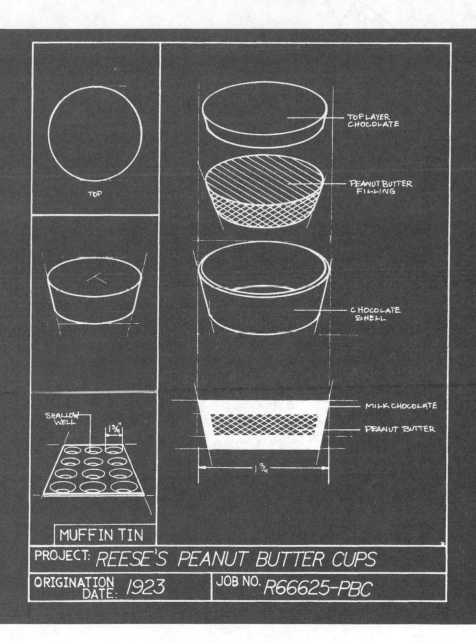

TOP

TOP LAYER
CHOCOLATE

PEANUT BUTTER
FILLING

CHOCOLATE
SHELL

MILK CHOCOLATE

PEANUT BUTTER

SHALLOW
WELL

1 3/4"

1 3/4

MUFFIN TIN

PROJECT: *REESE'S PEANUT BUTTER CUPS*

ORIGINATION
DATE: *1923*

JOB NO. *R66625-PBC*

SARA LEE
ORIGINAL CREAM
CHEESECAKE

☆　　✌　　💣　　✎　　🎱　　✂　　☞

In 1949 a bakery owner named Charles Lubin pioneered in the frozen-foods business when he invented a top-quality cream cheesecake for sale in supermarkets and restaurants. He named the cheesecake after his daughter, Sara Lee. Though skeptics believed that a frozen bakery item could not be sold in large grocery stores, Lubin's cheesecake was such a success that only two years later, in 1951, he opened the Kitchens of Sara Lee and began to add other items to his line. In the early 1950s Lubin experimented with, and introduced, the aluminum foil pan, which allowed his products to be baked, quickly frozen, and sold in the same container.

Today the Kitchens of Sara Lee produce more than 200 varieties of baked goods. And few people know that this diverse company has also been successful in manufacturing and marketing coffee, meats, and even pantyhose under the Hanes and Liz Claiborne labels.

CRUST

1½ cups fine graham-cracker crumbs (11 crackers, rolled)

¼ cup granulated sugar
½ cup (1 stick) butter, softened

FILLING

16 ounces cream cheese
1 cup sour cream
2 tablespoons cornstarch

1 cup granulated sugar
2 tablespoons butter, softened
1 teaspoon vanilla extract

TOPPING

¾ cup sour cream

¼ cup powdered sugar

1. Preheat the oven to 375°F.
2. For the crust, combine the graham-cracker crumbs, sugar, and butter, and mix well.
3. Press the mixture firmly into an ungreased 9-inch pie plate. Press flat onto bottom only.
4. Bake for 8 minutes, or until the edges are slightly brown. Reduce the oven temperature to 350°F.
5. For the filling, combine the cream cheese, sour cream, cornstarch, and sugar in the bowl of a mixer. Mix until the sugar has dissolved.
6. Add the butter and vanilla and blend until smooth. Be careful not to overmix, or the filling will become too fluffy and will crack when cooling.
7. Pour the filling over the crust.
8. Bake for 30 to 35 minutes, or until a knife inserted 1 inch from the edge comes out clean.
9. Cool for 1 hour.
10. For the topping, mix the sour cream and powdered sugar. Spread the mixture over the top of the cooled cheesecake. Chill or freeze until ready to eat.

TIDBITS

If you decide to freeze this cheesecake, defrost it for about an hour at room temperature before serving. You may also defrost slices in the microwave oven if you're in a hurry. (Impatience is a common cheesecake-craving affliction.) Set the microwave on high and zap as follows:

1 slice—15 seconds
2 slices—25 seconds
3 slices—40 seconds

Be sure to refreeze the remaining cheesecake after slicing.

•   •   •   •

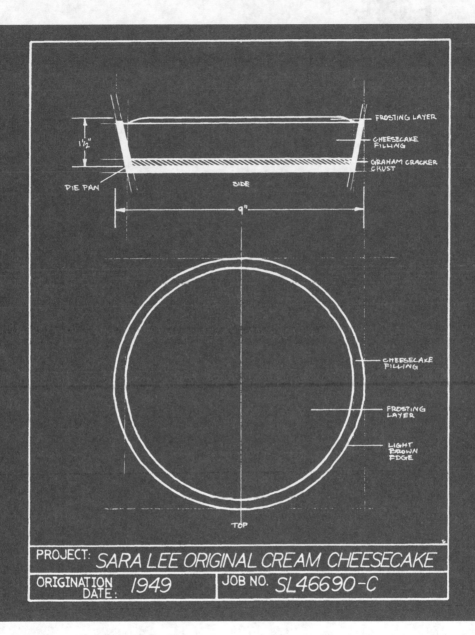

FROSTING LAYER

CHEESECAKE FILLING

GRAHAM CRACKER CRUST

1½"

PIE PAN

SIDE

9"

CHEESECAKE FILLING

FROSTING LAYER

LIGHT BROWN EDGE

TOP

PROJECT: SARA LEE ORIGINAL CREAM CHEESECAKE

ORIGINATION DATE: 1949

JOB NO. SL46690-C

TOP SECRET RECIPES

VERSION OF

SNICKERS
MUNCH BAR

It was only recently that the bigwigs at M&M/Mars, Inc. chose to capitalize on the company's bestselling candy bar, Snickers, by slapping the brand name on the peanut riddled, butter toffee Munch Bar. Despite the new moniker, the candy bar is the same simple, peanut-brittle recipe the company has used for decades, which makes it easy for us to clone with only four common ingredients, plus a candy thermometer. With this *Top Secret Recipe* you can produce the equivalent of 12 of these addictive candy bars in your own kitchen. Just be sure the dry-roasted peanuts you use are the salted kind, and watch that thermometer closely once the candy gets simmering.

2 cups salted dry-roasted peanuts *½ cup granulated sugar*
½ cup butter (1 stick) *¼ cup light corn syrup*

1. Spread peanuts out on a baking sheet and heat them up in your oven set on 300°F. This will warm up the peanuts so that they don't cool the candy too quickly when added later. There's no need to preheat the oven.
2. Melt the butter in a medium saucepan over medium/low heat.

3. Add sugar and corn syrup and simmer, stirring occasionally. Put a candy thermometer in the mixture and watch it closely.
4. When the mixture reaches 300°F, add the warm peanuts and stir well until all of the peanuts are coated with candy. Pour the candy onto the warm baking sheet and spread it flat. When the candy cools, break it into chunks and store it in a covered container.

• MAKES THE EQUIVALENT OF 12 1.5-OUNCE CANDY BARS.

•   •   •   •

TASTYKAKE BUTTERSCOTCH KRIMPETS

In 1914 Pittsburgh baker Philip J. Baur and Boston egg salesman Herbert T. Morris decided that there was a need for prewrapped, fresh cakes that were conveniently available at local grocers. The two men coined the name *Tastykake* for their new treats and were determined to use only the finest ingredients, delivered fresh daily to their bakery.

The founders' standards of freshness are still maintained. Tastykakes baked tonight are on the shelves tomorrow. That philosophy has contributed to substantial growth for the Tasty Baking Company. On its first day, the firm's sales receipts totaled $28.32; today the company boasts yearly sales of more than $200 million.

Among the top-selling Tastykake treats are the Butterscotch Krimpets, first created in 1927. Today, approximately 6 million Butterscotch Krimpets are baked each and every week.

CAKE
4 egg whites
1 16-ounce box golden pound cake mix
⅔ cup water

FROSTING
⅛ cup Nestlé Butterscotch Morsels (about 40 chips)
½ (1 stick) cup butter, softened
1½ cups powdered sugar

1. Preheat the oven to 325°F.
2. Beat the egg whites until thick.
3. Blend the egg whites with the cake mix and water.
4. Pour the batter into a greased 9 x 12-inch baking pan. Bake for 30 minutes, or until the top is golden brown and a toothpick inserted in the center comes out clean. Cool.
5. For the frosting, melt the butterscotch morsels in a microwave oven on high for 45 seconds. If you don't have a microwave oven, use a double boiler over hot, not boiling, water.
6. Mix the butter with the melted butterscotch. Add the powdered sugar. Blend with a mixer until the frosting has a smooth consistency.
7. Spread the frosting on top of the cooled pound cake.
8. Cut the cake into nine rows. Then make two cuts lengthwise. This should divide cake into twenty-seven equal pieces.

• Makes 27 cakes.

• • • •

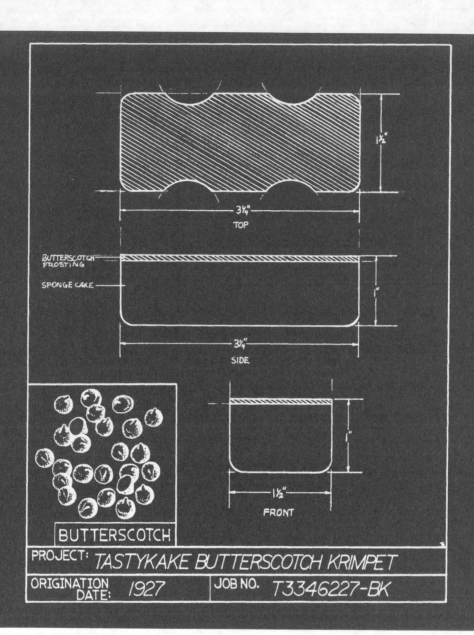

1½"

3¼"

TOP

BUTTERSCOTCH
FROSTING

SPONGE CAKE

1"

3¼"

SIDE

1"

1½"

FRONT

BUTTERSCOTCH

PROJECT: *TASTYKAKE BUTTERSCOTCH KRIMPET*

ORIGINATION DATE: *1927*

JOB NO. *T3346227-BK*

TASTYKAKE
PEANUT BUTTER
KANDY KAKES

☆ ✌ 💣 ✏ 🎱 ✂ ☞

Since it was founded in 1914, the Tasty Baking Company has continued to uphold its policy of controlled distribution to ensure freshness of its products. The company delivers only what it will sell promptly and removes cakes from the stores after just a few days in an effort to keep them from becoming stale.

As the years went by and delivery efficiency improved, transportation routes expanded from Philadelphia to New England, the Midwest, and the South. Mixing, baking, wrapping, and packaging of the products have changed from hand operations to sophisticated automated ones, cutting the production cycle from twelve hours to forty-five minutes, and loading time from five hours to forty-five minutes.

Peanut Butter Kandy Kakes made their debut in the early 1930s as *Tandy Takes*. The name was eventually changed, and the company claims you could make almost 8 million peanut butter sandwiches with the quantity of peanut butter used in Kandy Kakes each year.

4 egg whites
1 16-ounce box golden pound
    cake mix
⅔ cup water

1 cup peanut butter
½ cup powdered sugar
1 11.5-ounce bag Hershey milk-
    chocolate chips

1. Preheat the oven to 325°F.
2. Beat the egg whites until fluffy.
3. Blend the egg whites with the cake mix and water.
4. Pour tablespoon-size dollops of batter into each cup of a well-greased muffin tin. Bake for 10 minutes, or until a tooth-pick stuck in center of cake comes out clean. Make five batches. Clean muffin tin for later use. Do not grease.
5. Combine the peanut butter and sugar.
6. While the pound-cake rounds cool, heat the chocolate chips in a double boiler over low heat, stirring often. You can also melt them in a microwave oven set on high for 2 minutes, stirring once halfway through the heating time.
7. When the chocolate is soft, line the bottom half of each muffin-tin cup with shortening; then use a spoon to spread a thin layer of chocolate in each cup.
8. With your fingers, spread a thin layer of peanut butter over the chocolate.
9. Place a cake round on the peanut-butter layer.
10. Spread a layer of chocolate over the top of each cake, spreading to the sides to cover the entire surface.
11. Cool in the refrigerator for 10 minutes and turn out of the tin.

• MAKES 30 CAKES.

• • • •

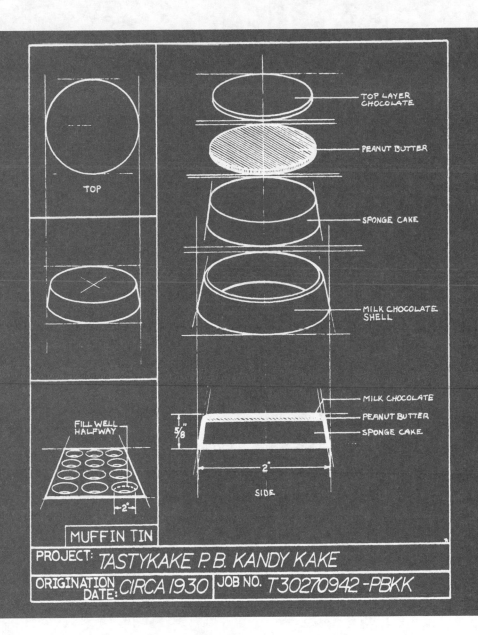

TOP

TOP LAYER
CHOCOLATE

PEANUT BUTTER

SPONGE CAKE

MILK CHOCOLATE
SHELL

MILK CHOCOLATE
PEANUT BUTTER
SPONGE CAKE

5/8"

2"

SIDE

FILL WELL
HALFWAY

2"

MUFFIN TIN

PROJECT: *TASTYKAKE P.B. KANDY KAKE*

ORIGINATION
DATE: *CIRCA 1930*

JOB NO. *T30270942-PBKK*

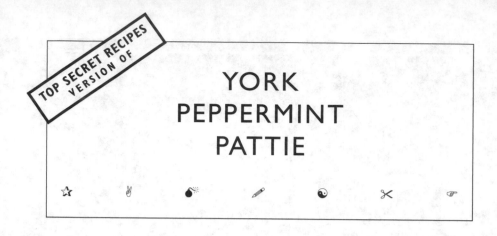

YORK PEPPERMINT PATTIE

In York, Pennsylvania, Henry C. Kessler first concocted this confection in the late 1930s at his candy factory, the York Cone Company. The company was originally established to make ice cream cones, but by the end of World War II, the peppermint patty had become so popular that the company discontinued all other products. In 1972, the company was sold to Peter Paul, manufacturers of Almond Joy and Mounds. Cadbury U.S.A. purchased the firm in 1978, and in 1988 the York Peppermint Pattie became the property of Hershey USA.

Many chocolate-covered peppermints had been made before the York Peppermint Pattie came on the market, but Kessler's version was firm and crisp, while the competition was soft and gummy. One former employee and York resident remembered the final test the patty went through before it left the factory. "It was a snap test. If the candy didn't break clean in the middle, it was a second."

For years, seconds were sold to visitors at the plant for fifty cents a pound.

1 egg white
4 cups powdered sugar
⅓ cup light corn syrup
½ teaspoon peppermint oil or
  extract

cornstarch for dusting
1 12-ounce bag semisweet
  chocolate chips

1. In a medium bowl, beat the egg white until frothy but not stiff. Don't use a plastic bowl for this.
2. Slowly add the powdered sugar while blending with an electric mixer set on medium speed.
3. Add the corn syrup and peppermint oil or extract and knead the mixture with your hands until it has the smooth consistency of dough. Add more powdered sugar if necessary, until mixture is no longer sticky.
4. Using a surface and rolling pin heavily dusted with cornstarch, roll out the peppermint dough until it is about ¼ inch thick.
5. Punch out circles of peppermint dough with a biscuit cutter or a clean can with a diameter of about 2½ inches. Make approximately 20, place them on plates or cookie sheets, and let them firm up in the refrigerator, about 45 minutes.
6. Melt the chocolate chips in a microwave set on high for 2 minutes. Stir halfway through the heating time. Melt thoroughly, but do not overheat.
7. Drop each patty into the chocolate and coat completely. Using a large serving fork, or 2 dinner forks, one in each hand, lift the coated patty from the chocolate. Gently tap the forks against the bowl to knock off the excess chocolate, and place each patty on wax paper.
8. Chill the peppermint patties until firm, about 30 minutes.

- MAKES 20 PEPPERMINT PATTIES.

TIDBITS

Being generous with the cornstarch will make it easier to work with the peppermint filling. Liberal dusting will ensure that your filling won't stick.

For your first batch, you'll find the dipping process smoother if you make smaller patties—about 1 inch in diameter. Try resting each pattie on a large serving fork, and tapping the fork against the side of the bowl to knock off excess chocolate after dipping.

• • • •

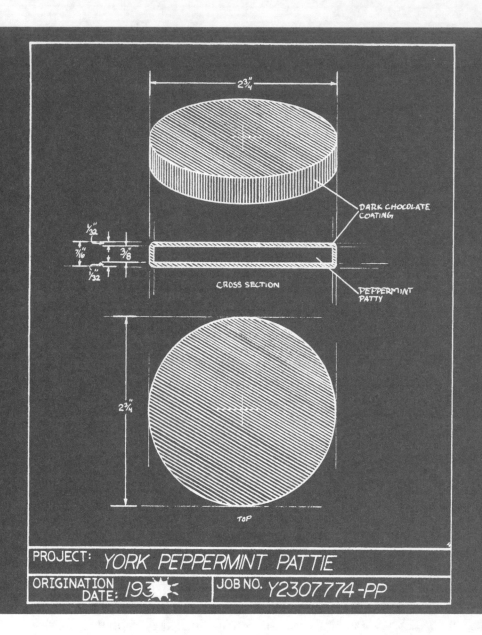

2¾"

DARK CHOCOLATE
COATING

1/32"
7/16"   3/8
1/32"

CROSS SECTION

PEPPERMINT
PATTY

2¾"

TOP

PROJECT: *YORK PEPPERMINT PATTIE*

ORIGINATION
DATE: *193*

JOB NO. *Y2307774-PP*

216

Introduction

The casual and fine-dining restaurant chains that are referred to as "full-service" in the food biz are the sole subject of this formula-cracking section. Just for clarity's sake, "full-service" excludes "quick-service" or "fast-food" restaurants. That means you won't find recipes here for Wendy's or Taco Bell or Burger King where you order your paper-wrapped food over a counter or from a drive-thru window.

At a full-service chain, you typically order from a menu while sitting down at a private table. You are usually waited on, you can order a beer, you can pay with a credit card, and you are expected to leave a tip. A full-service restaurant can be a steak-house, a family diner, a casual dinner house, a fancy restaurant, or extravagant theme chain.

Because the average American eats out 198 times a year or 4 times a week, chances are very good that you've noshed at one or more of the establishments referred to here. You may even be familiar with several of the dishes that inspired these recipes. That's good. Now you can take the *Top Secret Recipes* taste test. Compare what you make to the original menu item and you should find your version tastes just like the dish from these restaurant. To ensure that this is the case, I've tested the recipes numerous times. If my version didn't taste like the real dish, it didn't go in the book. Sure, the *Top Secret Recipes* version may not be prepared the exact same way as the original, but as long as the finished product is identical in taste, how we get to that point is inconsequential. Be aware that my intention here is not to steal the original recipe from the creators, only to duplicate the finished product as closely as possible, with ingredients you can find in any supermarket.

Just for fun, if you'd like to know if this smarty-pants author can really do what he says he can—create recipes that taste just like the real deal—take the Top Secret Challenge. Get some of these dishes to go, make the clone, put on some blindfolds, and give it the true taste test. If all goes well, you should have a tough time identifying the real product over the phony. My fingers are crossed.

APPLEBEE'S QUESADILLAS

☆   ✌   💣   ✏   ☯   ✂   ☞

Menu Description: "Two cheeses, bacon, tomatoes, onions & jalapeños grilled between tortillas with guacamole, sour cream & salsa."

When Bill and T. J. Palmer opened their first restaurant in Atlanta, Georgia, in 1980, they realized their dream of building a full-service, reasonably-priced restaurant in a neighborhood setting. They called their first place T.J. Applebee's Edibles & Elixirs, and soon began franchising the concept. In 1988 some franchisees bought the rights to the name and changed it to Applebee's Neighborhood Grill & Bar. By that time, there were 54 restaurants in the organization. Today there are over 650, making Applebee's one of the fastest-growing restaurant chains in the world.

According to waiters at the restaurant, the easy-to-make and slightly spicy quesadillas are one of the most popular appetizers on the Applebee's menu. The recipe calls for 10-inch or "burrito-size" flour tortillas, which can be found in most supermarkets, but any size can be used in a pinch. Look for the jalapeño "nacho slices" in the ethnic or Mexican food section of the supermarket. You'll find these in jars or cans. Cilantro, which is growing immensely in popularity, can be found in the produce section near the parsley, and is also called fresh coriander or Chinese parsley.

2 10-inch ("burrito-size") flour
   tortillas
2 tablespoons butter, softened
1/3 cup shredded Monterey Jack
   cheese
1/3 cup shredded Cheddar cheese
1/2 medium tomato, chopped
2 teaspoons diced onion

1 teaspoon diced canned jalapeño
   ("nacho slices")
1 slice bacon, cooked
1/4 teaspoon finely chopped fresh
   cilantro
dash salt

ON THE SIDE

sour cream
guacamole

salsa

1. Heat a large frying pan over medium heat.
2. Spread half of the butter on one side of each tortilla. Put one tortilla, butter side down, in the hot pan.
3. Spread the cheeses evenly onto the center of the tortilla in the pan. You don't have to spread the cheese all the way to the edge. Leave a margin of an inch or so all the way around.
4. Sprinkle the tomato, onion, and jalapeño over the cheese.
5. Crumble the slice of cooked bacon and sprinkle it over the other ingredients.
6. Sprinkle the cilantro and a dash of salt over the other ingredients.
7. Top off the quesadilla with the remaining tortilla, being sure that the buttered side is facing up.
8. When the bottom tortilla has browned, after 45 to 90 seconds, flip the quesadilla over and grill the other side for the same length of time.
9. Remove the quesadilla from the pan, and, using a sharp knife or pizza cutter, cut the quesadilla three times through the middle like a pizza, creating 6 equal slices. Serve hot with sour cream, guacamole, and salsa on the side.

- SERVES 1 OR 2 AS AN APPETIZER.

• • • •

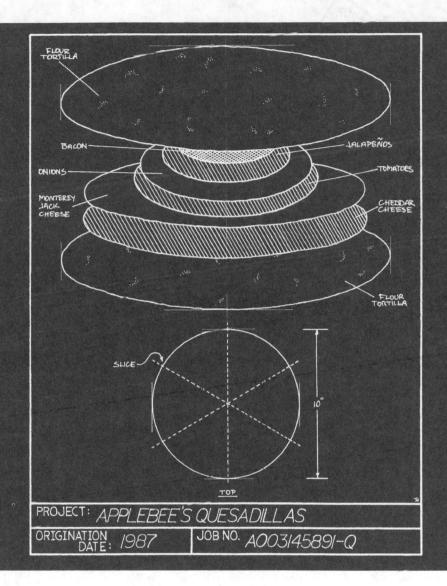

FLOUR TORTILLA

BACON

ONIONS

MONTEREY JACK CHEESE

JALAPEÑOS

TOMATOES

CHEDDAR CHEESE

FLOUR TORTILLA

SLICE

10"

TOP

PROJECT: APPLEBEE'S QUESADILLAS

ORIGINATION DATE: 1987

JOB NO. A003145891-Q

221

APPLEBEE'S TIJUANA "PHILLY" STEAK SANDWICH

Menu Description: "Lean shaved 'Philly' steak folded into a grilled tortilla roll with Monterey Jack & Cheddar, sautéed mushrooms, onions, tomatoes, bacon & jalapeños."

With the acquisition of 13 Rio Bravo Cantinas in 1994, Applebee's made its move into the competitive "Mexican casual dining sector." Perhaps it's the company's interest in Mexican food that inspired this Philadelphia-Tijuana hybrid sandwich. The steak, cheese, mushrooms, and onions give the sandwich a Philly taste, while the tomatoes, bacon, jalapeños, and the tortilla take you across the border.

I really like this newer addition to the menu, probably because I'm a big cheese-steak fan who also loves Mexican food. As you can see from this dish and the one before it, Applebee's has a knack for breathing new life into old sandwich concepts. I hope you'll find this one worth a try.

You shouldn't have any trouble locating the ingredients, except maybe the cilantro. It's becoming very popular so hopefully it will be easy to find. Just look in the produce section near the parsley, where it might also be called fresh coriander or Chinese parsley (not to be confused with Italian parsley). ¡Muy bien!

1 mushroom, diced
1 tablespoon plus ½ teaspoon
   butter, softened
salt

pepper
3 ounces chipped beef or 1 ½
   slices Steak-Umm frozen
   sandwich steaks

1/4 cup shredded Cheddar cheese
1/4 cup shredded Monterey Jack
    cheese
1 10-inch ("burrito-size") flour
    tortilla
1 heaping tablespoon diced
    tomato
1 teaspoon diced red onion
1/4 teaspoon finely chopped fresh
    cilantro
1 slice bacon, cooked

ON THE SIDE
shredded lettuce
sour cream
salsa

1. Sauté the mushroom in a small pan with 1/2 teaspoon butter and a dash of salt and pepper. The mushroom pieces should start to turn brown when they are done.
2. Break or cut the beef into bite-size pieces and grill it in another pan over medium heat until brown. Add a dash of salt and pepper. Drain off the fat.
3. Build your sandwich by first sprinkling both cheeses into the center of the tortilla. Keep in mind when adding the cheese that you will be folding in the sides like a burrito, so leave some room on each side.
4. Sprinkle the tomato, onion, sautéed mushroom, and cilantro over the cheese.
5. Crumble the bacon and sprinkle it over the cheese as well.
6. Sprinkle the cooked beef over the other ingredients, then add a bit more salt and pepper, if desired.
7. Fold the sides in, then use the 1 tablespoon butter to butter the top and bottom of the "sandwich" and grill it in a hot pan over medium heat for 2 minutes per side, or until the tortilla becomes golden brown and the cheese is melted.
8. Slice the "sandwich" in half diagonally and serve hot on a plate with shredded lettuce, sour cream, and salsa on the side.

• SERVES 1 AS AN ENTREE (CAN BE DOUBLED).

• • • •

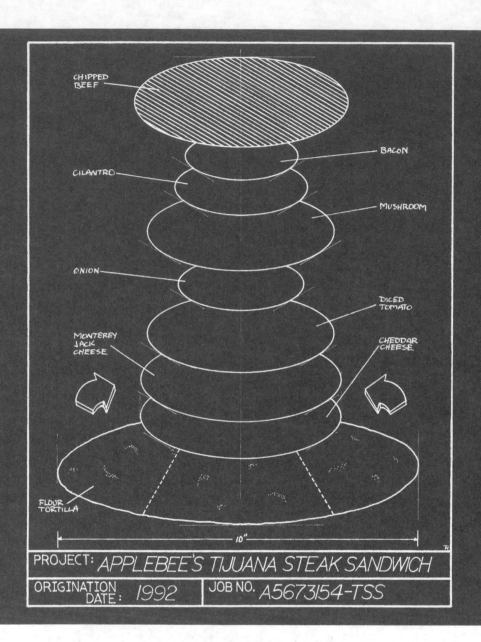

CHIPPED BEEF

BACON

CILANTRO

MUSHROOM

ONION

DICED TOMATO

MONTEREY JACK CHEESE

CHEDDAR CHEESE

FLOUR TORTILLA

10"

PROJECT: *APPLEBEE'S TIJUANA STEAK SANDWICH*

ORIGINATION DATE: *1992*

JOB NO. *A5673154-TSS*

BENNIGAN'S
BUFFALO CHICKEN
SANDWICH

☆　✌　💣　✎　☯　✂　☞

Menu Description: "Our spicy sauce tops a tender, fried, marinated chicken breast. Served with a tangy bleu cheese dressing."

When the first Bennigan's opened in Atlanta, Georgia, in 1976, it resembled an Irish pub. The green decor with brass accents, the Irish-style memorabilia hanging on the walls, and the upbeat friendly atmosphere made the establishment extremely popular, especially during St. Patrick's Day celebrations. Originally, the restaurant was best known for the bar, which served tasty appetizers and creative drinks, but that has since changed. As the restaurant chain expanded across the country, its menu grew to more than 50 items, making 220-outlet Bennigan's a popular casual dining stop.

If you're a big buffalo wings fan, as I am, you'll really dig this sandwich that puts the zesty flavor of hot wings between two buns. This recent addition to the Bennigan's menu has become a popular pick for the lunch or dinner crowd that likes its food on the spicy side. Feel free to double the recipe, but fry the chicken breasts one at a time.

oil for deep-frying
½ cup all-purpose flour
½ teaspoon salt
½ cup whole milk

1 boneless, skinless chicken breast
　half
1 hamburger bun
1 leaf green leaf lettuce

2 slices tomato
1 slice red onion
2 tablespoons Louisiana Hot
    Sauce or Frank's Red Hot

ON THE SIDE
bleu cheese dressing

1. Preheat the oil to 350°F in a deep fryer or a large frying pan over medium heat. Use just enough oil to cover the chicken breast.
2. Stir together the flour and salt in a medium bowl. Pour the milk into another medium bowl.
3. Trim the chicken of any fat. Cut the thin, pointed end off the breast. Pound on the chicken with a meat-tenderizing mallet to flatten the breast and shape it to fit better on the bun.
4. Dip the chicken in milk, then in the flour, being sure to coat the entire surface of the chicken. Take the coated chicken breast and repeat the process. Let the chicken sit in the refrigerator for 10 to 15 minutes.
5. Drop the chicken breast into the hot oil and fry for 10 minutes or until the outside becomes golden brown. Drain on paper towels.
6. As the chicken is frying, toast or grill the face of the hamburger bun until light brown.
7. The sandwich is served open face, so place the bun face up on the plate. On the face of the top bun place the leaf of lettuce.
8. On the lettuce stack two slices of tomato.
9. Separate the slice of red onion and place 2 to 3 rings of onion on the tomato slices.
10. When the chicken breast has cooked and drained, place it in a plastic container that has a lid. Pour the hot sauce into the container, put the lid on top, and shake gently to coat the chicken with hot sauce. Be sure to shake only enough to coat the chicken. If you shake too hard, the crispy coating will fall off the chicken.
11. Stack the chicken breast on the bottom half of the hamburger bun and place it on the plate beside the top half of the

sandwich. Serve open face, with bleu cheese dressing on the side.

- SERVES 1 AS AN ENTREE (CAN BE DOUBLED).

• • • •

TOP

TOP
BUN

GREEN
LEAF
LETTUCE

TOMATO
SLICES

RED
ONION

BUFFALO
CHICKEN

BOTTOM
BUN

4½"

SIDE

PROJECT: *BENNIGAN'S BUFFALO CHICKEN SAND.*

ORIGINATION DATE: *1990* JOB NO. *B45531355-BCS*

BENNIGAN'S
COOKIE MOUNTAIN
SUNDAE

Menu Description: "Four scoops of vanilla ice cream between two giant chocolate chip cookies. Drizzled with hot fudge and sprinkled with powdered sugar."

Bennigan's puts a twist on the traditional sundae with this sweet treat. Although this dessert was created for the Bennigan's menu, the original sundae has been with us since the turn of the century. Here's some cool history for you: This was a time when alternatives to alcohol were in high demand, so soda fountain proprietors began inventing new drinks. Ice cream sodas—scoops of ice cream combined with soda water and a squirt of flavored syrup—became so popular that Americans were enjoying them to the point of gluttony, especially on the Sabbath day. The treat was soon referred to as the "Sunday Soda Menace," and after Evanston, Illinois, became the first city to enact laws against selling ice cream sodas (shame!), the new prohibition was spreading nationwide. First alcohol, then sodas . . . you can bet a substitute was in order.

One day a soda fountain clerk, prohibited from selling sodas, served up a bowl of ice cream to a customer who requested a dribbling of chocolate syrup on the top. The fountain clerk, upon tasting the dish himself, found that he had discovered a new taste sensation, and soon the dessert was offered to everyone on Sundays only. Eventually that day of the week would be adopted as the name of the delicious ice-cream dish, with a bit of a spelling change to satisfy the scrutinizing clergy. The "soda-less soda" that we now call a sundae was born.

This recipe makes enough giant chocolate chip cookies for six or seven sundaes, but you don't have to serve them all at once. Store the cookies in an airtight container and assemble the sundaes as you need them . . . on any day of the week.

CHOCOLATE CHIP COOKIES

½ cup softened butter	½ teaspoon salt
¼ cup granulated sugar	½ teaspoon baking powder
¾ cup packed brown sugar	½ teaspoon baking soda
1 egg	1 cup semisweet chocolate chips
1 teaspoon vanilla	(6 ounces)
1 ¼ cups all-purpose flour	

½ gallon vanilla ice cream	powdered sugar
1 16-ounce jar hot fudge topping	

1. Preheat the oven to 350°F.
2. Make the cookies by creaming together the butter, sugars, egg, and vanilla in a medium-size bowl.
3. In a separate bowl, sift together the flour, salt, baking powder, and baking soda. Combine the dry ingredients with the butter mixture and mix well.
4. Add the chocolate chips and mix once more.
5. Roll the dough into golfball-size portions and place them 4 inches apart on an ungreased cookie sheet. With your hand, press down on the dough to flatten it to about ½ inch thick. You will likely have to use two cookie sheets for the 12 to 14 cookies the recipe will make. If you use the same cookie sheet for the second batch, be sure to let it cool before placing the dough on it.

6. Bake the cookies for 12 to 14 minutes or until they become a light shade of brown.

7. The cookies served with this dessert have a hole in the center so that when you pour on the hot fudge it flows down through the hole onto the ice cream in the middle. When you take the cookies out of the oven, use the opening of an empty glass soda or beer bottle like a cookie cutter to cut a 1-inch hole in the center of each cookie. Turn the bottle upside down and press the opening into the center of each cookie, rotating the bottle back and forth until the center of the cookie is cut out. Because the cookie centers will push into the bottle as you go, you'll have to rinse the bottle out before recycling. (If you prefer, you can punch holes in just half of the cookies; these will be the cookies that are stacked on top of the ice cream.)

8. When the cookies have cooled, take four small scoops (about ¼ cup each) of ice cream and arrange them on the top of one cookie that has been placed in the center of the serving plate.

9. Place another cookie on top of the ice cream.

10. Heat up the fudge in a microwave or in the top of a double boiler just long enough to soften the topping so that it is easy to pour. Pour 3 to 4 tablespoons of hot fudge over the top cookie. Let the fudge drizzle down the sides of the ice cream and through the hole that has been cut in the center of the top cookie.

11. Use a sifter or fine strainer to spread a dusting of powdered sugar onto the sundae and around the surface of the serving plate. Repeat with the remaining ingredients for the desired number of servings. The leftover ingredients (if any) can be saved for additional servings later.

- SERVES 6 TO 7.

•　•　•　•

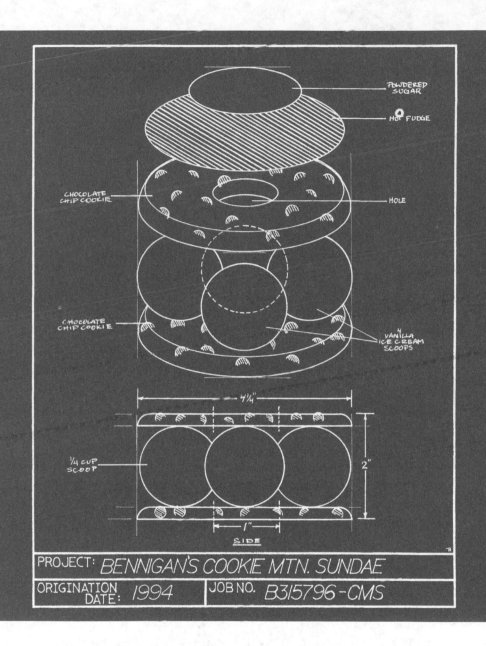

POWDERED
SUGAR

HOT FUDGE

CHOCOLATE
CHIP COOKIE

HOLE

CHOCOLATE
CHIP COOKIE

4
VANILLA
ICE CREAM
SCOOPS

4¼"

¼ CUP
SCOOP

2"

1"

SIDE

PROJECT: *BENNIGAN'S COOKIE MTN. SUNDAE*

ORIGINATION
DATE: *1994*

JOB NO. *B315796-CMS*

BIG BOY CLUB
SANDWICH

Menu Description: "Slices of turkey breast with bacon, tomato, lettuce and mayonnaise, stacked on toasted bread. Served with coleslaw."

When Bob Wian invented the first Big Boy double-decker hamburger in 1937, his restaurant business went through the roof. Soon a slew of imitators hit the market with their own giant-sized burgers: Bun Boy, Brawny Boy, Super Boy, Yumi Boy, Country Boy, Husky Boy, Hi-Boy, Beefy Boy, Lucky Boy, and many other "Boys" across the burger-crazed country.

By 1985 the Big Boy statues had become a common sight in front of hundreds of Bob's restaurants around the country. This was also the year the Marriott Corporation, which had purchased Bob's from a retiring Bob Wian in 1967, created a national ballot to decide whether the Big Boy character would stay or go. Thousands of voters elected to keep the tubby little tike, but his days were numbered. In 1992, Marriott chose to sell all of the Bob's Big Boys to an investment group. Those mostly West Coast Big Boys were later converted to Coco's or Carrow's restaurants, and there the Big Boy went bye-bye. The Elias Brothers, a Michigan-area franchiser for many years, purchased the Big Boy name from Marriott in 1987, and today is the sole Big Boy franchiser worldwide.

The Club Sandwich is one of Big Boy's signature sandwiches, and remains one of the most popular items on the menu since it was introduced in the mid-70s.

3 slices white or wheat bread
1 ½ tablespoons mayonnaise
1 lettuce leaf
1 slice Swiss cheese (optional)

2 ounces deli-sliced turkey breast
2 slices tomato
3 slices bacon, cooked

1. Toast the slices of bread.
2. Spread the mayonnaise evenly on one face of each slice of toast.
3. Build the sandwich by first stacking the lettuce leaf on the mayonnaise on one slice of toast. You will most likely have to cut or fold the lettuce so that it fits.
4. The Swiss cheese goes on next. This is an optional step since I've been served the original sandwich with the cheese, but the description of the sandwich and the photograph in the menu exclude it.
5. On the Swiss cheese, if you use it, stack the slices of turkey. Fold over the slices and arrange them neatly.
6. Stack a piece of toast, mayo side down, onto the turkey.
7. On top of the toast, arrange the tomato slices.
8. Lay the bacon, side by side, onto the tomatoes.
9. Top off the sandwich with the last piece of toast, mayo side down.
10. Slice the sandwich with two diagonal cuts from corner to corner, in an "x."
11. Push a toothpick down through the center of each triangular sandwich quarter. Spin each slice around 180° so that the center of the sandwich is now pointed out. Serve with French fries or with coleslaw arranged in the center of the plate of sandwich pieces.

- SERVES 1 AS AN ENTREE (CAN BE DOUBLED).

• • • •

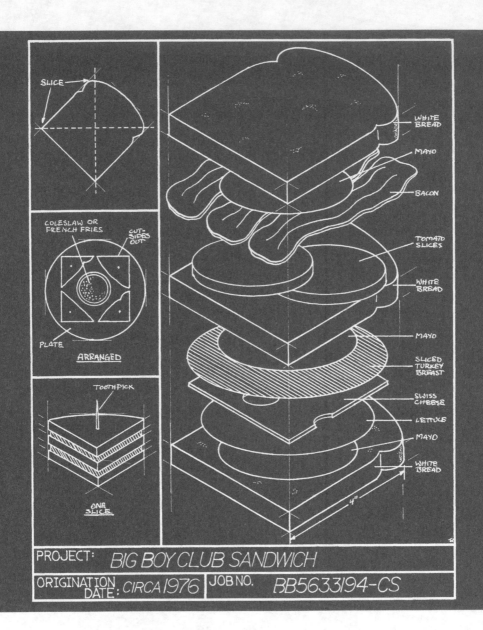

SLICE

COLESLAW OR
FRENCH FRIES

CUT-
SIDES
OUT

PLATE

ARRANGED

TOOTHPICK

**ONE
SLICE**

WHITE
BREAD

MAYO

BACON

TOMATO
SLICES

WHITE
BREAD

MAYO

SLICED
TURKEY
BREAST

SWISS
CHEESE

LETTUCE

MAYO

WHITE
BREAD

4"

PROJECT: *BIG BOY CLUB SANDWICH*

ORIGINATION DATE: *CIRCA 1976* JOB NO. *BB5633194-CS*

BIG BOY CREAM OF BROCCOLI SOUP

Menu Description: "Our famous Big Boy soups and chili are made fresh daily from fresh vegetables, pure cream and only the finest ingredients."

In 1936, Bob Wian had to make the painful decision to sell his cherished 1933 DeSoto roadster to buy a ten-stool lunch counter from a pair of elderly ladies in Glendale, California. He named his new restaurant Bob's Pantry, and went to work behind the counter himself. Receipts from his first day totaled only twelve dollars. But with the creation of a new hamburger just the next year, and a name change to Bob's Big Boy, business took off. Within three years Bob had expanded his first store and built another location in Los Angeles. In 1948 Bob Wian was voted mayor of Glendale.

A cup of the broccoli soup makes a great first course or a nice partner to a sandwich. I first designed this recipe using frozen broccoli, but the frozen stuff just isn't as tasty as a big bunch of firm, fresh broccoli. So go shopping, and get chopping.

Served in a large bowl, this soup can be a small meal in itself, or it serves four as an appetizer. Try it with a pinch of shredded Cheddar cheese on top.

4 cups chicken broth
1 large bunch broccoli, chopped
   (3 cups)
½ cup diced onion
1 bay leaf

¼ teaspoon salt
dash ground pepper
¼ cup all-purpose flour
2 ounces ham (⅓ cup diced)
½ cup heavy cream

1. Combine the chicken broth, broccoli, onion, bay leaf, salt, and pepper in a large saucepan over high heat. When the broth comes to a boil, turn down the heat and simmer, covered, for 30 minutes. The vegetables will become tender.
2. Remove the bay leaf and discard. Transfer a little more than half of the broth and vegetable mixture to a blender or food processor. Mix on low speed for 20 to 30 seconds. This will finely chop the vegetables to nearly a purée. (Be careful blending hot liquids. You may want to let the mixture cool a bit before transferring and blending it.)
3. Pour the blended mixture back into the saucepan over medium/low heat. Add the flour and whisk until all lumps have dissolved.
4. Add the diced ham and the cream to the other ingredients and continue to simmer for 10 to 15 minutes or until the soup is as thick as you like it.

- Serves 4 as an appetizer or 2 as an entree.

TIDBITS

Because some ham is much saltier than others, I was conservative on the amount of salt in this recipe. You may find that you need more.

•   •   •   •

BIG BOY ORIGINAL DOUBLE-DECKER HAMBURGER CLASSIC

☆   ✌   💣   ✎   ☯   ✂   ☞

Menu Description: "¼ pound of 100% pure beef in two patties with American cheese, crisp lettuce and our special sauce on a sesame seed bun."

Bob Wian's little ten-stool diner, Bob's Pantry, was in business only a short time in Glendale, California, before establishing a following of regular customers—among them the band members from Chuck Foster's Orchestra. One February night in 1937, the band came by after a gig as they often did to order a round of burgers. In a playful mood, bass player Stewie Strange sat down on a stool and uttered, "How about something different for a change, Bob?" Bob thought it might be funny to play along and serve up Stewie a burger he could barely get his mouth around. So Bob cut a bun into three slices, rather than the usual two, and stacked on two hamburger patties along with lettuce, cheese, and his special sauce. When Stewie tasted the huge sandwich and loved it, every band member wanted his own!

Just a few days later, a plump little six-year-old named Richard Woodruff came into the diner and charmed Bob into letting him do odd jobs in exchange for a burger or two. He often wore baggy overalls and had an appetite that forced the affectionate nickname "Fat Boy."* Bob thought it was the perfect name

---

*Please understand that these are not my choice of words to describe young Richard Woodruff. I prefer the more socially sensitive terms: "Weight-blessed Adolescent," or "Young Adult with a Thinness Deficit." However, I do realize that neither of these descriptions would be a good name for a hamburger.

for his new burger, except the name was already being used as a trademark for another product. So the name of the new burger, along with Bob's booming chain of restaurants, was changed to "Big Boy." The company's tradename Big Boy character is from a cartoonist's napkin sketch of "fat boy," little Richard Woodruff.

The Big Boy hamburger was the first of the double-decker hamburgers. McDonald's Big Mac, the world's best-known burger that came more than 30 years later, was inspired by Bob Wian's original creation. See if you can get your mouth around it.

¼ pound ground beef
1 ½ tablespoons mayonnaise
1 teaspoon relish
1 teaspoon tomato sauce
1 sesame seed hamburger bun

top half of additional hamburger
   bun
salt
¼ cup shredded lettuce
1 slice American cheese

1. Prepare the hamburger patties by dividing the beef in half and pressing each ⅛ pound of beef into a round patty that measures approximately 4 inches across. Because these patties are so thin, you may find them easier to cook if you press them out on waxed paper, and freeze them first. You may want to make several of these patties at once when you first purchase the ground beef, then cook them as you need them.
2. Combine the mayonnaise, relish, and tomato sauce in a small cup or bowl. This is the "secret sauce."
3. Use a serrated knife to cut the top off of the extra bun. You want to leave about a ½-inch, double-faced slice.
4. Toast the faces of the buns on a griddle or in a frying pan over medium heat.
5. When the buns are toasted, use the same pan to cook the beef patties. Cook the patties for about 2 minutes per side or until done, being sure to lightly salt each patty.
6. Build the burger by spreading half of the sauce on a face of

the middle bun, and the other half on the face of the bottom bun.

7. Stack the lettuce on the sauce on the bottom bun.
8. Stack the cheese on the lettuce.
9. Place one beef patty on the cheese.
10. The middle bun goes next with the sauce-coated side facing up.
11. Stack the other beef patty on the middle bun.
12. Finish the burger off with the top bun. You can microwave the burger for 10 to 15 seconds if you want to warm up the buns.

* SERVES 1 AS AN ENTREE (CAN BE DOUBLED).

• • • •

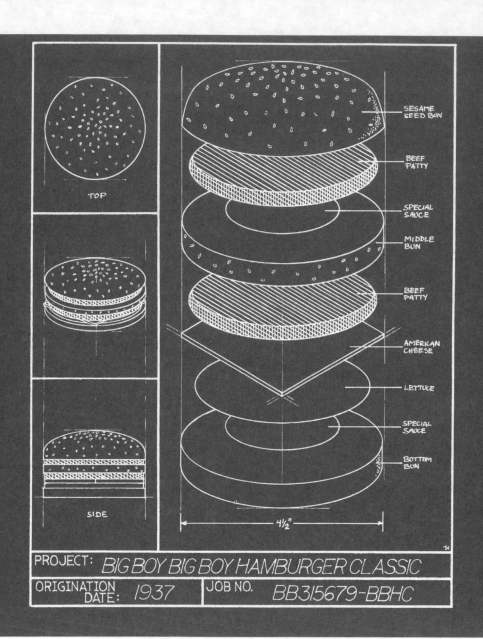

TOP

SIDE

SESAME
SEED BUN

BEEF
PATTY

SPECIAL
SAUCE

MIDDLE
BUN

BEEF
PATTY

AMERICAN
CHEESE

LETTUCE

SPECIAL
SAUCE

BOTTOM
BUN

4½"

PROJECT: *BIG BOY BIG BOY HAMBURGER CLASSIC*

ORIGINATION DATE: *1937*

JOB NO. *BB315679-BBHC*

CALIFORNIA PIZZA KITCHEN ORIGINAL BBQ CHICKEN PIZZA

Menu Description: "Introduced in our first restaurant in 1985. With barbecued chicken, sliced red onion, cilantro, and smoked Gouda cheese."

In 1985, attorneys Larry Flax and Rick Rosenfield traded in their private practice, which included defending mob bosses and union officials, for a specialty pizza chain. These two "amateur chefs" say they were influenced by Wolfgang Puck, whose Spago restaurant in Los Angeles was the first to create pizza with unusual toppings. Now they have developed a niche somewhere between gourmet food and traditional Italian-style pizzas, creating what one magazine described as "designer pizza at off-the-rack prices." In addition to the pastas, soups, and salads on its nothing-over-ten-dollars menu, California Pizza Kitchen offers 25 unique pizza creations that reflect the current trends in dining. When Cajun food was in style, the Cajun chicken pizza was a top seller; today that item has been replaced with Southwestern pizza varieties.

As the menu explains, the Barbecued Chicken Pizza was one of the first pizzas served at California Pizza Kitchen. Ten years later it remained the top-selling pizza creation.

You can use this recipe to make your pizza with premade or packaged dough, but I highly recommend taking the time to make the dough yourself. You'll find that it's worth the extra work. This recipe took a lot of time to perfect, and if you prepare the dough one day ahead of time, the result should convince you never to use packaged dough again.

THE CRUST

⅓ cup plus 1 tablespoon warm
    water (105° to 115°F)
¾ teaspoon yeast
1 teaspoon sugar

1 cup bread flour
½ teaspoon salt
½ tablespoon olive oil

or

Commercial pizza dough or dough mix or One 10-inch unbaked
    commercial crust

THE TOPPING

1 boneless, skinless chicken
    breast half
½ cup Bullseye Original barbecue
    sauce
1 ½ teaspoons olive oil
1 cup shredded mozzarella

½ cup grated Gouda cheese
    (smoked, if you can find it)
½ cup sliced red onion
2 teaspoons finely chopped fresh
    cilantro*

1. If you are making a homemade crust, start the dough one day before you plan to serve the pizza. In a small bowl or measuring cup dissolve the yeast and sugar in the warm water. Let it sit for 5 minutes until the surface of the mixture turns foamy. (If it doesn't foam, either the yeast was too old—i.e., dead—or the water was too hot—i.e., you killed it. Try again.) Sift together the flour and salt in a medium bowl. Make a depression in the flour and pour in the olive oil and yeast mixture. Use a fork to stir the liquid, gradually drawing

*Found in the produce section near the parsley. Also known as fresh coriander or Chinese parsley.

in more flour as you stir, until all the ingredients are combined. When you can no longer stir with a fork, use your hands to form the dough into a ball. Knead the dough with the heels of your hands on a lightly floured surface for 10 minutes, or until the texture of the dough is smooth. Form the dough back into a ball, coat it lightly with oil, and place it into a clean bowl covered with plastic wrap. Keep the bowl in a warm place for about 2 hours to allow the dough to double in size. Punch down the dough and put it back into the covered bowl and into your refrigerator overnight. Take the dough from the refrigerator 1 to 2 hours before you plan to build the pizza so that the dough can warm up to room temperature.

If you are using a commercial dough or dough mix, follow the instructions on the package to prepare it. You may have to set some of the dough aside to make a smaller, 10-inch crust.

2. Cut the chicken breast into bite-size cubes and marinate it in ¼ cup of the barbecue sauce in the refrigerator for at least 2 hours.
3. When the chicken has marinated, preheat the oven to 500°F. Heat a small frying pan on your stove with about 1½ teaspoons of olive oil in it. Sauté the chicken in the pan for about 3 to 4 minutes or until done.
4. Form the dough into a ball and roll out on a floured surface until very thin and 10 inches in diameter. Put your pizza crust onto a baking sheet or pizza pan, and spread the remaining ¼ cup of barbecue sauce evenly over the pizza crust.
5. Sprinkle ½ cup of the mozzarella and all of the Gouda cheese over the sauce.
6. Add the chicken next.
7. The red onion goes next.
8. Sprinkle the remaining ½ cup mozzarella around the center of the pizza.
9. Cilantro goes on top of the mozzarella.
10. Bake the pizza for 10 to 12 minutes or until the crust is light brown.

11. When the pizza is done, remove it from the oven and make 4 even cuts across the pie. This will give you 8 slices.

• SERVES 2 AS AN ENTRÉE.

• • • •

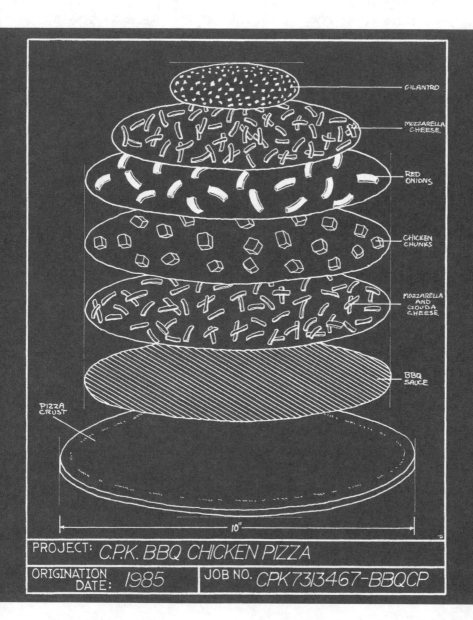

CILANTRO

MOZZARELLA CHEESE

RED ONIONS

CHICKEN CHUNKS

MOZZARELLA AND GOUDA CHEESE

BBQ SAUCE

PIZZA CRUST

10"

PROJECT: C.P.K. BBQ CHICKEN PIZZA

ORIGINATION DATE: 1985

JOB NO. CPK7313467-BBQCP

CALIFORNIA PIZZA KITCHEN SOUTHWESTERN BURRITO PIZZA

☆　✌　💣　✏　☯　✂　☞

Menu Description: "With grilled chicken breast marinated in lime and herbs, Southwestern black beans, fire-roasted mild chilies, sweet white onions and Cheddar cheese. Served with green tomatillo salsa and sour cream."

California Pizza Kitchen uses imported Italian wood-fired ovens to bake the specialty pizzas. These ovens reach temperatures over 800°F, allowing the pizzas to cook in just three minutes. This technique keeps ingredients from drying out so that the pizzas don't require as much cheese as in traditional recipes.

Unfortunately, most of us don't have wood-burning pizza ovens in our kitchens so I have designed these recipes to work in a conventional oven with a minimum of cheese. If you have a pizza stone, use it. If you have a hard time finding tomatillos (they look like small green tomatoes with a thin papery skin and are found in the produce section), you can use canned green salsa. Look for fresh cilantro in the produce section.

You have the option of using a store-bought crust or instant pizza dough, but I can't say enough about making the dough your-self from the recipe here. You just have to plan ahead, making the dough one day before you plan to bake the pizza. This way the dough will get to rest and will rise slowly in the refrigerator—a great technique the pros use.

THE CRUST

⅓ cup plus 1 tablespoon warm
    water (105° to 115°F)
¾ teaspoon yeast
1 teaspoon sugar
1 cup bread flour
½ teaspoon salt
½ tablespoon olive oil

or
1 10-inch unbaked commercial
    crust
or
commercial pizza dough or dough
    mix

MARINATED CHICKEN

1 tablespoon fresh lime juice
1 tablespoon plus 1 teaspoon
    olive oil
1 tablespoon soy sauce
2 cloves garlic, pressed
2 teaspoons chopped fresh
    cilantro
1 teaspoon salt
½ teaspoon crushed red pepper
    flakes
1 skinless, boneless chicken breast
    half

¾ cup canned refried black beans
1 tablespoon water
¼ teaspoon cayenne pepper
¼ cup sliced white onion
1 whole canned mild green chili
½ cup shredded Monterey Jack
    cheese
1 cup shredded Cheddar cheese

TOMATILLO SALSA (OPTIONAL)

¾ cup chopped tomatillos
    (about 4)
3 whole canned mild green chilies
    (4-ounce can)

¼ fresh jalapeño
2 tablespoons chopped onion
dash salt

ON THE SIDE

Sour cream

1. Prepare the crust following directions from step 1 on page
   242.
2. Make the marinade by combining the lime juice, 1 tablespoon
   olive oil, soy sauce, garlic, cilantro, salt, and pepper flakes in a

blender or in a small bowl with an electric mixer for only 5 seconds or so, just until the ingredients are well combined.

3. Cut the chicken into bite-size cubes, then marinate the chicken breast in the lime mixture for at least 2 hours.
4. When the chicken has marinated, heat up a small skillet with the remaining 1 teaspoon of olive oil over high heat. Cook the chicken in the pan for 2 to 4 minutes or until it is cooked through.
5. Mix the black beans with the water and cayenne pepper.
6. Roll out the pizza crust and place it on the baking sheet or pizza pan as in step 4, page 243. Preheat the oven to 475°F.
7. Spread the black bean mixture evenly over the crust.
8. Now arrange the chicken evenly over the black beans.
9. Spread the onions over the chicken.
10. Take the chili pepper and carefully slice it in half, crossways. Then slice the two halves into very thin strips. Sprinkle the chili over the onions.
11. Spread the Monterey Jack over the pizza.
12. Top it off with the Cheddar.
13. Cook the pizza for 12 to 15 minutes or until the crust begins to turn brown.
14. While the pizza cooks, combine all the ingredients for the tomatillo salsa in a food processor or blender. Run on low speed for about 15 seconds.
15. When the pizza is done, remove it from the oven and immediately make 4 even cuts through the middle, creating 8 slices of pizza. Serve with tomatillo salsa and sour cream on the side.

- SERVES 2 AS AN ENTREE.

• • • •

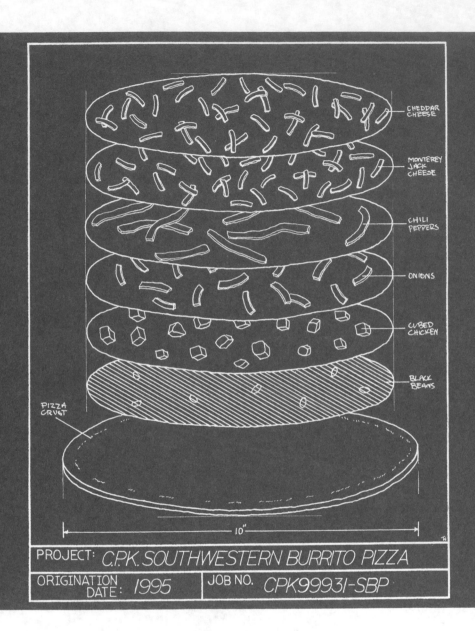

CHEDDAR CHEESE

MONTEREY JACK CHEESE

CHILI PEPPERS

ONIONS

CUBED CHICKEN

BLACK BEANS

PIZZA CRUST

10"

PROJECT: *C.P.K. SOUTHWESTERN BURRITO PIZZA*

ORIGINATION DATE: *1995*

JOB NO. *CPK99931-SBP*

CALIFORNIA PIZZA KITCHEN THAI CHICKEN PIZZA

☆   ✌   💣   ✏   ☯   ✂   ☞

Menu Description: "With pieces of chicken marinated in a spicy peanut-ginger and sesame sauce, green onions, bean sprouts, julienne carrots, cilantro and roasted peanuts."

After the first California Pizza Kitchen opened in Beverly Hills in 1985 success came quickly: there are currently 78 restaurants in 18 states. In 1992, huge food conglomerate PepsiCo paid over $70 million for a 70 percent share of the company—just eight years after Larry and Rick started the company. As for those two, well, they pocketed $18 million apiece, or around 70 times their initial investment in 1985.

Thai Chicken Pizza is one of the oldest varieties of pizza still on the menu, and remains a favorite. If you prefer, you can make this pizza with a store-bought package dough or dough mix, but I recommend making the crust yourself. If you decide to do that, make it one day ahead of time so that it can rise slowly in the refrigerator.

THE CRUST

⅓ cup plus 1 tablespoon warm
    water (105° to 115°F)
¾ teaspoon yeast
1 teaspoon granulated sugar
1 cup bread flour
½ teaspoon salt
½ tablespoon olive oil

or

commercial pizza dough or dough
    mix

or

1 10-inch unbaked commercial
    crust

PEANUT SAUCE

¼ cup creamy peanut butter
2 tablespoons teriyaki sauce (or
    marinade)
2 tablespoons hoisin
1 clove garlic, minced
½ teaspoon crushed red pepper
    flakes
1 tablespoon granulated sugar

1 tablespoon brown sugar
2 tablespoons water
2 teaspoons sesame oil
1 teaspoon soy sauce
1½ teaspoons minced onion
1 teaspoon minced gingerroot

TOPPINGS

1 boneless, skinless chicken breast
    half
1½ teaspoons olive oil
1¼ cups grated mozzarella
1 to 2 green onions

½ cup bean sprouts
½ carrot, julienned or grated
    (¼ cup)
2 teaspoons minced cilantro*
1 tablespoon chopped peanuts

1. Prepare the crust following the directions from step 1 on page 242.
2. Mix together the ingredients for the peanut sauce in a small bowl. Pour this mixture into a food processor or blender and blend for about 15 seconds or until the garlic, onion, and ginger are reduced to small particles. Pour this mixture into a small pan over medium heat and bring it to a boil. Cook for 1 minute. Don't cook too long or the sauce will become lumpy.

*Cilantro is found in the produce section of your supermarket, usually near the parsley.

(You may, instead, use a microwave for this step. Pour the mixture into a small microwavable bowl and heat for 1 to 2 minutes.) The peanut sauce should be darker now.

3. Slice the chicken into bite-size chunks.
4. Pour one-third of the peanut sauce over the chicken. Place in a sealed container in the refrigerator and marinate for at least 2 hours. I like to use a small resealable plastic bag for this. The chicken gets very well coated this way.
5. Heat 1 teaspoon of oil in a small pan over medium/high heat.
6. Cook the marinated chicken for 3 to 4 minutes in the pan.
7. Roll out your pizza crust and place on the baking sheet or pizza pan as in step 4, page 243. Preheat the oven to 475°F.
8. Spread a thin coating of the remaining peanut sauce (the stuff you *didn't* marinate the chicken in) on the pizza crust. You may have sauce left over.
9. Sprinkle 1 cup of the grated mozzarella over the peanut sauce.
10. Slice the green onion lengthwise into thin strips (julienne), then cut across the strips, slicing the onion into 2-inch matchstick strips. Spread the onions over the cheese.
11. Arrange the chicken on the pizza.
12. Next go the sprouts and the julienned carrots.
13. Sprinkle what's left of the mozzarella (¼ cup) just over the center area of the pizza.
14. Sprinkle the cilantro over the mozzarella, then the chopped nuts on top.
15. Bake the pizza for 10 to 12 minutes or until the crust turns light brown.
16. After removing the pizza from the oven, cut across it 4 times to make 8 slices.

• SERVES 2 AS AN ENTREE.

• • • •

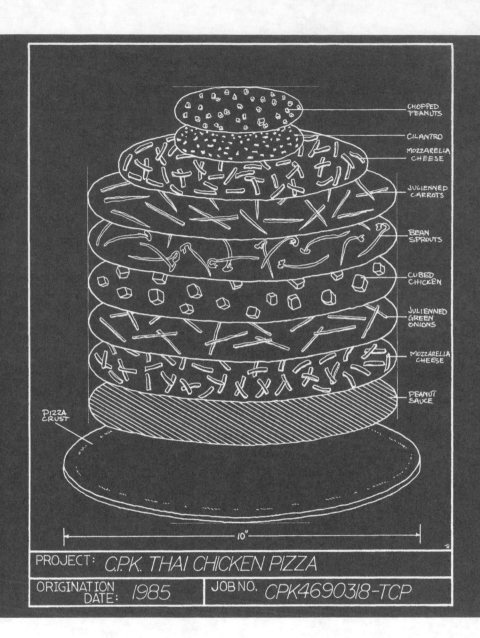

CHOPPED PEANUTS

CILANTRO

MOZZARELLA CHEESE

JULIENNED CARROTS

BEAN SPROUTS

CUBED CHICKEN

JULIENNED GREEN ONIONS

MOZZARELLA CHEESE

PEANUT SAUCE

PIZZA CRUST

10"

PROJECT: C.P.K. THAI CHICKEN PIZZA

ORIGINATION DATE: 1985

JOB NO. CPK4690318-TCP

TOP SECRET RECIPES
VERSION OF
CARNEGIE DELI
CLASSIC NEW YORK CITY
CHEESECAKE

☆   ✌   💣   ✎   ☯   ✂   ☞

Carnegie Deli's huge pastrami sandwiches were selected as the best in New York by *New York Magazine* in 1975, but it's the cheesecakes, which can be shipped anywhere in the country, that really put this famous deli on the map. The secret to accurately cloning a traditional New York cheesecake is in creating the perfect, not-too-sweet, sugar-cookie crust, and varying the baking temperature so that we get a nicely browned top before cooking the cheesecake through. Get ready for the best deli-style cheesecake to ever come out of your oven.

COOKIE CRUST

½ cup butter, softened
¼ cup granulated sugar
½ teaspoon vanilla
dash salt
1 egg
1 ½ cups flour

5 8-ounce packages cream
   cheese, softened
1 ⅓ cups sugar
2 teaspoons vanilla extract
4 teaspoons lemon juice
⅓ cup sour cream
2 tablespoons flour
3 eggs

1. Leave the butter and cream cheese out of the refrigerator for 30 to 60 minutes to soften. Make the crust by creaming together butter, $1/4$ cup sugar, $1/2$ teaspoon vanilla, and salt. Add 1 egg and mix well. Add $1 1/2$ cups flour and stir well to combine.
2. Preheat oven to 375°F, then press half of the dough onto the bottom of a 9-inch springform pan. Bake for 5 to 7 minutes or until edge of dough begins to turn light brown. Cool.
3. When the pan has cooled, take the remaining dough and press it around the inside edge of the pan. Don't go all the way up to the top though. Leave about a $1/2$-inch margin from the top of the pan.
4. Crank oven up to 500°F. Combine cream cheese, $1 1/3$ cups sugar, 2 teaspoons vanilla extract and lemon juice with an electric mixer in a large bowl until smooth. Mix in sour cream and 2 tablespoons flour. Add the eggs and mix on slow speed until combined.
5. Pour cream cheese filling into the pan and bake at 500°F for 10 minutes. Reduce heat to 350°F and bake for 30 to 35 minutes more, or until the center is firm. Cover and cool in refrigerator for several hours or overnight before serving.

• SERVES 8.

• • • •

CHEVYS
FRESH SALSA

☆ ✌ ✺ ✐ ☯ ✄ ☞

Chevys's concept of Fresh Mex® has made it one of the best Mexican restaurant chains in the country. You won't find any cans of food in the kitchen since every item on the menu is made daily with fresh ingredients. The restaurant claims it makes its heart-shaped tortillas each day, and this delicious, smoky salsa every hour. You can certainly taste that freshness in the salsa, along with the unique mesquite flavors that come from the restaurant's mesquite-fire grill.

For this clone you won't need a mesquite grill, just some mesquite liquid smoke flavoring and a hot barbecue grill. Oh, and you'll also need a food processor to get the right consistency. The original contains chipotle peppers, which is just another name for smoked red jalapeños. But if you get tired of hunting for the red jalapeños in your local supermarkets, just grab the green ones. They'll work fine. You'll need a total of ten peppers, which may seem like a lot, but their heat is tamed considerably when you grill 'em.

6 medium tomatoes
olive oil
10 jalapeños (red is best)
¼ medium Spanish
    onion
2 cloves garlic

2 tablespoons chopped fresh
    cilantro
2 teaspoons salt
2 tablespoons white vinegar
1 ½ teaspoons mesquite-flavored
    liquid smoke

1. Preheat your barbecue grill to high temperature.
2. Remove any stems from the tomatoes, then rub some oil over each tomato. You can leave the stems on the jalapeños for now.
3. Place the tomatoes on the grill when it's hot. After about 10 minutes, place all of the jalapeños onto the grill. In about 10 minutes you can turn the tomatoes and the peppers. When nearly the entire surface of the peppers has charred black, you can remove them from the grill. The tomatoes will turn black partially, but when the skin begins to come off they're done. Put the peppers and tomatoes on a plate and let them cool.
4. When the tomatoes and peppers have cooled, remove most of the skin from the tomatoes and place them into a food processor. Pinch the stem off the end of the peppers and place them into the food processor as well. Don't include the liquid left on the plate. Toss that out.
5. Add the remaining ingredients to the food processor and puree on high speed for 5 to 10 seconds or until the mixture has a smooth consistency.
6. Place the salsa into a covered container and chill for several hours or overnight while the flavors develop.

- MAKES 2 CUPS.

Nutrition Facts

SERVING SIZE—2 TABLESPOONS	FAT (PER SERVING)—0 G
TOTAL SERVINGS—16	CALORIES (PER SERVING)—10

• • • •

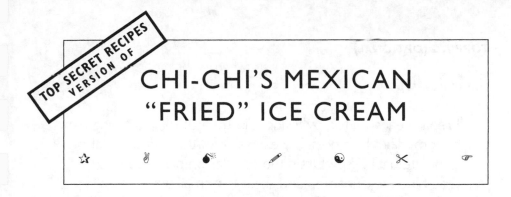

CHI-CHI'S MEXICAN "FRIED" ICE CREAM

Menu Description: "Our specialty! French Vanilla ice cream with a crunchy, crispy cinnamon coating. Served with your choice of honey, chocolate or strawberry topping."

Cooks at Chi-Chi's chain of Mexican restaurants are instructed to *not* memorize recipes for the dishes they make. Management says each chef is required to consult the company cookbooks every time they whip up a meal, so that each dish tastes exactly the same in every Chi-Chi's any time of the day. Perhaps it's that practice that has made Chi-Chi's the largest Mexican restaurant chain in the country.

This crispy-coated ice cream sundae is not exactly fried as you may expect by the name. The scoop of vanilla ice cream is actually rolled in cornflake crumbs that have been flavored with sugar and cinnamon, giving it the appearance and texture of being fried. It's a simple idea that tastes just great, and is well worth a try. Chi-Chi's calls this their "specialty" and claims it's the most requested dessert item on the menu.

½ cup vegetable oil
2 6-inch flour tortillas
½ teaspoon ground cinnamon
2 tablespoons sugar

¼ cup cornflake crumbs
2 large scoops vanilla ice cream
1 can whipped cream
2 maraschino cherries with stems

TOPPING (OPTIONAL)

honey   strawberry topping
chocolate syrup

1. Prepare each tortilla by frying it in the hot oil in a frying pan over medium/high heat. Fry each side of the tortilla for about 1 minute until crispy. Drain the tortillas on paper towels.
2. Combine the cinnamon and sugar in a small bowl.
3. Sprinkle half of the cinnamon mixture over both sides of the fried tortillas, coating evenly. Not all of the sugar mixture will stick to the tortillas, and that's okay.
4. Combine the other half of the cinnamon mixture with the cornflake crumbs in another small bowl. Pour the cornflake mixture into a wide, shallow bowl or onto a plate.
5. Place a large scoop of ice cream in the cornflake crumbs, and with your hands roll the ice cream around until the entire surface is evenly coated with cornflake crumbs. You should not be able to see the ice cream.
6. Place the ice cream scoop on the center of a cinnamon/sugar-coated tortilla.
7. Spray whipped cream around the base of the ice cream. Spray an additional pile of cream on top of the ice cream.
8. Put a cherry in the top pile of whipped cream. Repeat for the remaining scoop of ice cream. Serve with a side dish of honey, chocolate syrup, or strawberry topping, if desired.

- SERVES 2.

• • • •

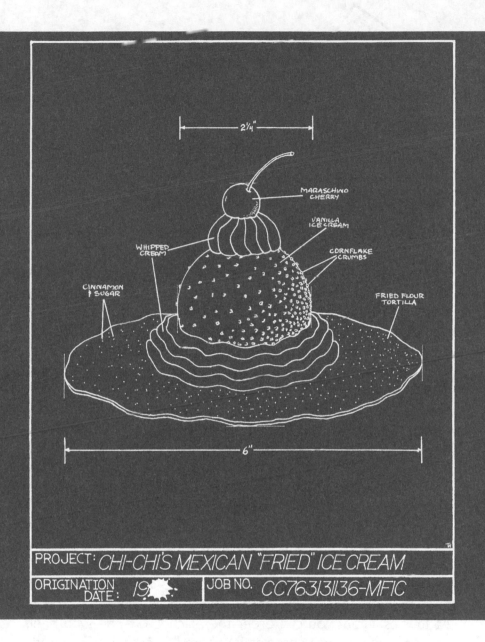

2¼"

MARASCHINO
CHERRY

VANILLA
ICE CREAM

WHIPPED
CREAM

CORNFLAKE
CRUMBS

CINNAMON
& SUGAR

FRIED FLOUR
TORTILLA

6"

PROJECT: *CHI-CHI'S MEXICAN "FRIED" ICE CREAM*

ORIGINATION
DATE: *19*

JOB NO. *CC76313136-MFIC*

CHI-CHI'S
NACHOS GRANDE

☆ ✌ 💣 ✏ ☯ ✂ ☞

Menu Description: "Seasoned beef, refried beans and cheese."

Marno McDermott was a successful Minneapolis restaurateur, opening a chain of Mexican restaurants in the seventies called Zapata's against the advice of skeptics who said he would never be able to sell Mexican food to the large population of Scandinavians in the area. Marno proved them wrong then, and once again in 1976, when he partnered with Max McGee, a former Green Bay Packer football player, to open the first Chi-Chi's in Richfield, Minnesota. The restaurant was built inside a deserted Kroger grocery store and became instantly famous for the intensely flavored and larger-than-usual portions of food. To keep volume high, Chi-Chi's designed a custom computer-driven system that clocks every aspect of service from the time each server enters an order to when the order is placed in front of customers. Special attention was given to the design of the menu's items as well, with each dish taking no more than nine minutes to prepare, even during the rush hours.

Since you're starting from scratch, this appetizer will probably take longer than nine minutes to make, but not by much. At the restaurant you can order the Nachos Grande with beef, chicken, seafood, or a combination; here I've described methods to recreate the beef and chicken versions. You can choose to make the nachos from store-bought tortilla chips or make them yourself with the recipe in "Tidbits." Personally I think the fresh, home-fried type tastes the best. If you're up for the task, amigos, I say give it a go.

BEEF NACHOS GRANDE

½ pound ground beef
1 teaspoon chili powder (Spanish blend)
½ teaspoon salt
½ teaspoon dried minced onion
⅛ teaspoon paprika
2 tablespoons water
8 "restaurant-style" corn tortilla chips

½ cup refried beans
1½ cups shredded Cheddar cheese
½ cup shredded Monterey Jack cheese
¼ cup diced onion
1 large red jalapeño (or green)

ON THE SIDE

sour cream
guacamole

salsa

1. Preheat the oven to 375°F.
2. Brown the ground beef in a skillet over medium heat. Use a spatula or fork to crumble the beef into small pieces as it cooks. When you no longer see pink in the meat, drain off the fat.
3. To the meat, add the chili powder, salt, dried onion, paprika, and water. Simmer over medium/low heat for 10 minutes.
4. If you are going to prepare your own tortilla chips, do that following the instructions in "Tidbits" while the meat is simmering.
5. Heat the refried beans in a small saucepan over low heat or in the microwave for about 2 minutes.
6. Mix the two cheeses together in a small bowl.
7. Arrange the tortilla chips on a baking sheet or an oven-safe ceramic plate. Spread about a tablespoon of refried beans on each chip.
8. Sprinkle a couple of tablespoons of spiced beef onto the beans on each chip. Press down on the beef to make a flat surface for the cheese.
9. Carefully pile a small handful of cheese on each chip.
10. Sprinkle a pinch of the diced onion over the cheese.

11. Place a slice of jalapeño on top of the onion.
12. Bake the chips for 8 to 10 minutes or until the cheese has melted. Serve with your choice of sour cream, guacamole, and salsa on the side.

CHICKEN NACHOS GRANDE

2 tablespoons lime juice
¼ cup water
1 tablespoon vegetable oil
¼ teaspoon liquid smoke
2 teaspoons vinegar
1 clove garlic, pressed
salt
pepper
1 boneless, skinless chicken breast
8 "restaurant style" corn tortilla
   chips

1 cup salsa
1½ cups shredded Cheddar
   cheese
½ cup shredded Monterey Jack
   cheese
¼ cup diced onion
1 large red jalapeño pepper
   (or green)

1. Combine the lime juice, water, oil, liquid smoke, vinegar, and garlic. Add a little salt and pepper and marinate the chicken in the mixture for at least 2 hours.
2. Grill the chicken on your preheated barbecue or stovetop grill or griddle for 4 to 5 minutes per side or until done. Dice the chicken. Preheat the oven to 375°F.
3. Instead of refried beans as in the previous recipe, spread 1 tablespoon of salsa on each of the eight chips. Sprinkle some chicken over the top and build the rest of the nacho the same way as the beef version: Cheeses, onion, then a jalapeño slice.
4. Bake for 8 to 10 minutes. Serve with sour cream, guacamole, and additional salsa on the side.

• SERVES 2 TO 4 AS AN APPETIZER.

TIDBITS

If you want to make your own tasty tortilla chips, buy some 6-inch corn tortillas and cut two of them twice—like a small pizza—into 4 equal triangular pieces (making a total of 8 slices). Drop the tortilla slices 4 at a time into a frying pan filled with about $\frac{1}{2}$ inch of oil that has preheated over medium heat. Chips should bubble rapidly and will only need to fry 30 to 45 seconds per side. They should become a bit more golden in color, and very crispy. Drain the chips on a rack or on some paper towels. Salt to taste.

• • • •

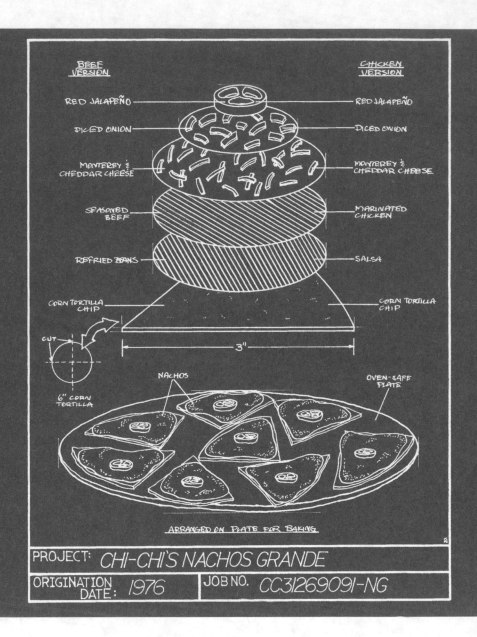

BEEF VERSION

CHICKEN VERSION

RED JALAPEÑO — RED JALAPEÑO

DICED ONION — DICED ONION

MONTERBY & CHEDDAR CHEESE — MONTEREY & CHEDDAR CHEESE

SEASONED BEEF — MARINATED CHICKEN

REFRIED BEANS — SALSA

CORN TORTILLA CHIP — CORN TORTILLA CHIP

CUT

3"

6" CORN TORTILLA

NACHOS

OVEN-SAFE PLATE

ARRANGED ON PLATE FOR BAKING

PROJECT: CHI-CHI'S NACHOS GRANDE

ORIGINATION DATE: 1976

JOB NO. CC3126909I-NG

264

CHI-CHI'S SWEET CORN CAKE

Chi-Chi's cofounder Marno McDermott named his restaurant chain after his wife Chi Chi. He claims the name is quite memorable as it translates in Spanish into something a lot like "hooters" in English. The *Minneapolis Star* quoted McDermott in 1977 shortly after the first Chi-Chi's opened in Richfield, Minnesota, "English-speaking patrons remember it because it's catchy. And the Spanish-speaking customers are amused. Either way it doesn't hurt business."

One of the side dishes included with several of the entrees at Chi-Chi's is the Sweet Corn Cake. It's sort of like cornbread but much softer and sweeter, almost like corn pudding. You'll find it goes well with just about any Mexican dish. The recipe incorporates a *bain marie* or water bath—a technique of baking used commonly for custards and mousses to keep them from cracking or curdling. This is done by simply placing the covered baking pan of batter into another larger pan filled with a little hot water before baking.

½ cup (1 stick) butter, softened
⅓ cup masa harina*
¼ cup water
1 ½ cups frozen corn, thawed
¼ cup cornmeal

⅓ cup sugar
2 tablespoons heavy cream
¼ teaspoon salt
½ teaspoon baking powder

*A Mexican corn flour used to make tortillas. It is usually found in Latin-American groceries and in the supermarket next to the flour.

1. Preheat the oven to 375°F.
2. Blend the butter in a medium bowl with an electric mixer until creamy. Add the masa harina and water to the butter and beat until well combined.
3. Put the defrosted corn into a blender or food processor and, with short pulses, coarsely chop the corn on low speed. You want to leave several whole kernels of corn. Stir the chopped corn into the butter and masa harina mixture. Add the cornmeal to the mixture. Combine.
4. In another medium bowl, mix together the sugar, cream, salt, and baking powder. When the ingredients are well blended, pour the mixture into the other bowl and stir everything together by hand.
5. Pour the corn batter into an ungreased 8 x 8-inch baking pan. Smooth the surface of the batter with a spatula. Cover the pan with aluminum foil. Place this pan into a 13 x 9-inch pan filled one-third of the way up with hot water. Bake for 50 to 60 minutes or until the corn cake is cooked through.
6. When the corn cake is done, remove the small pan from the larger pan and let it sit for at least 10 minutes. To serve, scoop out each portion with an ice cream scoop or rounded spoon.

• SERVES 8 TO 10 AS A SIDE DISH.

•   •   •   •

CHI-CHI'S TWICE GRILLED BARBECUE BURRITO

☆   ✌   💣   ✒   ☯   ✂   ☞

Menu Description: "Grilled steak or chicken wrapped in a flour tortilla with cheese and sautéed vegetables. Then the burrito is basted with spicy barbecue sauce and grilled again. Served with Spanish rice and sweet corn cake."

This dish bursts with the Southwestern flavors that have become so popular lately. Southwestern dishes like fajitas and specialty burritos are the latest rage in the restaurant industry, and now more chains than ever are creating their own spicy, Southwestern-style goodies.

I think you'll really enjoy this one. Chi-Chi's has taken fajita-style grilled beef, rolled it up like a burrito, grilled it again, and then smothered it with smoky barbecue sauce. The dish has quickly become a favorite menu item at Chi-Chi's and a favorite for people tiring of the same old Mexican food. Fire up the grill and give this zesty recipe a try.

MARINADE

⅓ cup water	2 teaspoons vinegar
¼ cup lime juice	2 teaspoons soy sauce
1 large clove garlic, pressed or grated	½ teaspoon liquid smoke
2 tablespoons vegetable oil	½ teaspoon chili powder
	½ teaspoon cayenne pepper

1 teaspoon salt	dash of onion powder
¼ teaspoon pepper	¼ cup shredded cheddar cheese
	¼ cup shredded monterey jack cheese

1 pound sirloin steak	2 tablespoons vegetable oil
1 red bell pepper, sliced	2 10-inch flour tortillas
1 green bell pepper, sliced	3 tablespoons Bullseye original
1 Spanish onion, sliced	barbecue sauce

1. Combine all of the ingredients for the marinade in a small bowl. Set aside ¼ cup of the marinade. Store it in a sealed container in the fridge until you need it. Marinate the steak in the refrigerator with the remaining marinade for several hours. Overnight is best. Be sure the steak isn't too thick. If it's more than ½ inch thick, slice it thinner.
2. Grill the steak on a hot barbecue or preheated stovetop grill for 4 to 5 minutes per side or until done. Cook less for a rarer steak, longer if you want it well done.
3. While the steak grills, sauté the peppers and onion in 1 tablespoon of vegetable oil over high heat. When the vegetables are tender, add the ¼ cup of marinade you set aside. Continue sautéing the vegetables until they brown.
4. When the steak is done, slice it into long strips that are no more than ½ inch thick and ½ inch wide. Keep the grill on.
5. Lay the tortillas in a hot pan over low heat to make them warm and pliable. Turn them as they heat up. It should only take a few seconds to get the tortillas warm enough to bend without cracking. Lay each warm tortilla on a clean surface and fill each one with equal portions of grilled steak. Position the steak near the bottom edge of the burrito with about a 1-inch "margin."
6. Combine the two shredded cheeses. Sprinkle half of the cheese blend over the meat on each tortilla.

7. Take half of the sautéed peppers and onions and split it between the two burritos, laying it on the steak.
8. Roll the burrito by folding the bottom up and over the filling. Fold in the sides, and then roll the filling up over twice, being careful to make a neat little package.
9. Rub 1 teaspoon of vegetable oil over the entire surface of each burrito.
10. Put the burritos, seam side down, back on your barbecue grill set on medium heat for 1 to 2 minutes. When the bottom of the burrito begins to char, turn the burritos over. By now the tortilla should be stiff and crunchy making it easy to roll the burrito over without the filling falling out. Grill the tops of the burritos for 1 to 2 minutes more, or until the surface begins to char.
11. Transfer the burritos from the grill to two serving plates with the seam side down. Coat the top of each burrito with 1 to 1½ tablespoons of barbecue sauce.
12. Split the remaining peppers and onions and spread them over the top of the two burritos.

• SERVES 2 AS AN ENTREE.

• • • •

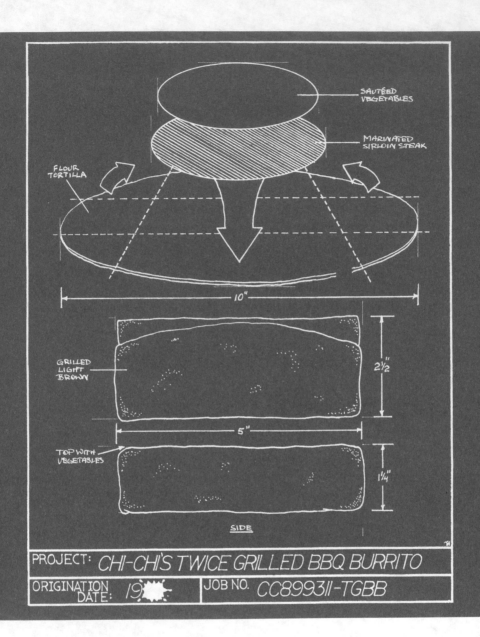

SAUTÉED
VEGETABLES

MARINATED
SIRLOIN STEAK

FLOUR
TORTILLA

10"

GRILLED
LIGHT
BROWN

2½"

5"

TOP WITH
VEGETABLES

1¼"

SIDE

PROJECT: *CHI-CHI'S TWICE GRILLED BBQ BURRITO*

ORIGINATION
DATE: *19*

JOB NO. *CC899311-TGBB*

270

CHILI'S FAJITAS
FOR TWO

☆ ✌ 💣 ✏ ☯ ✂ ☞

Menu Description: "A pound of steak, chicken or combination on a sizzling skillet. Peppers available w/Fajitas upon request."

Chili's is perhaps the restaurant most responsible for introducing the famous finger food known as fajitas to the mass market. Company CEO Norman Brinker discovered the dish at a small restaurant on a visit to San Antonio, Texas. When Chili's put the item on its menu in the early eighties, sales immediately jumped a whopping 25 percent. One company spokesperson told Spirit magazine, "I remember walking into one of the restaurants after we added them to the menu and all I could see were wisps of steam coming up from the tables. That revolutionized Chili's."

Today Chili's serves more than 2 million pounds of fajitas a year. If all of the flour tortillas served with those fajitas were laid end-to-end, they'd stretch from New York to New Zealand, on the other side of the earth!

Today just about every American knows what fajitas are— the Southwestern-style grilled chicken, beef, or seafood, served sizzling on a cast iron skillet. And everyone has their own method of arranging the meat and onions and peppers in a soft tortilla with globs of pico de gallo, cheese, guacamole, lettuce, sour cream, and salsa. The tough part is trying to roll the thing up and take a bite ever so gracefully without squeezing half of the filling out the backside of the tortilla onto the plate, splattering your clean clothes, while goo goes dripping down your chin. This recipe is guaranteed to be as delicious and messy as the original.

MARINADE

¼ cup fresh lime juice
⅓ cup water
2 tablespoons vegetable oil
1 large clove garlic, pressed
3 teaspoons vinegar
2 teaspoons soy sauce

½ teaspoon liquid smoke
1 teaspoon salt
½ teaspoon chili powder
½ teaspoon cayenne pepper
¼ teaspoon ground black pepper
dash onion powder

2 boneless, skinless chicken breast
   halves or 1 pound top sirloin
   or a combination of 1 chicken
   breast half and ½ pound
   sirloin
1 Spanish onion, sliced
1 tablespoon vegetable oil

1 teaspoon soy sauce
2 tablespoons water
½ teaspoon lime juice
dash ground black pepper
dash salt

ON THE SIDE

½ cup pico de gallo
½ cup grated Cheddar cheese
½ cup guacamole
½ cup sour cream

1 cup shredded lettuce
6 to 8 six-inch flour tortillas
salsa

1. Combine all of the ingredients for the marinade in a small bowl. Soak your choice of meat in the marinade for at least 2 hours. If you are just using the sirloin, let it marinate overnight, if possible.
2. When the meat has marinated, preheat your barbecue or stovetop grill to high.
3. Preheat a skillet over medium/high heat. Sauté the onion slices in the oil for 5 minutes. Combine the soy sauce, water, and lime juice in a small bowl and pour it over the onions. Add the black pepper and continue to sauté until the onions are translucent and dark on the edges (4 to 5 more minutes). Salt to taste.
4. While the onions are sautéing, grill the meat for 4 to 5 minutes per side or until done.

5. While the meat and onions are cooking, heat up another skillet (cast iron if you have one) over high heat. This will be your sizzling serving pan.
6. When the meat is done remove it from the grill and slice it into thin strips.
7. Remove the extra pan from the heat and dump the onions and any liquid into it. If you've made it hot enough the onions should sizzle. Add the meat to the pan and serve immediately with pico de gallo, Cheddar cheese, guacamole, and sour cream arranged on a separate plate on a bed of shredded lettuce. Steam the tortillas in a moist towel in the microwave for 30 seconds and serve on the side. Serve salsa also, if desired.

Assemble fajitas by putting the meat into a tortilla along with your choice of condiments. Roll up the tortilla and scarf out.

- SERVES 2 AS AN ENTREE.

TIDBITS

At Chili's, bell peppers are optional with this dish. If you like peppers, combine a small sliced green or red bell pepper with the onion, and sauté the vegetables together. Follow the rest of the steps as described.

•   •   •   •

INTERNATIONAL HOUSE OF PANCAKES BANANA NUT PANCAKES

☆　　✌　　💣　　✐　　☯　　✂　　☞

Menu Description: "Four banana-flavored pancakes garnished with fresh banana and chopped pecans. Served with banana-flavored syrup."

You'll find sixteen varieties of pancakes on the IHOP menu, including one of the newest flavors: pumpkin pancakes. IHOP claims to sell over 400,000 pancakes each day. That's a lot of pancakes. So many, in fact, that if all of those flapjacks were served up on one plate, it would make a giant stack taller than the Sears Tower in Chicago. And probably much tastier.

According to servers, of all the pancake flavors and varieties, the Banana Nut Pancakes are one of the most often requested. I've included a recipe for the banana-flavored syrup here, but you can use any flavor syrup, including maple, on these babies.

BANANA SYRUP

½ cup corn syrup
½ cup sugar
½ cup water

¼ teaspoon banana extract or
　flavoring

PANCAKES

1 1/4 cups all-purpose flour
1 1/2 cups buttermilk
1 egg
1/4 cup vegetable oil
2 tablespoons sugar
1 teaspoon baking powder

1 teaspoon baking soda
1/2 tablespoon banana extract or
    flavoring
1/4 teaspoon salt
2/3 cup chopped pecans
1 banana

1. Make the banana syrup first by combining all the syrup ingredients—except for the banana extract—in a small saucepan over high heat, stirring occasionally. When the mixture begins to boil, remove it from the heat and stir in the banana extract.

2. In a large bowl, combine all the ingredients for the pancakes except the pecans and the banana. Use an electric mixer to blend until smooth.

3. Heat a large frying pan or griddle over medium heat, and coat it with butter or nonstick cooking spray when hot.

4. Pour 1/4-cup dollops of batter into the pan. Realize the batter will spread out to about 4 inches across, so leave enough room if you are cooking more than one at a time. Granted, some pans may only hold one or two at a time. Sprinkle about 1/2 tablespoon pecans into the center of each pancake immediately after you pour the batter so that the nuts are "cooked in."

5. Cook the pancakes for 1 to 2 minutes per side or until golden brown.

6. Slice the banana, divide it up, and serve it on top of a stack of 3 to 4 pancakes with the remaining chopped pecans divided and sprinkled on top of each stack.

• SERVES 3 TO 4.

•   •   •   •

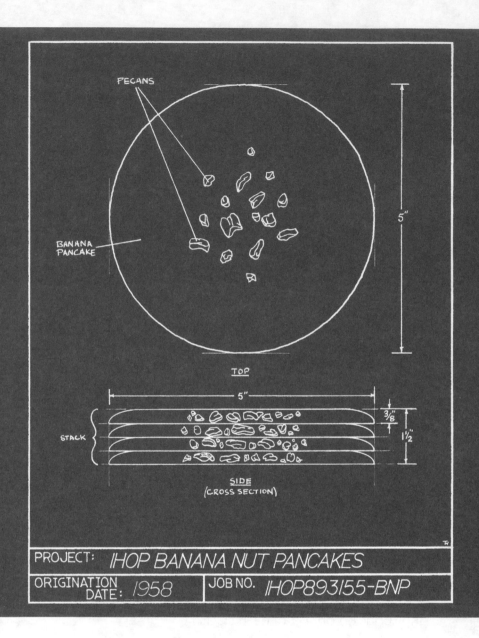

PECANS

5"

BANANA
PANCAKE

TOP

5"

STACK

SIDE
(CROSS SECTION)

3/8"

1½"

PROJECT: *IHOP BANANA NUT PANCAKES*

ORIGINATION
DATE: *1958*

JOB NO. *IHOP893155-BNP*

INTERNATIONAL HOUSE OF PANCAKES CHEESE BLINTZ

☆　　　✌　　　💣　　　✏　　　☯　　　✂　　　☞

Menu Description: "Crepe-style pancakes filled with a blend of cheeses with strawberry preserves and sour cream."

Detroit's mayoral candidate Sharon McPhail and Detroit schools superintendent David Snead often dined in the city's hottest spot for power breakfasts—the local IHOP. Perhaps it was that first little something in common that eventually led to the two exchanging vows in front of 1,800 guests in a 1995 wedding ceremony. It was dubbed Detroit's "wedding of the year." That particular IHOP, which just happens to be owned by singer Anita Baker's husband, Walter Bridgforth, has seen a 200 percent jump in business.

　　You'll enjoy this simple recipe for crepes, which, when filled with cheese, become delicious blintzes. The restaurant uses a type of cheese that is similar to soft farmer's cheese, but you can make this with cream cheese, or even with yogurt that has been strained to make it thicker. Any way you decide to go, you're in for a treat.

CREPES

1 ½ cups all-purpose flour
2 cups milk
3 tablespoons butter, melted
2 tablespoons granulated sugar
2 eggs

½ teaspoon vanilla
½ teaspoon baking powder
½ teaspoon salt

butter (for pan)

FILLING

1 cup cottage cheese
1 cup soft farmer cheese or
   softened cream cheese
   (see Tidbits)

¼ cup powdered sugar
¼ teaspoon vanilla

ON THE SIDE

sour cream
strawberry preserves

powdered sugar

1. Use an electric mixer to blend together all the crepe ingredients except the butter for the pan in a large bowl. Blend just until smooth. The batter will be very thin.
2. Combine the filling ingredients in a medium bowl and mix by hand. Keep the filling nearby.
3. Preheat a 10-inch frying pan over medium heat. (This size pan tapers to about 8 inches at the bottom.) When the pan is hot, add about ½ teaspoon of butter.
4. When the butter has melted, pour ⅓ cup of batter into the pan. Swirl the batter so that it entirely coats the bottom of the pan. Cook for 1 ½ to 2 minutes or until golden brown on one side.
5. Use a spatula to lift an edge of the crepe. Grab it with your finger, slip the spatula underneath, and quickly flip it over. Cook for another 1 ½ minutes or until a bit lighter shade of brown than the first side, then slide it out of the pan. Repeat with the rest of the batter and stack the finished crepes on top of each other to keep them warm.

6. Heat the cheese filling in the microwave for 1 to 2 minutes or until it is hot.
7. When ready to fill the crepes, place each crepe, dark side down, on a plate. Pour 2 to 3 tablespoons of cheese filling across the center of the crepe. Fold the sides in and turn the entire blintz over (to hide the seam) onto a serving plate. You can use a knife to cut the rounded ends off the blintzes if you like. Repeat with the remaining blintzes.
8. Serve 2 to 3 blintzes on a plate with a dollop of sour cream and 2 dollops of strawberry preserves carefully arranged on the plate next to the blintzes. Sprinkle the blintzes with powdered sugar.

- SERVES 3 TO 4 (10 TO 12 BLINTZES).

TIDBITS

If you would like to make this recipe with a lowfat or nonfat filling, replace the cream cheese or farmer's cheese with strained yogurt—a yogurt solid that is thick like cheese. To make it, pour a cup of lowfat or nonfat yogurt into a coffee filter placed inside a strainer. Put the strainer over a bowl and into the refrigerator for 4 to 5 hours so that all of the liquid whey strains out of the yogurt. What you have left in the strainer is a thick, nutritious yogurt cheese that can be used in place of cream cheese or sour cream in this recipe and many others.

• • • •

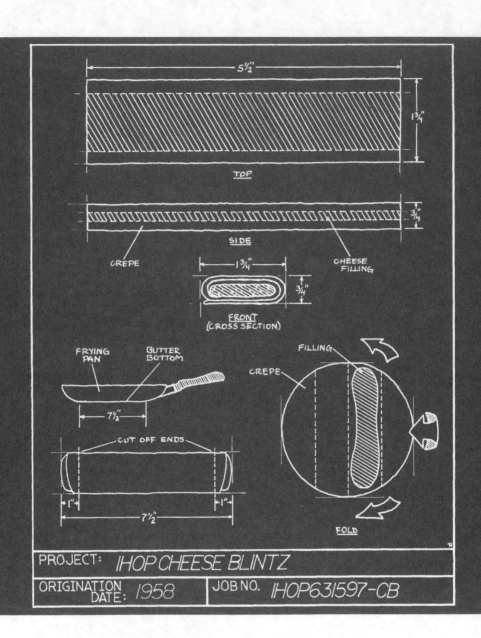

5½"

1¾"

TOP

¾"

SIDE

CREPE

CHEESE
FILLING

1¾"

¾"

FRONT
(CROSS SECTION)

FRYING
PAN

BUTTER
BOTTOM

7½"

FILLING

CREPE

CUT OFF ENDS

1"

1"

7½"

FOLD

PROJECT: IHOP CHEESE BLINTZ

ORIGINATION
DATE: 1958

JOB NO. IHOP631597-CB

280

INTERNATIONAL HOUSE OF PANCAKES FRENCH TOAST

Menu Description: "Six triangular slices with powdered sugar."

Now in its 38th year, IHOP has become one of the recognized leaders for breakfast dining, serving up thousands of omelettes, waffles, blintzes, and pancakes each and every day.

Among the popular morning meals is IHOP's classic French toast. You'll notice the addition of a little bit of flour to the batter to make this version of French toast more like the dish you get at the restaurant. The flour helps to create a thicker coating on the bread, almost like a tender crepe on the surface, keeping the bread from becoming too soggy.

2 eggs
1/2 cup milk
1 teaspoon vanilla
3 tablespoons all-purpose flour

1/8 teaspoon salt
3 teaspoons butter
6 slices thick-sliced French bread
1 tablespoon powdered sugar

ON THE SIDE
butter

pancake syrup

1. Beat the eggs in a large shallow bowl.
2. Add the milk, vanilla, flour, and salt to the eggs. Beat the mixture with an electric mixer. Be sure all the flour is well combined.
3. Heat a large skillet over medium heat. When the surface is hot, add about a teaspoon of butter.
4. Dip the bread, a slice at a time, into the batter, being sure to coat each side well. Drop the bread into the hot pan (as many as will fit at one time) and cook for 2 to 3 minutes per side or until the surface is golden brown. Repeat with the remaining pieces of bread.
5. Cut each piece of toast in half diagonally. Arrange six halves of the toast on two plates by neatly overlapping the slices. Sprinkle about $\frac{1}{2}$ tablespoon of powdered sugar over the tops of the toast slices on each plate. Serve with butter and syrup on the side.

- SERVES 2 (CAN BE DOUBLED).

• • • •

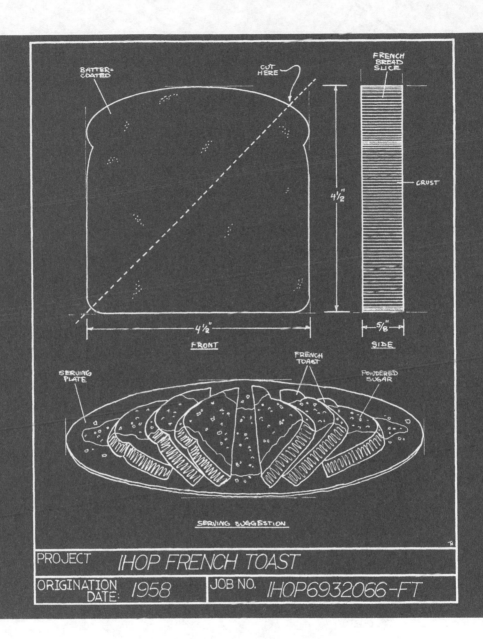

BATTER-COATED

CUT HERE

FRENCH BREAD SLICE

CRUST

4½"

FRONT

4½"

SIDE

⅝"

SERVING PLATE

FRENCH TOAST

POWDERED SUGAR

SERVING SUGGESTION

PROJECT	IHOP FRENCH TOAST	
ORIGINATION DATE: 1958	JOB NO.	IHOP6932066-FT

LONE STAR
STEAKHOUSE & SALOON
AMARILLO CHEESE FRIES

☆　✌　💣　✏　☯　✂　☞

Menu Description: "Lone Star fries smothered in Monterey Jack and Cheddar cheese, topped with bacon and served with ranch dressing."

Growth by this newcomer to the steakhouse segment has been phenomenal. So far, there are over 160 Lone Stars across the country, most of them in the East and Midwest. There are even four in Australia. The company is the fastest growing steakhouse chain in the country, and if you don't have one near you yet, you probably will soon.

Amarillo Cheese Fries are made with thick-sliced unpeeled potatoes. The recipe here is created from scratch, using freshly sliced potatoes. But, if this is one of those days when you just don't feel up to slicing and frying some russets, you can also use a bag of frozen steak fries. Just be aware that those will likely be made from peeled potatoes, unlike the real thing that is served at the restaurant. I've also included a cool recipe for homemade ranch dressing to dip the fries in, if you decide you'd like to make yours from scratch.

3 unpeeled russet potatoes
4 to 6 cups vegetable oil for
　frying
1 cup shredded Cheddar cheese

1 cup shredded Monterey Jack
　cheese
3 slices bacon, cooked
⅓ cup ranch dressing

1. Slice the potatoes into wide rectangular slices. They should be about ¼ inch thick and ¾ inch wide. You should end up with around 12 to 15 slices per potato. Keep the potato slices immersed in water until they are ready to fry so that they don't turn brown.
2. Heat the oil in a deep fryer or deep pan to 350°F. Dry the potato slices on paper towels and fry them for 1 minute in the hot oil. This is the blanching stage. Remove the potatoes from the oil and drain until they cool, about 10 minutes.
3. When the potato slices are cool, fry them for 5 more minutes or until they are a light golden brown. Drain.
4. Preheat your oven to 375°F, then arrange the fries on an oven-safe plate.
5. Sprinkle the Cheddar cheese over the fries.
6. Sprinkle the Monterey Jack cheese over the Cheddar.
7. Crumble the cooked bacon and sprinkle it over the cheese.
8. Bake the fries in the oven for 5 minutes or until the cheese has melted. Serve hot with bottled ranch dressing or make your own with the recipe offered here.

- SERVES 4 TO 6 AS AN APPETIZER OR SNACK.

TIDBITS

You can also make this recipe using a 32-ounce bag of store-bought frozen steak fries. Just cook them following the directions on the bag, adding the toppings in the last 5 minutes of baking.

If you want to make your own ranch dressing for dipping instead of buying it at the store, here is a good recipe that I came up with:

RANCH DRESSING

¼ cup mayonnaise
1 tablespoon buttermilk
½ teaspoon sugar
¼ teaspoon vinegar
¼ teaspoon garlic powder
¼ teaspoon finely chopped
    fresh dill

¼ teaspoon finely chopped fresh
    parsley
⅛ teaspoon onion powder
dash salt
dash paprika

Combine all of the ingredients in a small bowl and let them chill for an hour or two.

•   •   •   •

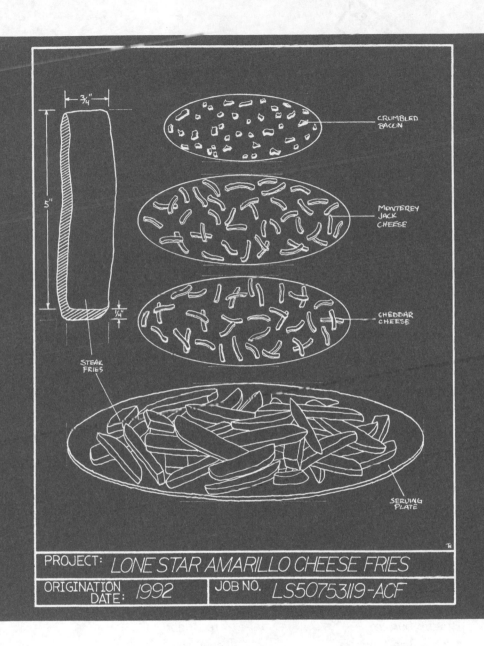

CRUMBLED BACON

MONTEREY JACK CHEESE

CHEDDAR CHEESE

STEAK FRIES

SERVING PLATE

PROJECT: *LONE STAR AMARILLO CHEESE FRIES*

ORIGINATION DATE: *1992*

JOB NO. *LS50753119-ACF*

MARIE CALLENDER'S BANANA CREAM PIE

☆ ✌ 💣 ✏ ☯ ✂ ☞

Menu Description: "Fresh ripe bananas in our rich vanilla cream, topped with fresh whipped cream or fluffy meringue."

Bakers get to work by 5 A.M. at Marie Callender's to begin baking over 30 varieties of pies. Huge pies. Pies that weigh nearly three pounds apiece. The fresh, creamy, flaky, delicious pies that have made Marie Callender's famous in the food biz. On those mornings about 250 pies will be made at each of the 147 restaurants. Modest, I suppose, when compared with Thanksgiving Day when the stores can make up to 3,500 pies each.

For now though, we'll start with just one—banana cream pie with flaky crust, whipped cream, and slivered almonds on top. This recipe requires that you bake the crust unfilled, so you will have to use a pie weight or other oven-safe object to keep the crust from puffing up. Large pie weights are sold in many stores, or you can use small metal or ceramic weights (sold in packages) or dried beans on the crust which has first been lined with aluminum foil or parchment paper.

¼ cup butter
¼ cup shortening
1 ¼ cups all-purpose flour
1 tablespoon sugar

¼ teaspoon salt
1 egg yolk
2 tablespoons ice water
½ teaspoon vinegar

FILLING

⅔ cup sugar
¼ cup cornstarch
½ teaspoon salt
2¾ cups whole milk

4 egg yolks, beaten
1 tablespoon butter
2 teaspoons vanilla
2 ripe bananas, sliced

TOPPING

1 can whipped cream

¼ cup slivered almonds

1. Beat together the butter and shortening until smooth and creamy and chill until firm.
2. Sift together the flour, sugar, and salt in a medium bowl.
3. Using a fork, cut the butter and shortening into the dry ingredients, until the mixture has a consistent texture. Mix egg yolk, ice water, and vinegar into the dough, then form it into a ball and refrigerate it for 1 hour so that it will be easier to work with.
4. Preheat the oven to 450°F. When the dough has chilled, roll it out and press it into a 9-inch pie plate.
5. Press parchment paper or aluminum foil into the crust and weight the crust down with a ceramic pie weight or another pie pan filled with dried beans. This will prevent the crust from puffing up and distorting. Bake for 15 minutes, then remove the weight or pan filled with beans and prick the crust with a fork to allow steam to escape. Bake for another 5 to 10 minutes, or until the crust is golden brown. Let the crust cool.
6. Make the filling by sifting together the sugar, cornstarch, and salt into a medium saucepan.
7. Blend the milk, eggs, and butter in a medium bowl, then add the mixture to the dry ingredients and cook over medium heat stirring constantly for 6 to 8 minutes or until the mixture boils and thickens, then cook for 1 minute more.
8. Remove the filling from the heat, and mix in the vanilla.
9. Put plastic wrap on the surface of the filling and let it cool to

about room temperature. The plastic wrap will prevent the top of the filling from becoming gummy.

10. When the filling has cooled, remove the plastic wrap and add the sliced bananas. Stir.

11. Pour the filling into the pie shell and chill for a couple of hours before serving. Slice across the pie 3 times to make 6 large slices. Serve each slice topped with fresh whipped cream and slivered almonds.

- SERVES 6.

• • • •

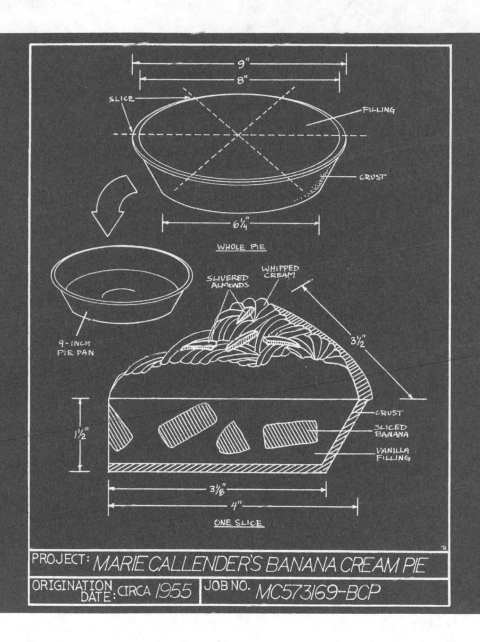

9"

8"

SLICE

FILLING

CRUST

6¼"

WHOLE PIE

9-INCH PIE PAN

SLIVERED ALMONDS

WHIPPED CREAM

3½"

CRUST

SLICED BANANA

VANILLA FILLING

1½"

3⅛"

4"

ONE SLICE

PROJECT: *MARIE CALLENDER'S BANANA CREAM PIE*

ORIGINATION DATE: CIRCA *1955*

JOB NO. *MC573169-BCP*

MARIE CALLENDER'S CHICKEN POT PIE

Menu Description: "Tender chunks of chicken with seasonings and vegetables."

All the Marie Callender's restaurants try to maintain a homestyle ambiance, kind of like being at Grandma's house for dinner. The wallcoverings reflect styles of the thirties and forties and are complemented by dark mahogany-stained, wood-paneled walls and brass fixtures. You'll also find old-fashioned furnishings, many of them throwbacks to the forties, the time of this restaurant chain's founding fifty years ago.

The menu, which features meatloaf, pot roast, and country fried steak, reflects a satisfying homestyle cuisine that today is all too rare. If you wondered whether a company that is known for its great dessert pies could make a great pot pie . . . it can.

For this recipe, try to use small 16-ounce casserole dishes that measure 4 or 5 inches across at the top. Any casserole dishes that come close to this size will probably work; the yield will vary depending on what size dishes you decide to use.

CRUST
1 ½ cups all-purpose flour
¾ teaspoon salt
2 egg yolks

3 tablespoons ice water
⅔ cup cold butter

FILLING

1 cup sliced carrots (3 carrots)	5 tablespoons all-purpose flour
1 cup sliced celery (1 stalk)	2½ cups chicken broth
2 cups frozen peas	⅔ cup milk
1 cup chopped white onion	½ teaspoon salt
4 boneless, skinless chicken breast halves	dash pepper
	1 egg, beaten
4 tablespoons butter	

1. Prepare the crust by sifting together the flour and salt in a medium bowl. Make a depression in the center of the flour with your hand.
2. Put the yolks and ice water into the depression. Slice the butter into tablespoon-size portions and add it into the flour depression as well.
3. Using a fork, cut the wet ingredients into the dry ingredients. When all of the flour is moistened, use your hands to finish combining the ingredients. This will ensure that the chunks of butter are well blended into the dough. Roll the dough into a ball, cover it with plastic wrap and put it into the refrigerator for 1 to 2 hours. This will make the dough easier to work with.
4. When the dough has chilled, preheat the oven to 425°F and start on the filling by steaming the vegetables. Steam the carrots and celery for 5 minutes in a steamer or a saucepan with a small amount of water in the bottom. Add the frozen peas and onions and continue to steam for an additional 10 to 12 minutes or until the carrots are tender.
5. Prepare the chicken by poaching the breasts in lightly salted boiling water for 8 to 10 minutes.
6. In a separate large saucepan, melt the butter over medium heat, remove from the heat, then add the flour and whisk together until smooth. Add the chicken broth and milk and continue stirring over high heat until the mixture comes to a boil. Cook for an additional minute or so until thick, then reduce the heat to low.

7. Cut the poached chicken into large bite-size chunks and add them to the sauce. Add the salt and a dash of pepper.
8. Add the steamed vegetables to the sauce and simmer the mixture over medium/low heat for 4 to 5 minutes.
9. As the filling simmers, roll out the dough on a floured surface. Use one of the casserole dishes you plan to bake the pies in as a guide for cutting the dough. The filling will fit four 16-ounce casserole dishes perfectly, but you can use just about any size single-serving casserole dishes or oven-safe bowls for this recipe. Invert one of the dishes onto the dough and use a knife to cut around the rim. Make the cut about a half-inch larger all of the way around to give the dough a small "lip," which you will fold over when you cover the pie. Make four of these.
10. Spoon the chicken and vegetable filling into each casserole dish and carefully cover each dish with the cut dough. Fold the edge of the dough over the edge of each dish and press firmly so that the dough sticks to the outer rim. Brush some beaten egg on the dough on each pie.
11. Bake the pies on a cookie sheet for 30 to 45 minutes or until the top crust is light brown.

• SERVES 4.

•   •   •   •

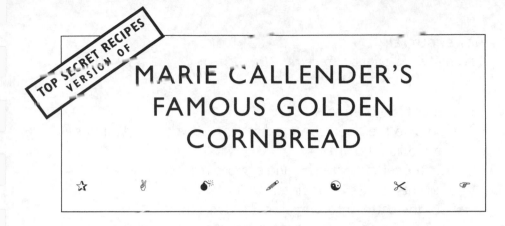

MARIE CALLENDER'S FAMOUS GOLDEN CORNBREAD

The American restaurant business has been shaped by many young entrepreneurs, so determined to realize their dreams of owning a hot dog cart or starting a restaurant that they sell everything they own to raise cash. Food lore is littered with these stories, and this one is no exception. This time the family car was sold to pay for one month's rent on a converted World War II army tent, an oven, refrigerator, rolling pin, and some hand tools. It was 1948, and that's all that Marie Callender and her family needed to make enough pies to start delivering to restaurants in Long Beach, California.

It was pies that started the company, but soon the bakeries became restaurants and they started serving meals. One of my favorites is the Famous Golden Cornbread and whipped honey butter that comes with many of the entrees. What makes this cornbread so scrumptious is its cake-like quality. The recipe here requires more flour than traditional cornbread recipes, making the finished product soft and spongy just like Marie's.

1 ¼ cups all-purpose flour
¾ cup cornmeal
2 teaspoons baking powder
⅓ cup sugar

¾ teaspoon salt
1 ¼ cups whole milk
¼ cup shortening
1 egg

HONEY BUTTER

½ cup (1 stick) butter, softened   ⅓ cup honey

1. Preheat the oven to 400°F.
2. Combine the flour, cornmeal, baking powder, sugar, and salt in a medium bowl.
3. Add the milk, shortening, and egg and mix only until all the ingredients are well combined.
4. Pour the batter into a greased 8 × 8-inch pan.
5. Bake for 25 to 30 minutes or until the top is golden brown. Let the cornbread cool slightly before slicing it with a sharp knife into 9 pieces.
6. For the honey butter, use a mixer on high speed to whip the butter and honey together until smooth and fluffy.

- MAKES 9 PIECES.

•   •   •   •

OLIVE GARDEN HOT ARTICHOKE-SPINACH DIP

☆   ✌   💣   ✏   🎱   ✂   ☞

Menu Description: "A creamy hot dip of artichokes, spinach and parmesan with pasta chips."

It's interesting to note that just about every aspect of the Olive Garden restaurants was developed from consumer research conducted in a corporate think tank by the General Mills corporation. Restaurant-goers were questioned about preferences such as the type of food to be served, the appearance and atmosphere of the restaurant, even the color of the candle holders on each table. The large tables and the comfy chairs on rollers that you see today at the Olive Garden restaurants came out of these vigorous research sessions.

I'm not sure if this dish came from those sessions, but according to servers at the Olive Garden, the Hot Artichoke-Spinach Dip is one of the most requested appetizers on the menu. The restaurant serves the dip with chips made from fried pasta, but you can serve this version of the popular appetizer with just about any type of crackers, chips, or toasted Italian bread, like bruschetta.

½ cup frozen chopped spinach, thawed

1 cup chopped artichoke hearts (canned or frozen and thawed)

8 ounces cream cheese

½ cup grated Parmesan cheese

½ teaspoon crushed red pepper flakes

¼ teaspoon salt

⅛ teaspoon garlic powder

dash ground pepper

ON THE SIDE

crackers   *sliced, toasted bread*

chips

1. Boil the spinach and artichoke hearts in a cup of water in a small saucepan over medium heat until tender, about 10 minutes. Drain in a colander when done.
2. Heat the cream cheese in a small bowl in the microwave set on high for 1 minute. Or, use a saucepan to heat the cheese over medium heat just until hot.
3. Add the spinach and artichoke hearts to the cream cheese and stir well.
4. Add the remaining ingredients to the cream cheese and combine. Serve hot with crackers, chips, or toasted bread for dipping.

- SERVES 4 AS AN APPETIZER.

TIDBITS

It's easy to make a lighter version of this dip by using a reduced fat cream cheese in the same measurement.

•   •   •   •

OLIVE GARDEN
ITALIAN SALAD DRESSING

☆ ✌ 💣 ✐ ☯ ✂ ☞

In the 1970s, food conglomerate General Mills set out to expand its growing restaurant business. A research team was organized to study the market, and to conduct interviews with potential customers on what they would want in a restaurant. Seven years later, in 1982, the first Olive Garden restaurant opened its doors in Orlando, Florida. Today it is the number one Italian restaurant chain in the country with over 470 stores.

One of the favorites at the Olive Garden is an item that isn't even mentioned in the menu: the Italian salad dressing served on the house salad that comes with every meal. The dressing became so popular that the chain now sells it by the bottle "to go" in each restaurant. Now you can make a version of the dressing for yourself that tastes just like the original, but will cost much less. The secret to thickening this dressing is to use dry pectin, a natural ingredient often used to thicken jams and jellies. Pectin can be found in most stores in the aisle with baking and cooking supplies or near the canning items.

½ cup white vinegar
⅓ cup water
⅓ cup vegetable oil
¼ cup corn syrup
2½ tablespoons grated Romano cheese

2 tablespoons dry pectin
2 tablespoons beaten egg or egg substitute
1¼ teaspoons salt
1 teaspoon lemon juice
½ teaspoon minced garlic

¼ teaspoon dried parsley flakes   *pinch of crushed red pepper*
pinch of dried oregano   *flakes*

1. Combine all of the ingredients with a mixer on medium speed or in a blender on low speed for 30 seconds. Chill at least 1 hour. Serve over mixed greens or use as a marinade.

• MAKES 1½ CUPS.

•   •   •   •

OUTBACK STEAKHOUSE BLOOMIN' ONION

☆　　✌　　💣　　✏　　☯　　✂　　☞

Menu Description: "An Outback Ab-original from Russell's Marina Bay."

If you go to an Outback Steakhouse expecting exotic Aussie prairie food that someone like Crocodile Dundee would have enjoyed, you're gonna be a bit disappointed, mate. Except for a little Australia-themed paraphernalia on the walls, like boomerangs and pictures of kangaroos, the restaurant chain is about as "down under" as McDonald's is Irish. The three founders, Tim Gannon, Chris Sullivan, and Bob Basham, are all U.S. boys. And the menu, which is about 60 percent beef, contains mainly American fare with cute Australian names like The Melbourne, Jackeroo Chops, and Chicken on the Barbie.

The founders say they chose the Aussie theme because "Most Australians are fun-loving and gregarious people and very casual people. We thought that's exactly the kind of friendliness and atmosphere we want to have in our restaurants."

In only six years, Outback Steakhouse has become our number one steakhouse chain—in part because of the Bloomin' Onion: a large, deep-fried onion sliced to look like a flower in bloom that was created by one of the restaurant's founders. What makes this appetizer so appealing besides its flowery appearance is the onion's crispy spiced coating, along with the delicious dipping sauce, cleverly presented in the center of the onion.

Although the restaurant uses a special device to make the slicing process easier, you can make the incisions with a sharp knife. It just takes a steady hand and a bit of care.

DIPPING SAUCE

½ cup mayonnaise
2 teaspoons ketchup
2 tablespoons cream-style
    horseradish
¼ teaspoon paprika

¼ teaspoon salt
⅛ teaspoon dried oregano
dash ground black pepper
dash cayenne pepper

THE ONION

1 egg
1 cup milk
1 cup all-purpose flour
1 ½ teaspoons salt
1 ½ teaspoons cayenne pepper
½ teaspoon ground black pepper
1 teaspoon paprika

¼ teaspoon dried oregano
⅛ teaspoon dried thyme
⅛ teaspoon cumin
1 jumbo sweet yellow or white
    onion (¾ pound or more)
vegetable oil for frying

1. Prepare the dipping sauce by combining all of the ingredients in a small bowl. Keep the sauce covered in your refrigerator until needed.
2. Beat the egg and combine it with the milk in a medium bowl big enough to hold the onion.
3. In a separate bowl, combine the flour, salt, peppers, paprika, oregano, thyme, and cumin.
4. Now it's time to slice the onion—this is the trickiest step. First slice ¾ inch to 1 inch off the top and bottom of the onion. Remove the papery skin. Use a thin knife to cut a 1-inch diameter core out of the middle of the onion. Now use a very sharp, large knife to slice the onion several times down the center to create the "petals" of the completed onion. First slice through the center of the onion to about three-fourths of the way down. Turn the onion 90° and slice it again in an "x" across the first slice. Keep slicing the sections in half, very carefully, until you've cut the onion 16 times. Do not cut

down to the bottom. The last 8 slices are a little hairy, just use a steady hand and don't worry if your onion doesn't look like a perfect flower. It'll still taste good.

5. Spread the "petals" of the onion apart. The onion sections tend to stick together, so you'll want to separate them to make coating easier. To help separate the "petals," plunge the onion into boiling water for 1 minute, and then into cold water.

6. Dip the onion in the milk mixture, and then coat it liberally with the dry ingredients. Again separate the "petals" and sprinkle the dry coating between them. Once you're sure the onion is well-coated, dip it back into the wet mixture and into the dry coating again. This double dipping makes sure you have a well-coated onion because some of the coating tends to wash off when you fry. Let the onion rest in the refrigerator for at least 15 minutes while you get the oil ready.

7. Heat oil in a deep fryer or deep pot to 350°F. Make sure you use enough oil to completely cover the onion when it fries.

8. Fry the onion right side up in the oil for 10 minutes or until it turns brown.

9. When the onion has browned, remove it from the oil and let it drain on a rack or paper towels.

10. Open the onion wider from the center so that you can put a small dish of the dipping sauce in the center. You may also use plain ketchup.

- SERVES 2 TO 4 AS AN APPETIZER OR SNACK.

• • • •

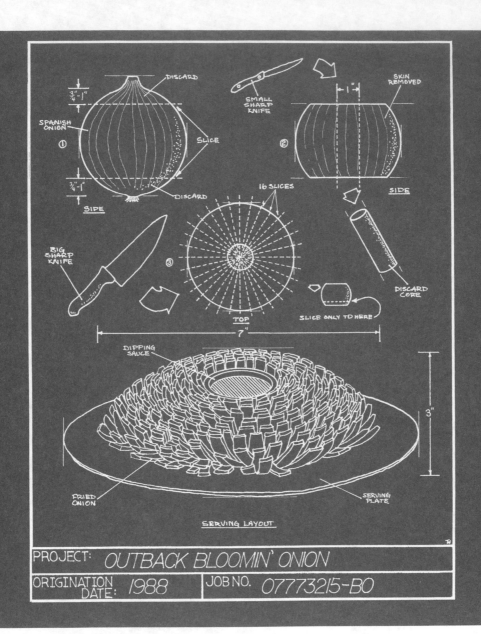

DISCARD

SMALL SHARP KNIFE

SPANISH ONION

① $\frac{3}{4}"-1"$

SLICE

$\frac{3}{4}"-1"$

DISCARD

SIDE

② SKIN REMOVED

1"

SIDE

16 SLICES

BIG SHARP KNIFE

③

TOP

7"

SLICE ONLY TO HERE

DISCARD CORE

DIPPING SAUCE

3"

FRIED ONION

SERVING PLATE

SERVING LAYOUT

PROJECT:	*OUTBACK BLOOMIN' ONION*	
ORIGINATION DATE: *1988*	JOB NO. *07773215-BO*	

OUTBACK STEAKHOUSE
GOLD COAST
COCONUT SHRIMP

☆   ✌   💣   ✏   ☯   ✂   ☞

Menu Description: "Six colossal shrimp dipped in beer batter, rolled in coconut, deep-fried to a golden brown and served with marmalade sauce."

The three founders of Outback Steakhouse are an experienced lot of restaurateurs. Tim Gannon, Chris Sullivan, and Bob Basham had each worked for the Steak & Ale chain of restaurants at one time or another, as well as other large casual dining chains. When the three got together and decided they wanted to open a few restaurants in the Tampa, Florida, area, they had modest ambitions.

Basham told *Food & Beverage* magazine, "We figured if we divided up the profits with what we thought we could make out of five or six restaurants, we could have a very nice lifestyle and play a lot of golf." The first six restaurants opened within 13 months. Eight years later the chain had grown to over 300 restaurants, and the three men now have a very, very nice lifestyle indeed.

Coconut Shrimp is a sweet and crispy fried appetizer not found on most other menus, especially with the delicious marmalade sauce. Outback servers claim it's a top seller.

At the restaurant chain, you get six of these shrimp to serve two as an appetizer, but since we're taking the time to make the batter and use all of that oil, I thought I'd up the yield to a dozen shrimp to serve four as an appetizer. If you don't want to make that many, you can use the same recipe with fewer shrimp and save the leftover batter to make more later or just toss it out.

1 cup flat beer	1/2 teaspoon salt
1 cup self-rising flour	12 jumbo shrimp
2 cups sweetened coconut flakes	vegetable oil for frying
(1 7-ounce package)	paprika
2 tablespoons sugar	

MARMALADE SAUCE (FOR DIPPING)

1/2 cup orange marmalade	dash salt
2 teaspoons stone-ground	
mustard (with whole-grain	
mustard seed)	
1 teaspoon prepared horseradish	

1. For the batter, use an electric mixer to combine the beer, flour, 1/2 cup coconut flakes, sugar, and salt in a medium-size bowl. Mix well, then cover and refrigerate at least 1 hour.
2. Prepare your marmalade sauce by combining all four ingredients in a small bowl. Cover and refrigerate this for at least 1 hour as well.
3. Prepare the shrimp by deveining and peeling off the shell back to the tail. Leave the last segment of the shell plus the tailfins as a handle.
4. When the batter is ready, preheat oil in a deep pot or deep fryer to about 350°F. Use enough oil to completely cover the shrimp. Pour the remainder of the coconut into a shallow bowl.
5. Be sure the shrimp are dry before battering. Sprinkle each shrimp lightly with paprika before the next step.
6. Dip one shrimp at a time into the batter, coating generously. Drop the battered shrimp into the coconut and roll it around so that it is well coated.
7. Fry four shrimp at a time for 2 to 3 minutes or until the shrimp become golden brown. You may have to flip the shrimp over halfway through cooking time. Drain on paper

towels briefly before serving with marmalade sauce on the side.

- SERVES 1 AS AN APPETIZER.

• • • •

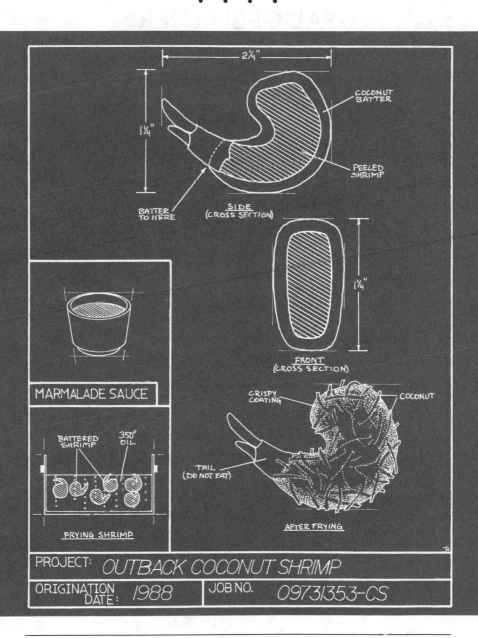

COCONUT BATTER

PEELED SHRIMP

2¼"

1¼"

BATTER TO HERE

SIDE
(CROSS SECTION)

1¼"

FRONT
(CROSS SECTION)

MARMALADE SAUCE

BATTERED SHRIMP

350° OIL

FRYING SHRIMP

CRISPY COATING

COCONUT

TAIL
(DO NOT EAT)

AFTER FRYING

PROJECT: OUTBACK COCONUT SHRIMP

ORIGINATION DATE: 1988

JOB NO. 0973I353-CS

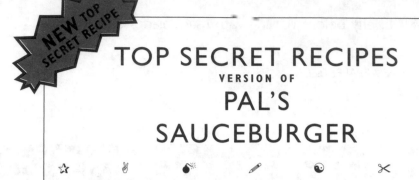

TOP SECRET RECIPES
VERSION OF
PAL'S
SAUCEBURGER

Here's a simple, great-tasting burger from a small, yet beloved, Tennessee-based hamburger chain famous for its quirky buildings and simple, tasty food. Established in 1956 by Pal Barger, this 17-unit fast-service chain has been making a name for itself by recently winning the Malcolm Baldrige National Quality Award and performing admirably in markets among huge chains such as McDonald's, Burger King, and Wendy's. The signature sandwich from this little drive-thru comes slathered with a simple sauce—a combination of ketchup, mustard, and relish—that makes quick production of scores of these tasty sandwiches a breeze when the line of cars grows long, as it often does.

⅛ pound ground beef
1 small hamburger bun
salt

2 tablespoons ketchup
1 teaspoon sweet pickle relish
½ teaspoon yellow mustard

1. Pat out the ground beef until about the same diameter as the bun. If you like, you can freeze this patty ahead of time to help keep the burger from falling apart when you cook it.
2. Brown or toast the faces of the top and bottom buns. You can do this in a frying pan over medium heat or by toasting them in the oven (or toaster oven).

3. As the buns are browning, grill the hamburger patty, in a hot frying pan over medium heat. Salt the meat generously.
4. Combine the ketchup, relish, and mustard in a small bowl.
5. When the meat is cooked to your liking, place it on the face of the bottom bun.
6. Slather the sauce on the face of the top bun and place it onto the meat.

• MAKES 1 BURGER.

TIDBITS

To multiply this recipe, use this handy multiplier for the sauce:

Sauce for 2 burgers:	¼ cup ketchup	2 teaspoons relish	1 teaspoon mustard
Sauce for 4 burgers:	½ cup ketchup	4 teaspoons relish	2 teaspoons mustard
Sauce for 6 burgers:	¾ cup ketchup	2 tablespoons relish	1 tablespoon mustard

• • • •

PIZZA HUT ORIGINAL STUFFED CRUST PIZZA

☆　　✌　　💣　　✏　　◉　　✂　　☞

Menu Description: "This unique thinner crust has a ring of cheese baked into the edge so you get cheese in the very last bite of every slice."

Brothers Dan and Frank Carney have dear old Mom to thank for helping them to become founders of the world's largest pizza chain. It was in 1958 that a family friend approached the two brothers with the idea of opening a pizza parlor, and it was the brothers' mother who lent them the $600 it took to purchase some second-hand equipment and to rent a small building. There, in the Carneys' hometown of Wichita, Kansas, the first Pizza Hut opened its doors. By 1966, there were 145 Pizza Hut restaurants doing a booming business around the country with the help of the promotional musical jingle "Putt-Putt to Pizza Hut." Today the chain is made up of more than 10,000 restaurants, delivery–carry out units, and kiosks in all 50 states and 82 foreign countries.

Introduced in 1995, the Stuffed Crust Pizza, which includes sticks of mozzarella string cheese loaded into the crust before cooking, increased business at Pizza Hut by 37 percent. Because the outer crust is filled with cheese, the chain designed a special dough formula that does not rise as high as the original. It's best to prepare your Top Secret Recipe version of this delicious crust a day before you plan to cook the pizza so that the dough can rest while the gluten in the flour forms a texture just like the original.

CRUST

¾ cup warm water (105° to
    115°F)
1 tablespoon sugar
1¼ teaspoons yeast

2¼ cups bread flour
1½ teaspoons salt
1½ tablespoons olive oil

SAUCE

1 15-ounce can tomato sauce
¼ cup water
1 teaspoon sugar
¼ teaspoon dried oregano
¼ teaspoon dried basil leaves
¼ teaspoon dried thyme

¼ teaspoon garlic powder
¼ teaspoon salt
⅛ teaspoon ground black pepper
1 bay leaf
dash onion powder
½ teaspoon lemon juice

8 1-ounce mozzarella string
    cheese sticks

1½ cups shredded mozzarella

TOPPINGS (YOUR CHOICE OF . . .)

pepperoni slices, chopped onions, sliced mushrooms, sliced black olives,
    sliced jalapeños (nacho slices), sliced green peppers, pineapple
    chunks, Italian sausage, sliced tomatoes, sliced ham, anchovies

1. First prepare the dough for the crust. I suggest you prepare the crust one day prior to baking the pizza. To get the best dough you need to allow it to rise in your refrigerator overnight. This procedure will produce a great commercial-style crust.

    Combine the warm water, sugar, and yeast in a small bowl or measuring cup and stir until the yeast and sugar have dissolved. Let the mixture sit for about 5 minutes. Foam should begin building up on the surface. If it doesn't, either the water was too hot or the yeast was dead. Throw it out and start again.

2. In a large bowl, sift together the flour and salt. Make a depression in the center of the flour and pour in the yeast mixture. Add the oil.

3. Use a fork to stir the liquid in the center of the flour. Slowly draw in more flour, a little bit at a time, until you have to use your hands to completely combine all of the ingredients into a ball.

4. Dust a clean, flat surface with flour, and with the heel of your hands, knead the dough on this surface until it seems to have a smooth, consistent texture. This should take around 10 minutes. Rub a light coating of oil on the dough, then put it into a tightly covered container and in a warm place to rise for 2 hours or until it has doubled in size. When it has doubled in size, punch the dough down, put it back into the covered container and into the refrigerator overnight. If you don't have time for that, you can use the crust at this point. But without the long rest it just won't have the same texture as the original.

5. You can prepare the pizza sauce ahead of time as well, storing it in the refrigerator until you are ready to make the pizza. Simply combine the tomato sauce, water, and sugar with the spices and lemon juice in a small saucepan over medium heat. Heat the sauce until it starts to bubble, then turn the heat down and simmer, covered, for 30 to 60 minutes until it reaches the thickness you like. When the sauce has cooled, store it in the refrigerator in a tightly sealed container.

6. About an hour or so before you are ready to make your pizza, take the dough out of the refrigerator so that it will warm up to room temperature.

    Preheat the oven to 475°F.

    Roll the dough out on a floured surface until it is 18 inches across. Put the dough on a pizza pan that has either been greased or has a sprinkling of cornmeal on it. This will prevent your pizza from sticking. Score the pizza dough several times with a fork so that it doesn't bubble up when baked.

7. Place a ring of the string cheese sticks, end to end, around the edge of the dough, an inch in from the edge.

8. Use water on your fingertips or on a brush to moisten the outer edge of the dough, all of the way around so that it will stick when folded over. Fold the dough up and over the

cheese and press it down onto itself, sealing it tightly. Form a nice, round crust as you seal the cheese inside. Lightly brush the top of the folded dough with olive oil all of the way around the edge.

9. Now spread about a cup of the pizza sauce on the crust (you will likely have enough sauce left over for another pie later). As you spread the sauce onto the crust, be sure to spread sauce all of the way to the folded edge, enough to hide that seam you made when folding the crust over the cheese.

10. Spread the toppings other than pepperoni, sausage, ham, and olives on the pizza sauce. Sprinkle the shredded mozzarella onto the sauce and any olives or meat toppings you wish on top of the cheese.

11. Bake the pizza for 12 to 16 minutes or until the crust begins to turn dark brown and the cheese develops dark spots.

12. Slice the pizza 4 times through the center, making 8 slices.

• SERVES 3 TO 4.

• • • •

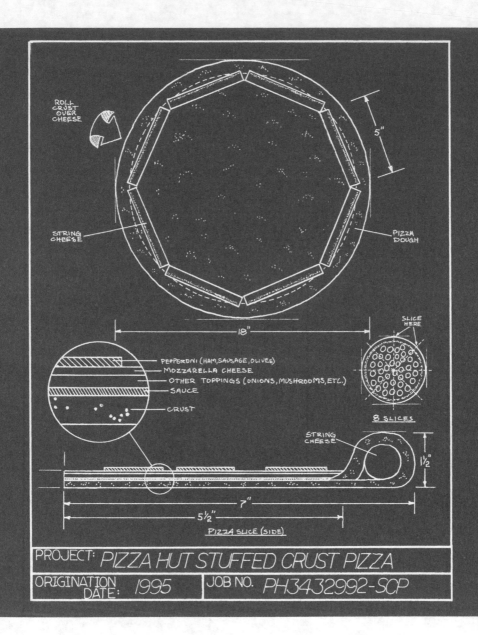

ROLL CRUST OVER CHEESE

5"

STRING CHEESE

PIZZA DOUGH

18"

PEPPERONI (HAM, SAUSAGE, OLIVES)
MOZZARELLA CHEESE
OTHER TOPPINGS (ONIONS, MUSHROOMS, ETC.)
SAUCE
CRUST

SLICE HERE

8 SLICES

STRING CHEESE

1½"

7"

5½"

PIZZA SLICE (SIDE)

PROJECT: PIZZA HUT STUFFED CRUST PIZZA

ORIGINATION DATE: 1995

JOB NO. PH3432992-SCP

314

RUBY TUESDAY
SONORA CHICKEN PASTA

☆　　✌　　💣　　✏　　☯　　✂　　☞

Menu Description: "Penne pasta tossed in a spicy Southwestern cheese sauce, topped with grilled chicken, spicy black beans, scallions and more."

If you like pasta, black beans, and chicken, you'll love having it all swimming together in this spicy cheese sauce. The chicken is prepared over an open grill, then sliced before laying it over a bed of pasta and cheese sauce. The black beans and peppers give this dish a decidedly Southwestern flair.

1 pound Velveeta cheese spread
    (or one 16-ounce jar Cheez
    Whiz)
1/2 cup heavy cream
2 tablespoons minced red chili
    pepper
4 tablespoons green chili pepper
    (1/2 pepper), minced
4 tablespoons minced onion
1 clove garlic, minced
2 teaspoons olive oil
2 tablespoons water
1/2 teaspoon salt
2 teaspoons sugar

1/2 tablespoon vinegar
1/4 teaspoon cumin
1 15-ounce can black beans
dash paprika
4 boneless, skinless chicken breast
    halves
vegetable oil
dash dried thyme
dash dried summer savory
1 16-ounce box penne pasta
1 tablespoon butter
2 Roma (plum) tomatoes,
    chopped
2 to 4 green onions, chopped

1. Prepare the barbecue or preheat your stovetop grill.
2. Combine the cheese spread with the cream in a small saucepan over medium/low heat. Stir the cheese often until it melts and becomes smooth.
3. Sauté the red chili pepper and 2 tablespoons green chili pepper, 2 tablespoons onion, and ½ clove garlic in the olive oil for a couple minutes then add the water to the pan so that the peppers do not scorch. Simmer another 2 minutes or until the water has cooked off.
4. When the cheese is smooth, add the sautéed vegetables, ¼ teaspoon salt, sugar, vinegar, and cumin. Leave on low heat, stirring occasionally, until the other ingredients are ready.
5. Pour the entire can of beans with the liquid into a small saucepan over medium heat. Add the remaining green chili pepper, onions, garlic, a pinch of salt, and a dash of paprika. Bring the beans to a boil, stirring often, then reduce the heat to low and simmer until everything else is ready. By this time the beans will have thickened and the onions will have become transparent.
6. Rub the chicken breasts lightly with oil, then season with salt, thyme, and savory.
7. Cook the breasts on a hot grill for 5 minutes per side or until done. When they have cooked thoroughly, remove them from the grill and use a sharp knife to slice each breast into ½ -inch slices, so that they are easier to eat. Retain the shape of the chicken breast by keeping the slices in order with one hand as you slice.
8. As the chicken cooks, prepare the pasta in a large pot filled with 3 to 4 quarts of boiling water. Cook the pasta for 12 to 14 minutes or until tender. Drain the pasta in a colander, and toss with the butter.
9. When everything is ready, spoon one-fourth of the pasta onto each plate.
10. Pour about ⅓ cup of cheese sauce over the pasta.
11. Carefully add a sliced breast of chicken, being sure to maintain its shape as you lay the slices on the bed of pasta.

12. Spread ⅓ cup of the black beans over the chicken.
13. Sprinkle ¼ cup of chopped tomatoes on the beans.
14. Sprinkle about 1 tablespoon of green onions on the tomatoes and serve immediately. Salt to taste.

• SERVES 4 AS AN ENTREE.

TIDBITS

You can make a lighter version of this meal by using the lower fat version of the Cheez Whiz or Velveeta cheese spreads.

•　•　•　•

RUBY TUESDAY
STRAWBERRY TALLCAKE
FOR TWO

Menu Description: "Three layers of light and airy sponge cake and strawberry mousse, drenched in strawberry sauce, topped with vanilla ice cream, fresh strawberries and whipped cream."

The Strawberry Tallcake is a signature, trademarked item for Ruby Tuesday. It's pretty big, so plan on sharing it. This copycat recipe requires that you bake the sponge cake in a large, shallow pan—I use a cookie sheet that has turned-up edges to hold in the batter. And you might find the strawberry mousse that is used to frost the cake makes a great, simple-to-make dessert on its own.

STRAWBERRY MOUSSE AND SAUCE

1 10-ounce package frozen
   strawberries in syrup
1¾ cups water

1 3-ounce package strawberry
   Jell-O
1 cup heavy cream

SPONGE CAKE

5 eggs, separated
1½ cups sugar
½ cup cold water
2 teaspoons vanilla

1½ cups all-purpose flour
½ teaspoon baking powder
½ teaspoon salt
½ teaspoon cream of tartar

12 to 18 scoops vanilla ice cream
   (½ gallon)

½ pint fresh strawberries, sliced
1 can whipped cream

1. Defrost the frozen strawberries and pour the entire package, including the syrup, into a blender or food processor and purée for 10 to 15 seconds until smooth.
2. Combine the strawberry purée with 1½ cups of the water in a small saucepan over medium heat.
3. When the strawberry mixture comes to a boil, add the entire package of Jell-O, stir to dissolve, and remove the pan from the heat to cool.
4. When the strawberry mixture has cooled to room temperature, divide it in half into two medium bowls.
5. Beat the whipping cream until it is thick and forms peaks. Fold the cream into one of the bowls of the strawberry mixture until well combined. This is your strawberry mousse. Cover and chill.
6. To the other bowl, add the remaining ¼ cup of water. This is the strawberry syrup. Cover and chill this mixture as well.
7. Preheat the oven to 350°F.
8. Beat the egg yolks until they turn creamy and a much lighter shade of yellow.
9. Add the sugar and blend it well into the yolks.
10. Add the water and vanilla and combine well with the yolk mixture.
11. Sift together the flour, baking powder, and salt, and add it to the yolk mixture. Mix well until the batter is smooth.
12. In a separate bowl, beat the egg whites until smooth, then add the cream of tartar. Continue beating until the whites are stiff and form peaks.
13. Fold the egg whites into the batter and mix slowly just until well combined.
14. Pour the batter into an ungreased 17 x 11-inch cookie sheet (with turned-up edges all the way around) and bake for 25 to 30 minutes or until the top of the sponge cake is a light brown color.
15. When the cake has cooled and the mousse has firmed up, you are ready to assemble the cake. First divide the cake into three even sections by cutting down the width of the cake twice with a sharp knife. Be sure the cake has come loose

from the pan. You may need to use a spatula to unstick the cake sections.

16. Divide the mousse in half and spread each half onto two sections of the cake. Carefully place the layers on top of each other so that the mousse has been sandwiched in the middle between the three layers. This cake can be stored in the refrigerator for several days until you need it.

17. When you are ready to assemble the dessert, slice the cake into 6 even sections. Put a slice into a medium-sized bowl (or a large goblet if you have one), then arrange 2 to 3 scoops of vanilla ice cream around the cake. Pour a sixth (just over $\frac{1}{4}$ cup) of the strawberry sauce over the top of the cake and ice cream, sprinkle some sliced strawberries on top, then cover the thing with whipped cream. Repeat with the remaining servings.

• MAKES SIX 2-PERSON SERVINGS.

•   •   •   •

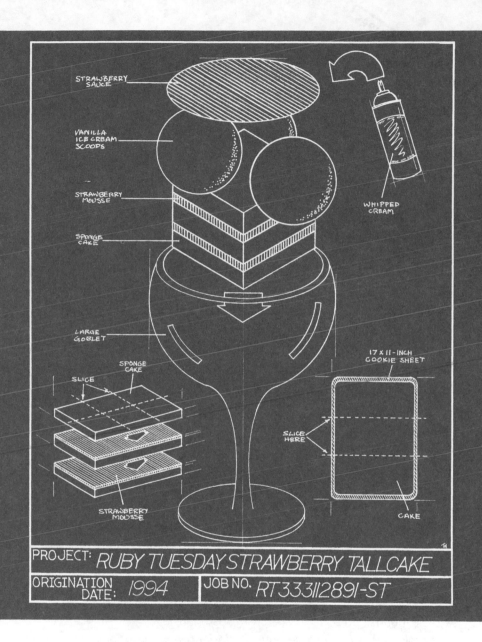

STRAWBERRY SAUCE

VANILLA ICE CREAM SCOOPS

STRAWBERRY MOUSSE

SPONGE CAKE

WHIPPED CREAM

LARGE GOBLET

SPONGE CAKE

SLICE

STRAWBERRY MOUSSE

17 x 11 - INCH COOKIE SHEET

SLICE HERE

CAKE

PROJECT: RUBY TUESDAY STRAWBERRY TALLCAKE

ORIGINATION DATE: 1994

JOB NO. RT33112891-ST

RUTH'S CHRIS
STEAK HOUSE
CREAMED SPINACH

☆　✌　💣　✏　☯　✂　☞

"Ruth's Chris Steak House" is such a difficult name to spit out that a restaurant critic suggested it be used as a sobriety test. Surely anyone who could say the name three times fast couldn't possibly be intoxicated. But the hard-to-say name has probably worked well for the steakhouse chain; it is surely a memorable one. The name came from the first restaurant that Ruth purchased in 1965 called Chris Steak House. When she opened a second restaurant with that same name, the previous owner, Chris Matulich, tried to sue her. She won the case, but to avoid future lawsuits she put her name in front of the original and it became the tongue twister we know today.

The delicious creamed spinach served at Ruth's Chris inspired this recipe that has just a hint of cayenne pepper in it for that Louisiana zing. The recipe requires a package of frozen spinach to make it convenient, but you can use the same amount of fresh spinach if you prefer.

1 10-ounce package frozen
　　chopped spinach
2 tablespoons butter
1½ tablespoons all-purpose flour
½ cup heavy cream

¼ teaspoon salt
dash pepper
dash nutmeg
dash cayenne pepper

1. Cook the spinach following the directions on the package. Drain and squeeze all the liquid from the spinach when it's done.
2. Melt the butter in a saucepan over medium heat. Be careful not to burn it.
3. Add the flour to the melted butter and stir until smooth.
4. Add the cream and heat for 2 to 3 minutes or until the sauce thickens. Stir constantly so that sauce does not burn.
5. Add the spinach, salt, pepper, nutmeg, and cayenne. Cook for 2 to 4 minutes, stirring often. Serve hot.

- SERVES 4 AS A SIDE DISH.

• • • •

SHONEY'S
HOT FUDGE CAKE

Menu Description: "Vanilla ice cream between two pieces of devil's food cake. Served with hot fudge, creamy topping and a cherry."

One of Shoney's signature dessert items is this Hot Fudge Cake, a dessert worshipped by all who taste it. It's such a simple recipe for something that tastes so good. To make construction of this treat simpler for you, the recipe calls for a prepackaged devil's food cake mix like that which you can find in just about any supermarket baking aisle. Bear in mind when you shop for ingredients for this recipe that the vanilla ice cream must come in a box, so that the ice cream slices can be arranged properly between the cake layers. Leftovers can be frozen and served up to several weeks later.

1 18.25-ounce box devil's food
    cake mix
3 eggs
1 1/3 cups water
1/3 cup vegetable oil
1 half-gallon box vanilla ice cream
    (must be in a box)

1 16-ounce jar chocolate fudge
    topping
1 can whipped cream
12 maraschino cherries

1. Mix the batter for the cake as instructed on the box of the cake mix by combining cake mix, eggs, water, and vegetable oil in a large mixing bowl.

2. Measure only 4 cups of the batter into a well-greased 13 x 9-inch baking pan. This will leave about 1 cup of batter in the bowl, which you can discard or use for another recipe, such as cupcakes.
3. Bake the cake according to the box instructions. Allow the cake to cool completely.
4. When the cake has cooled, carefully remove it from the pan, and place it right side up onto a sheet of waxed paper. With a long knife (a bread knife works great) slice horizontally through the middle of the cake, and carefully remove the top.
5. Pick up the waxed paper with the bottom of the cake still on it, and place it back into the baking pan.
6. Take the ice cream from the freezer and, working quickly, tear the box open so that you can slice it like bread.
7. Make six ¾-inch-thick slices and arrange them on the cake bottom in the pan. Cover the entire surface of the cake with ice cream. You will most likely have to cut 2 of the ice cream slices in half to make it all fit. Hey, it's a puzzle . . . that melts!
8. When you have covered the entire bottom cake half with ice cream slices, carefully place the top half of the cake onto the ice cream layer. You now have ice cream sandwiched between the two halves of your cake. Cover the whole pan with plastic wrap or foil and pop it into your freezer for a couple hours (it will keep well in here for weeks as long as you keep it covered).
9. When you are ready to serve the dessert, slice the cake so that it will make 12 even slices—slice lengthwise twice and crosswise three times. You may not want to slice what you won't be serving at the time so that the remainder will stay fresh. Leave the cake you are using out for 5 minutes to defrost a bit.
10. Heat up the fudge either in a microwave or in a jar immersed in a saucepan of water over medium/low heat.
11. Pour the fudge over the cake slices and to each add a small mountain of whipped cream.

12. Top off each cake with a cherry stuck into the center of the whipped cream.

- SERVES 12.

• • • •

MARASCHINO CHERRY

WHIPPED CREAM

¾"

HOT FUDGE

¾"

1"

¾"

2½"

3"

VANILLA ICE CREAM

DEVIL'S FOOD CAKE

ASSEMBLED

PROJECT: *SHONEY'S HOT FUDGE CAKE*

ORIGINATION DATE: 19

JOB NO. *S46312672-HFC*

T.G.I. FRIDAY'S JACK DANIEL'S GRILL SALMON

☆   ✌   💣   ✏   ☯   ✂   ☞

The glaze that is brushed over this salmon is one of the most scrumptious sauces you will ever taste on fish, or just about any other meat. T.G.I. Friday's introduced the glaze in 1997 and it became the company's most successful new product launch. I was encouraged to figure out how to clone the stuff when the *Oprah Winfrey Show* requested a re-creation of the glaze for an appearance. This recipe is the result of hard work, and darn accurate at that. Plus, when the glaze is brushed over salmon, it makes for a very healthy meal.

While the fat count here may seem high compared to other recipes in the book, don't be too concerned. That fat, which comes from the salmon, is called Omega-3 fatty acids, and it is a beneficial type of fat found in fish and nuts. Research has shown that Omega-3 fatty acids can actually prevent heart disease and lower cholesterol.

As for the sauce, you will find it is very versatile. You can brush it on almost any type of fish, as well as ribs, chicken, and beef. It also keeps very well for long periods of time if stored in the refrigerator in a sealed container.

GLAZE

1 head of garlic	3 tablespoons lemon juice
1 tablespoon olive oil	3 tablespoons minced white
⅔ cup water	onion
1 cup pineapple juice	1 tablespoon Jack Daniel's
¼ cup teriyaki sauce	whiskey
1 tablespoon soy sauce	1 tablespoon crushed pineapple
1⅓ cups dark brown sugar	¼ teaspoon cayenne pepper

4 ½-pound fresh Atlantic salmon fillets	salt
fat-free butter-flavored spray or spread	pepper

1. Preheat the oven to 325°F.
2. To roast the garlic for the glaze, cut about ½-inch off the top of the garlic head. Cut the roots so that the garlic will sit flat. Remove most of the papery skin from the garlic, but leave enough so that the cloves stay together. Place the head of garlic in a small casserole dish or baking pan, drizzle the olive oil over it, and cover it with a lid or foil. Bake for 1 hour. Remove the garlic and let it cool until you can handle it.
3. Combine the water, pineapple juice, teriyaki sauce, soy sauce, and brown sugar in a medium saucepan over medium/high heat. Stir occasionally until the mixture boils, then reduce the heat until the mixture is just simmering.
4. Squeeze the sides of the head of garlic until the pasty roasted garlic is squeezed out. Measure 2 teaspoons into the saucepan and whisk to combine. Add the remaining glaze ingredients to the pan and stir.
5. Let the mixture simmer for 40 to 50 minutes or until the glaze has reduced by about one-third and is thick and syrupy. Make sure it doesn't boil over. When the glaze is done, cover the saucepan and set it aside until the fish is ready.
6. To cook the fish, preheat your barbecue or kitchen grill to

medium/high heat. Remove any skin or bones from the fillets. Brush the entire surface of each fillet with a light coating of the fat-free butter-flavored spread or spray. Lightly salt and pepper both sides of the fillets and place them on the hot grill at a slight angle, so that grill marks will be made at an angle on the fish. Cook each fillet for 2 to 4 minutes, then turn them over, placing them back on the grill at an angle once again. After 2 to 4 minutes, turn the fish over at a different angle so that the grill marks will criss-cross. Cook 2 to 4 minutes more, flip again, and cook until done. The entire cooking time should be somewhere between 8 to 15 minutes depending on the thickness of your fillets and the heat of the grill. Be careful not to burn the fish, and quickly move the fish away from any flare-ups.

7. When the fillets are done, remove them from the grill and spoon a generous portion of glaze over each one. Serve hot with a baked potato and vegetables, if desired.

- SERVES 4 AS AN ENTRÉE.

Nutrition Facts

SERVING SIZE—1 FILLET   FAT (PER SERVING)—16.5G
TOTAL SERVINGS—4   CALORIES (PER SERVING)—525

• • • •

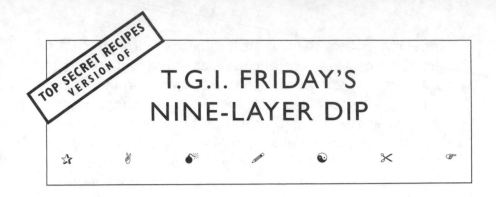

T.G.I. FRIDAY'S NINE-LAYER DIP

☆　　✌　　💣　　✏　　☯　　✂　　☞

Menu Description: "Refried Beans, cheddar cheese, guacamole, black olives, seasoned sour cream, green onions, tomatoes and cilantro. Served with tortilla chips and fresh salsa."

When the first T.G.I. Friday's opened in New York City in 1965 as a meeting place for single adults, *Newsweek* and *The Saturday Evening Post* reported that it was the beginning of the "singles age." Today the restaurant's customers have matured, many are married, and they bring their children with them to the more than 300 Friday's across the country and around the world.

The Nine-Layer Dip is one of the often requested appetizers on the T.G.I. Friday's menu. This dish will serve half a dozen people easily, so it's perfect for a small gathering, or as a snack. Don't worry if there's only a couple of you—leftovers can be refrigerated for a day or two. Cilantro, also called fresh coriander or Chinese parsley, can be found in the produce section of most supermarkets near the parsley.

⅔ cups sour cream
⅛ teaspoon cumin
⅛ teaspoon cayenne pepper
⅛ teaspoon paprika
dash salt
1 16-ounce can refried beans
1 cup shredded Cheddar cheese

½ cup guacamole (made fresh or frozen, thawed)
¼ cup sliced black olives
2 green onions, chopped (¼ cup)
1 medium tomato, chopped
1 teaspoon chopped fresh cilantro

1. Combine the sour cream, cumin, cayenne pepper, paprika, and salt in a small bowl and mix well. Set aside.
2. Heat the refried beans until hot, using a microwave or in a saucepan over medium heat.
3. When the beans are hot, spread them over the center of a serving platter or in a shallow dish.
4. Sprinkle ½ of the cheese evenly over the beans.
5. Spread the guacamole over the cheese.
6. Sprinkle the sliced olives over the guacamole.
7. Spread the seasoned sour cream over the olives.
8. Sprinkle the green onions, then the tomatoes evenly over the sour cream layer.
9. Finish up by sprinkling the remainder of the cheese over the tomatoes, and topping the dip off with the cilantro. Serve the dip with tortilla chips and a side of your favorite salsa.

- SERVES 4 TO 8 AS AN APPETIZER OR SNACK.

• • • •

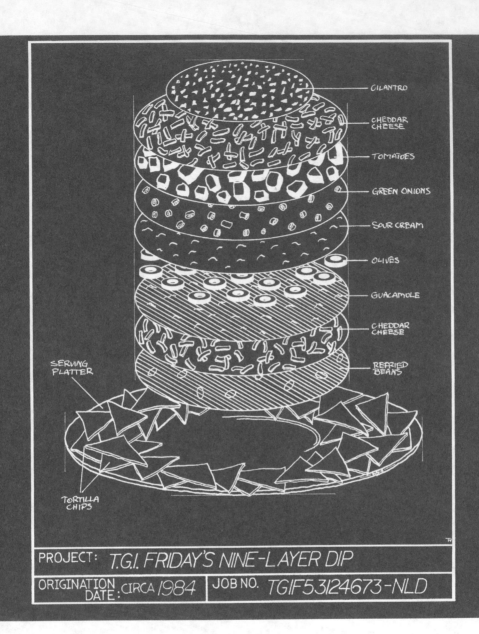

CILANTRO

CHEDDAR CHEESE

TOMATOES

GREEN ONIONS

SOUR CREAM

OLIVES

GUACAMOLE

CHEDDAR CHEESE

REFRIED BEANS

SERVING PLATTER

TORTILLA CHIPS

PROJECT: *T.G.I. FRIDAY'S NINE-LAYER DIP*

ORIGINATION DATE: CIRCA *1984*

JOB NO. *TGIF53124673-NLD*

T.G.I. FRIDAY'S
POTATO SKINS

Menu Description: "Loaded with cheddar cheese and bacon. Served with sour cream and chives."

Perfume salesman Alan Stillman was a single guy in New York City in 1965, looking for a way to meet women who lived in his neighborhood. He figured a hip way to get their attention: buy a broken-down beer joint in the area, jazz it up, and call it "The T.G.I.F." to attract the career crowd. Within a week, police had to barricade the area to control the crowds flocking to Alan's new restaurant. The restaurant made $1 million in its first year—a lot of dough back then. Soon restaurants were imitating the concept across the country.

In 1974 T.G.I. Friday's invented an appetizer that would also be imitated by many others in the following years. Today Potato Skins are still the most popular item on the T.G.I. Friday's menu, with nearly 4 million orders served every year. The recipe has the added benefit of providing you with leftover baked potato ready for mashing or to use in another dish.

4 medium russet potatoes
⅓ cup sour cream
1 tablespoon snipped fresh chives
¼ cup (½ stick) butter, melted

1 ½ cups shredded Cheddar cheese
5 slices bacon, cooked

1. Preheat the oven to 400°F. Bake the potatoes for 1 hour. Let the potatoes cool down enough so that you can touch them.
2. As the potatoes are baking, make the sour cream dip by mixing the sour cream with the chives. Place the mixture in a covered container in your refrigerator.
3. When the potatoes are cool enough to handle, make 2 lengthwise cuts through each potato, resulting in three ½- to ¾-inch slices. Discard the middle slices or save them for a separate dish of mashed potatoes. This will leave you with two potato skins per potato.
4. With a spoon, scoop some of the potato out of each skin, being sure to leave about ¼ inch of potato inside of the skin.
5. Brush the entire surface of each potato skin, inside and outside, with the melted butter.
6. Place the skins on a cookie sheet, cut side up, and broil them for 6 to 8 minutes or until the edges begin to turn dark brown.
7. Sprinkle 2 to 3 tablespoons of Cheddar cheese into each skin.
8. Crumble the cooked bacon and sprinkle 1 to 2 teaspoons of the bacon pieces onto the cheese.
9. Broil the skins for 2 more minutes or until the cheese is thoroughly melted. Serve hot, arranged on a plate surrounding a small bowl of the sour cream dip.

- SERVES 2 TO 4 AS AN APPETIZER OR SNACK.

•　•　•　•

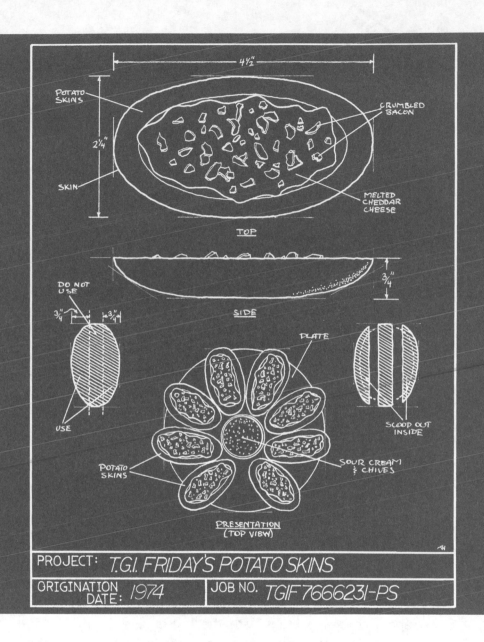

4½"

POTATO
SKINS

CRUMBLED
BACON

2¼"

SKIN

MELTED
CHEDDAR
CHEESE

TOP

SIDE

¾"

DO NOT
USE

¾" ¾"

PLATE

SCOOP OUT
INSIDE

USE

POTATO
SKINS

SOUR CREAM
& CHIVES

PRESENTATION
(TOP VIEW)

PROJECT: T.G.I. FRIDAY'S POTATO SKINS

ORIGINATION
DATE: 1974

JOB NO. TGIF 7666231-PS

335

THE CHEESECAKE FACTORY KEY LIME CHEESECAKE

Just 15 minutes after the very first Cheesecake Factory opened in Beverly Hills back in 1978, the lines began forming. Here's their cheesecake twist on the delicious Key lime pie. Since Key limes and Key lime juice can be hard to find, this recipe uses standard lime juice, which can be purchased bottled or squeezed fresh. If you can find Key lime juice, bear in mind that Key limes are more tart, and use only half as much juice. This recipe also requires a springform pan. If you don't have one, you can use two 9-inch pie pans and make two smaller cheesecakes.

1¾ cups graham cracker crumbs
5 tablespoons butter, melted
1 cup plus 1 tablespoon sugar
3 8-ounce packages cream
    cheese, softened

1 teaspoon vanilla
½ cup fresh lime juice (about 5
    limes)
3 eggs
whipped cream

1. Preheat the oven to 350°F. Make the crust by combining the graham cracker crumbs with the butter and 1 tablespoon sugar in a medium bowl. Stir well enough to coat all of the crumbs with the butter. Keep it crumbly.
2. Press the crumbs onto the bottom and about one half of the way up the sides of an 8-inch springform pan. You don't want the crust to form all the way up the back of each slice of

cheesecake. Bake the crust for 5 minutes, then set it aside until you are ready to fill it.

3. In a large mixing bowl combine the cream cheese, I cup sugar, and vanilla. Mix with an electric mixer until smooth.

4. Add the lime juice and eggs and continue to beat until smooth and creamy.

5. Pour the filling into the pan. Bake for 60 to 70 minutes. If the top of the cheesecake is turning light brown, it's done. Remove from the oven and allow it to cool.

6. When the cheesecake has come to room temperature, put it into the refrigerator. When the cheesecake has chilled, remove the pan sides and cut the cake into 3 equal pieces. Serve with a generous dollop of whipped cream on top.

• SERVES 8.

• • • •

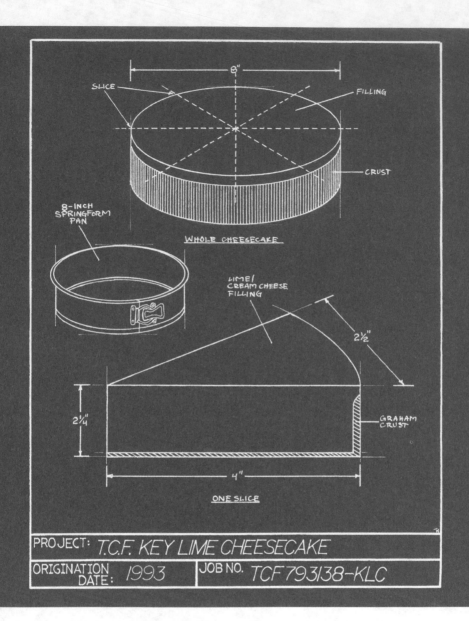

8"

SLICE

FILLING

CRUST

8-INCH
SPRINGFORM
PAN

WHOLE CHEESECAKE

LIME/
CREAM CHEESE
FILLING

2½"

2¼"

GRAHAM
CRUST

4"

ONE SLICE

PROJECT: T.C.F. KEY LIME CHEESECAKE

ORIGINATION
DATE: 1993

JOB NO. TCF 793138-KLC

THE CHEESECAKE FACTORY PUMPKIN CHEESECAKE

☆　　✌　　💣　　✏　　☯　　✂　　☞

While most restaurant chains attempt to keep their menus simple so as to not tax the kitchen, the Cheesecake Factory's menu contains more than 200 items. Perhaps it's the time spent reading the 17-page menu that leads to the one- and two-hour waits for a table that customers not only expect, but cheerfully endure for lunch or dinner, or just for a taste of the delicious Pumpkin Cheesecake or any of the other 40 cheesecake selections.

Use an 8-inch springform pan for this recipe. If you don't have one, you should get one. They're indispensable for thick, gourmet cheesecake and several other scrumptious desserts. If you don't want to use a springform pan, this recipe will also work with two 9-inch pie plates. You'll just end up with two smaller cheesecakes.

1 ½ cups graham cracker crumbs
5 tablespoons butter, melted
1 cup plus 1 tablespoon sugar
3 8-ounce packages cream
　　cheese, softened
1 teaspoon vanilla

1 cup canned pumpkin
3 eggs
½ teaspoon cinnamon
¼ teaspoon nutmeg
¼ teaspoon allspice
whipped cream

1. Preheat the oven to 350°F.
2. Make the crust by combining the graham cracker crumbs with the melted butter and 1 tablespoon sugar in a medium bowl. Stir well enough to coat all of the crumbs with the butter, but not so much as to turn the mixture into paste. Keep it crumbly.
3. Press the crumbs onto the bottom and about two-thirds of the way up the sides of the springform pan. You don't want the crust to form all of the way up the back of each slice of cheesecake. Bake the crust for 5 minutes, then set it aside until you are ready to fill it.
4. In a large mixing bowl combine the cream cheese, 1 cup sugar, and vanilla. Mix with an electric mixer until smooth.
5. Add the pumpkin, eggs, cinnamon, nutmeg, and allspice and continue to beat until smooth and creamy.
6. Pour the filling into the pan. Bake for 60 to 70 minutes. The top will turn a bit darker at this point. Remove from the oven and allow the cheesecake to cool.
7. When the cheesecake has come to room temperature, put it into the refrigerator. When the cheesecake has chilled, remove the pan sides and cut the cake into 8 equal pieces. Serve with a generous portion of whipped cream on top.

• SERVES 8.

•   •   •   •

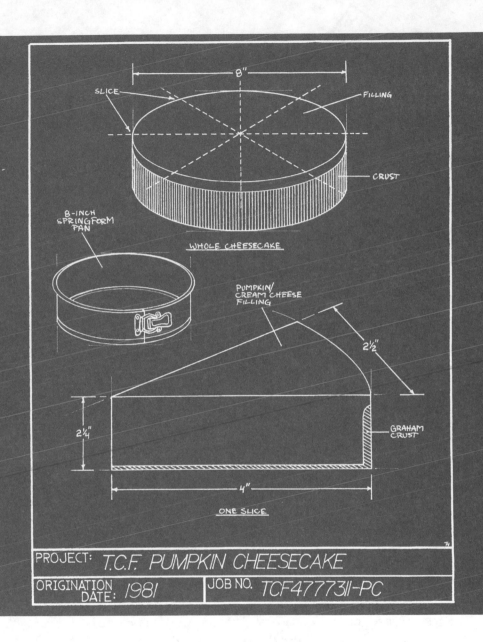

8"

SLICE

FILLING

CRUST

8-INCH
SPRINGFORM
PAN

WHOLE CHEESECAKE

PUMPKIN/
CREAM CHEESE
FILLING

2½"

2¼"

GRAHAM
CRUST

4"

ONE SLICE

PROJECT: T.C.F. PUMPKIN CHEESECAKE

ORIGINATION
DATE: 1981

JOB NO. TCF4777311-PC

341

TONY ROMA'S
WORLD FAMOUS RIBS

☆ ✌ 💣 ✏ ☯ ✂ ☞

Tony Roma had already been in the restaurant business for many years when he opened Tony Roma's Place in North Miami, Florida, in 1972. This casual diner featured food at reasonable prices, nightly live entertainment and the house specialty—baby back ribs. Soon, customers were traveling from miles away to get a taste of the succulent, mouth-watering ribs. One rib-lover came from Texas in 1976: Clint Murchison, Jr., a Texas financier and owner of the Dallas Cowboys. After sampling the baby backs, and claiming they were the best he'd ever tasted, he struck up a deal with Tony to purchase the majority of the U.S. rights to the company and planned for a major expansion. Today that plan has been realized with nearly 150 Tony Roma's restaurants in the chain pulling in over $250 million per year.

The famous barbecue ribs served at the restaurant have been judged the best in America at a national rib cook-off and have won more than 30 awards at other state and local competitions. The secret to the tender, melt-in-your-mouth quality of the ribs at Tony Roma's is the long, slow-cooking process. Here is the *Top Secret Recipes* version of the cooking technique. Three varieties of the famous barbecue sauce are found on pages 344, 346, and 348. Note that the restaurant uses pork baby back ribs for the Original Baby Backs recipe, and pork spare ribs for the Carolina Honeys and Red Hots. Of course *you* can use these sauces interchangeably on the ribs *you* like best, including beef ribs.

THE TECHNIQUE

4 pounds baby back pork ribs or
4 pounds pork spareribs

barbecue sauce for coating (See recipes on pages 348, 344, and 346)

1. Often when you buy ribs at the butcher counter, you get a full rack of ribs that wouldn't fit on a plate. Usually you just have to cut these long racks in half to get the perfect serving size (about 4 to 6 rib bones per rack). You'll likely have 4 of these smaller racks at about a pound each.
2. Preheat the oven to 300°F.
3. Tear off 4 pieces of aluminum foil that are roughly 6 inches longer than the ribs.
4. Coat the ribs, front and back, with your choice of barbecue sauce. Place a rack of ribs, one at a time, onto a piece of foil lengthwise and wrap it tightly.
5. Place the ribs into the oven with the seam of the foil wrap facing up. Cook for 2 to 2½ hours, or until you see the meat of the ribs shrinking back from the cut ends of the bones by about ½ inch. This long cooking time will ensure that the meat will be very tender and fall off the bone.
6. Toward the end of the cooking time, prepare the barbecue.
7. Remove the ribs from the foil and smother them with additional barbecue sauce. Be sure to save some sauce for later.
8. Grill the ribs on the hot barbecue for 2 to 4 minutes per side, or just until you see several spots of charred blackened sauce. Watch for flames and do not burn!
9. When the ribs are done, use a sharp knife to slice the meat between each bone about halfway down. This will make it easier to tear the ribs apart when they are served.

    Serve the ribs piping hot with additional sauce on the side, if desired.

- SERVES 2 TO 4 AS AN ENTREE.

TIDBITS

If you've got time to marinate these ribs in advance, do it. I've found these ribs are extraordinary when they've been soaking in barbecue sauce for 24 hours before cooking. Just prepare the ribs in the foil as described in the recipe and keep them in your fridge. Toss them, foil and all, into the oven the next day, 2 to 2½ hours before you plan to scarf out.

TONY ROMA'S
ORIGINAL BABY BACKS

☆　✌　🔥　✒　☯　✂　☞

Menu Description: "Our house specialty and award-winning ribs. Lean, tender, meaty pork ribs cut from the choicest tenderloin and basted with our original barbecue sauce. So tender the meat practically falls off the bone."

This is the sauce that made the chain famous. This version of the sauce uses a ketchup base, vinegar, dark corn syrup, and a bit of Tabasco for a slight zing. The chain uses their sauce on baby back ribs and has started selling it by the bottle in each restaurant. Now you can make a version of your own that is less costly than the bottled brand, and can be used on any cut of ribs, or even chicken.

BARBECUE SAUCE

I cup ketchup
I cup vinegar
½ cup dark corn syrup
2 teaspoons sugar

½ teaspoon salt
¼ teaspoon garlic powder
¼ teaspoon onion powder
¼ teaspoon Tabasco pepper
　　　sauce

4 pounds baby back pork ribs

1. Combine all of the ingredients for the barbecue sauce in a saucepan over high heat. Use a whisk to blend the ingredients until smooth.
2. When the mixture comes to a boil, reduce the heat and simmer uncovered.
3. In 30 to 45 minutes, when the mixture thickens, remove it from the heat. If you want a thicker sauce, heat it longer. If you make the sauce too thick, thin it with more vinegar.

4. Use baby back ribs and the cooking technique from page 342 to complete the recipe.

• SERVES 2 TO 4 AS AN ENTREE.

• • • •

BONE
(DO NOT EAT)

8"

RIB MEAT

4"

½"   TOP

SLATHERED
WITH SAUCE

8"

1¼"

HALF
RACK

SIDE

SIX
BONES

PROJECT: *TONY ROMA'S ORIGINAL BABY BACKS*

ORIGINATION DATE: *1972*

JOB NO. *TR69031057-0BB*

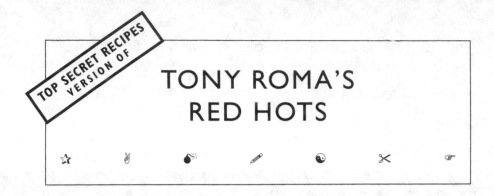

TONY ROMA'S
RED HOTS

Menu Description: "Some like it hot! Tender, meaty ribs basted with our spicy red hot sauce made with five types of peppers."

If you like your sauces especially spicy, this is the recipe for you. Five different peppers go into this one, including crushed red pepper, red bell pepper, Tabasco, cayenne pepper, and ground black pepper. The restaurant serves this one on pork spareribs, but you can slather it on any type of ribs, chicken, and steaks.

BARBECUE SAUCE

1 cup ketchup
1 cup vinegar
½ cup dark corn syrup
2 tablespoons molasses
½ tablespoon finely diced red bell pepper
2 teaspoons sugar
1 teaspoon liquid smoke

½ teaspoon salt
½ teaspoon crushed red pepper flakes
½ teaspoon Tabasco pepper sauce
¼ teaspoon cayenne pepper
¼ teaspoon ground black pepper
¼ teaspoon garlic powder
¼ teaspoon onion powder

4 pounds pork spareribs

1. Combine all of the ingredients for the barbecue sauce in a saucepan over high heat. Use a whisk to blend the ingredients until smooth.
2. When the mixture comes to a boil, reduce the heat and simmer uncovered.

3. In 30 to 45 minutes, when the mixture thickens, remove it from the heat. If you want a thicker sauce, cook it longer. If you make the sauce too thick, thin it with more vinegar.
4. Use pork spareribs and the cooking technique from page 342 to complete the recipe.

- SERVES 2 TO 4 AS AN ENTREE.

• • • •

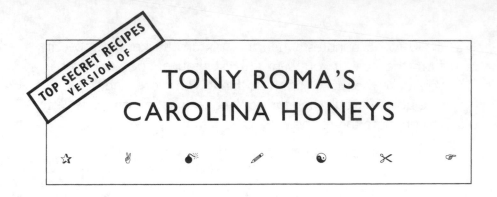

TONY ROMA'S
CAROLINA HONEYS

Menu Description: "Tender select-cut pork spare ribs basted with our special-recipe sauce. Nothing could be finer..."

This smoky sauce is perfectly sweetened with honey and molasses, and bites just a bit with pepper sauce. Smother pork spareribs with this sauce, as they do at the restaurant chain. Also use it on baby back ribs and beef spare ribs along with the slow-cooking technique. It's good with chicken, too.

BARBECUE SAUCE

I cup ketchup
I cup vinegar
1/2 cup molasses
1/2 cup honey
I teaspoon liquid smoke

1/2 teaspoon salt
1/4 teaspoon garlic powder
1/4 teaspoon onion powder
1/4 teaspoon Tabasco pepper
   sauce

4 pounds pork spare ribs

1. Combine all of the ingredients for the barbecue sauce in a saucepan over high heat. Blend the ingredients with a whisk until smooth.
2. When the mixture comes to a boil, reduce the heat and simmer uncovered.
3. In 30 to 45 minutes, when the mixture thickens, remove it from the heat. If you overcook it and make the sauce too thick, thin it with more vinegar.

4. Use pork spareribs and the cooking technique from page 342 to complete the recipe.

- SERVES 2 TO 4 AS AN ENTREE.

• • • •

BEVERAGES

Introduction

Today I've been drinking the world's number one beverage, but I can't give you the recipe. Unless you already know how to combine two hydrogen atoms with one oxygen atom in abundance, you'll have to settle for drinking it out of a bottle or straight off the tap.

What I can give you, though, is a bunch of recipes to duplicate the taste of the other drinks we hold dear, including several iced versions for the second most popular beverage in the world: tea. You'll recognize many of these products because it would be nearly impossible to exist in civilization on this planet without being reminded several times each day that you absolutely must drink these wonderful drinks. And that you will enjoy them. And that when you are thirsty again you will come back for more.

It's true that this book includes clone recipes for some of the most successful products in the world—those drinks you've enjoyed since birth—with long, remarkable histories and huge profits. But a collection such as this would not be complete without also including copycat formulas for the newer, trendier drinks that have garnered more recent worship.

You'll learn how to re-create your favorite sodas using the old soda-fountain technique: adding flavored syrup to cold soda water. This is also where you get the secret to mixing a *Dairy Queen Blizzard* clone of your own at home so that the ice cream won't get too runny when you stir in all the chunks. If you like coffee, you'll find out what secret ingredients will copy a *Starbucks Frappuccino* and the instant *General Foods International Coffees*.

So grab a straw and dive on in. As with all the other *Top Secret Recipes* books, measure carefully and follow the directions precisely. In no time at all you'll soon be downing a duplicate of your favorite drink, from your favorite glass, while sitting in your favorite chair.

A&W
CREAM SODA

☆   ✌   💣   ✏   ☯   ✂   ☞

Sure, Roy Allen and Frank Wright are better known for their exquisite root beer concoction sold first from California drive-up stands under the A&W brand name. But these days the company makes a darn good vanilla cream soda as well. And the formula is one that we can easily clone at home just by combining a few simple ingredients. Most of the flavor comes from vanilla, but you'll also need a little lemonade flavor Kool-Aid unsweetened drink mix powder. This mix comes in .23-ounce packets and provides the essential citric acid that gives this soda clone the necessary tang of the real thing. Once you make the syrup, let it cool down in the fridge, then just combine the syrup with cold soda water in a 1 to 4 ratio, add a little ice, and get sipping.

1 ⅓ cups granulated sugar
⅛ teaspoon Kool-Aid lemonade
    unsweetened drink mix
1 cup very hot water
1 cup corn syrup

½ teaspoon plus ¼ teaspoon
    vanilla extract

10 cups cold soda water

1. Dissolve the sugar and Kool-Aid drink mix in the hot water in a small pitcher.
2. Add the corn syrup and vanilla extract and stir well. Cover and chill syrup until cold.
3. When the syrup is cold, pour ¼ cup syrup into 1 cup cold soda water. Stir gently, add ice, and serve.

• MAKES 10 10-OUNCE SERVINGS.

• • • •

7-ELEVEN
CHERRY SLURPEE

Put on a big red smile. Now you can make your own version of the popular convenience store slush we know by the excruciating brain throb that follows a big ol' gulp. You must have a blender to make this clone of 7-Eleven's Slurpee, and enough room to stick that blender into your freezer to get it nice and thick. This recipe gets close to the original with Kool-Aid mix and a little help from cherry extract, but you can make this drink with any flavor Kool-Aid mix (if you decide to make some variations, don't worry about adding extract). This recipe makes enough to fill one of those giant 32-ounce cups you find at the convenience store. Now if we could just figure out how to make those funky spoon-straws.

2 cups cold club soda
½ cup sugar
¼ teaspoon plus ⅛ teaspoon
   Kool-Aid cherry-flavored
   unsweetened drink mix

½ teaspoon cherry extract
2½ cups crushed ice

1. Pour 1 cup of the club soda into a blender. Add the sugar, Kool-Aid mix, and cherry extract. Blend this until all of the sugar is dissolved.
2. Add the crushed ice and blend on high speed until the drink is a slushy, smooth consistency, with no remaining chunks of ice.
3. Add the remaining club soda and blend briefly until mixed.

You may have to stop the blender and use a long spoon to stir up the contents.

4. If necessary, put the blender into your freezer for ½ hour. This will help thicken the slurpee. After ½ hour remove blender from freezer and, again, blend briefly to mix.

• MAKES 1 32-OUNCE DRINK (OR 2 16-OUNCERS).

• • • •

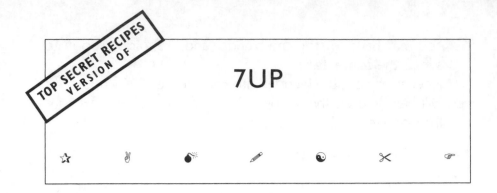

7UP

It was the perfect drink for a Great Depression. In 1929, the United States slipped into a giant economic slump, and a new lemon-lime soda with an attitude-adjusting additive was rolled out. The drink's slogan, "Takes the Ouch Out of the Grouch," referred to lithium, a powerful drug used to treat manic depression and prevent mood swings. Lithium was added to every serving of 7UP until the mid-1940s.

The soda wasn't called 7UP at first. The drink, created by Charles Leiper Grigg, was originally called Bib-Labeled Lithiated Lemon-Lime Soda, but that name, and even the abbreviated version, BLLLLS, was too long.

Today, no one can agree on the origin of the name 7UP. Some theorize that it came from the number of ingredients in the soda, while others say it came from the size of the 7-ounce bottles in which the drink was first sold. There are even theories that the name came from a popular card game at the time called 7UP, or from a cattle brand Charlie Grigg saw one day.

During the sugar rationing of World War II, 7UP was especially popular with bottlers since it used less sugar than other soft drinks. In 1967, the company introduced the famous "uncola" ads, with an image of the drink served in an upside-down bell-shaped cola glass. That campaign continued through the 70s with deep-throated actor Geoffrey Holder explaining the secret of the drink to be the "uncola nut."

The slogan "follow the liter" was later developed to announce 7UP's new packaging in 1-liter bottles. Soon afterward, every major soft drink label was selling their sodas in metric bottles.

In 1986, the Seven Up Company merged with the Dr Pepper Company, creating the world's third-largest soft drink company behind Coca-Cola and Pepsi.

Now you can make a home clone for this refreshing citrus beverage in no time at all. Just add lemon and lime juice to a syrup solution, along with a little Kool-Aid lemonade drink mix for that special tang (thanks to included citric acid), and you're almost there. When the syrup has cooled, you just mix it into some cold soda water in a 1 to 4 ratio. And that's it. You've just made this clone of 7UP yours.

I cup plus 1 tablespoon
   granulated sugar
I cup corn syrup
½ teaspoon Kool-Aid lemonade
   unsweetened drink mix
1 ¼ cups very hot water

I tablespoon bottled lime juice
2 teaspoons bottled lemon juice

11 cups cold soda water

1. Combine sugar, corn syrup, and lemonade drink mix in a medium pitcher or bowl. Add hot water and stir until sugar has dissolved and syrup is clear.
2. Add lime juice and lemon juice and stir. Cover and chill for several hours until cold.
3. To make the soda, add ¼ cup of cold syrup to 1 cup of cold soda water (1 to 4 ratio). Stir gently, drop in some ice, and serve.

• MAKES 11 10-OUNCE SERVINGS.

• • • •

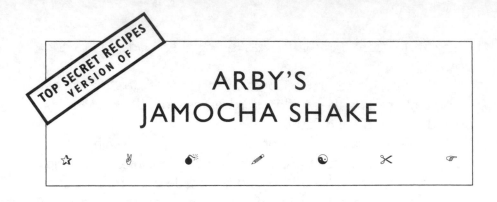

ARBY'S JAMOCHA SHAKE

Okay, wash out the blender; this one's been begging to be cloned for years now. Arby's famous Jamocha Shake was one of the first frozen coffee drinks to gain popularity, even before Starbucks pummeled us with Frappuccinos. This thick drink is actually more milk shake than coffee drink, but if you like the original, you'll love this easy-to-make clone that serves two.

1 cup cold coffee
1 cup low-fat milk
3 tablespoons granulated sugar

3 cups vanilla ice cream
3 tablespoons chocolate syrup

1. Combine the coffee, milk, and sugar in a blender and mix on medium speed for 15 seconds to dissolve the sugar.
2. Add the ice cream and chocolate syrup, then blend on high speed until smooth and creamy. Stop blender and stir mixture with a spoon if necessary to help blend ingredients.
3. Pour drink into two 16-ounce glasses and serve.

• MAKES 2 LARGE DRINKS.

• • • •

ARIZONA
GREEN TEA WITH GINSENG
AND HONEY

☆　　✌　　💣　　✐　　☻　　✄　　☞

Hard to believe it takes only one regular-sized green tea bag to make an entire 2-quart clone of the popular iced tea in the foam green bottles. Ah, but it's true. Find the liquid ginseng for this recipe in your local health food store, and try to get American ginseng if you can because the Chinese stuff tastes kinda nasty.

2 quarts (8 cups) water
1 Lipton green tea bag
½ cup sugar
2 tablespoons honey

3 tablespoons lemon juice
¼ teaspoon ginseng extract
　(American ginseng)

1. Heat water in a large saucepan until it boils. Turn off heat, put the teabag in the water, then cover the pan and let the tea steep for 1 hour.
2. Pour the sugar and honey into a 2-quart pitcher. Pour the tea into the pitcher and stir to dissolve sugar.
3. Add lemon juice and ginseng and stir. Cool and serve.

• MAKES 2 QUARTS.

•　•　•　•

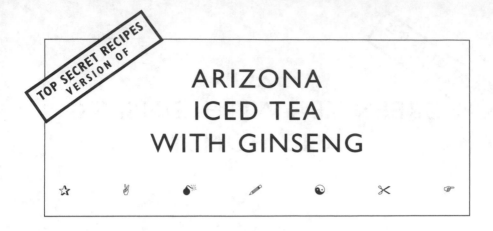

ARIZONA
ICED TEA
WITH GINSENG

When John Ferolito and Don Vultaggio pondered a name for a new line of canned iced teas, all they had to do was look at a map of the United States. They wanted to name their iced tea after a hot place where a cold can of iced tea was worshipped. Originally they picked "Santa Fe," but soon ditched the name of the city and settled on a state: AriZona, complete with an uppercase "Z" in the middle for kicks. The secret to the duo's early success was largely in their creative packaging decisions. If you think the tea's great chilled, the company claims you can also sip it hot by simply zapping a cupful in the microwave.

2 quarts (8 cups) water
1 Lipton tea bag (black tea)
⅔ cup sugar

2 tablespoons lemon juice
¼ teaspoon ginseng extract
    (American ginseng)

1. Heat water in a large saucepan until it boils. Turn off heat, put the teabag in the water, then cover the pan and let the tea steep for 1 hour.
2. Pour the sugar into a 2-quart pitcher. Pour the tea into the pitcher and stir to dissolve sugar.
3. Add lemon juice and ginseng and stir. Cool and serve.

• MAKES 2 QUARTS.

You can find liquid ginseng, usually in dropper bottles, in your local health food store. Be sure to get American ginseng if you have a choice. Some of the Chinese ginseng tastes too bitter for this tea.

•   •   •   •

BASKIN-ROBBINS
PEACH SMOOTHIE

Dairy Queen's got twice as many stores, but Baskin-Robbins is still the country's second-largest ice cream chain with around 2,500 outlets spread across the nation. And, naturally, when the chain known for its 31 flavors of ice cream noticed the smoothie craze building in 1997, it hopped right on board with its own selection made from sherbet or vanilla fat-free frozen yogurt. In the stores, servers use a pineapple juice concentrate for this smoothie, but we can still get a great clone by using the more popular canned pineapple juice found in any supermarket. As for the peaches, you may want to let them thaw a bit and then chop them up so you can get a more accurate measure.

1 cup pineapple juice
¾ cup frozen peaches, sliced

1 scoop fat-free vanilla frozen
   yogurt
3 or 4 ice cubes

Combine all ingredients in a blender and blend on high speed until all the ice is crushed and the drink is smooth.

• MAKES 1 16-OUNCE DRINK.

• • • •

BASKIN-ROBBINS STRAWBERRY BANANA SMOOTHIE

☆   ✌   💣   ✏   ☯   ✂   ☞

It was in 1953 that the now-famous "31 Flavors" sign was introduced, burdening customers with the dilemma of having to decide which of so many great ice cream flavors they would choose. The number 31 was picked to suggest that a new flavor could be selected every day of the month. The company has come up with around one thousand flavors so far. And as with their most famous flavor, Rocky Road, many other Baskin-Robbins flavor creations would be often imitated—among them Pralines and Cream and Jamoca Almond Fudge.

This recipe for a smoothie is very similar to the previous clone, the only difference being a reduction in strawberries and the addition of half of a ripe banana. You may want to chop up those frozen strawberries (especially the big 'uns) to make measuring easier and more accurate.

1 cup Kern's strawberry nectar
½ cup frozen whole strawberries,
    chopped
1 scoop fat-free vanilla frozen
    yogurt

½ ripe banana
3 or 4 ice cubes

Combine all ingredients in a blender and blend on high speed until all the ice is crushed and the drink is smooth.

• MAKES 1 16-OUNCE DRINK.

• • • •

CINNABON
MOCHALATTA CHILL

☆　　✌　　💣　　✏　　☯　　✂　　☞

If you want your refreshing caffeine buzz kicked up with a nice chocolate rush, try this clone for Cinnabon's Mochalatta Chill. Brew some strong coffee and let it cool off, then get out the half-and-half and chocolate syrup. The real thing from Cinnabon is made with Ghirardelli chocolate syrup, but Hershey's syrup, which can be found everywhere, works great for this delicious duplicate.

1 cup double-strength coffee, cold
  (see Tidbits)
1 cup half-and-half
½ cup Hershey's chocolate syrup

GARNISH
whipped cream

Combine all ingredients in a small pitcher. Stir well or cover and shake. Pour over ice in two 16-ounce glasses, and top with whipped cream.

- MAKES 2 LARGE DRINKS.

TIDBITS

Make double-strength coffee in your coffee maker by adding half the water suggested by the manufacturer. Allow coffee to chill in the refrigerator before using it in this recipe.

•　•　•　•

COCA-COLA

☆　　　✌　　　💣　　　✒　　　☯　　　✂　　　☞

When Atlanta pharmacist John Pemberton whipped up his first cocaine-laced drink he was actually cloning Vin Mariani, a coca leaf–infused red wine that had been selling successfully in Europe since 1863. John's version—called "Pemberton's French wine coca"—had cocaine and wine in it too, but John added kola nut extract to give the drink additional kick (as if it needed it) from the stimulant alkaloid caffeine. Shortly after John had perfected his new drink, local Prohibition hit Atlanta in 1886, and the booze had to come out. The wine was replaced with sugar syrup to make it sweet along with some citric acid for tang, and the name of the new drink was changed to "Coca-Cola," representing the beverage's two very stimulating ingredients. As enthusiasm for cocaine-based tonics waned toward the end of the century, Coca-Cola manufacturers were again forced to ditch another key ingredient. By 1903, the cocaine in Coca-Cola had to come out too.

Although it was a major change to the recipe, removing cocaine from Coca-Cola didn't alter the beverage enough to keep it from becoming the world's number one fountain and bottled soft drink over the years. People enjoyed the drink for its refreshing taste. And, the drink did, after all, still contain enough caffeine to provide a sufficient spring to the step. The drink's success spawned many clones from competitors with only slight variations on the formula's top secret taste, but none, including Pepsi, would become as big a phenomenon as Coke. Many recipes were floating around at the time. It is well documented that John sold several copies of the original recipe along with shares in his company to help him through the morphine addiction and poverty that plagued his later years. John died at age 57 in 1888 from stomach cancer before knowing the enormous success of his creation.

Although the drink is 99 percent sugar water, that other 1 percent is the key to the drink's unique taste. The tangy citrus flavors, from lime juice, citrus oils, and citric acid (today the citric acid has been replaced with phosphoric acid), was used by John to overcome the inherent unpleasant bitterness of cocaine and caffeine. Even after removing the coca from the drink, it was still necessary to conceal the ghastly flavor of kola nut caffeine from the taste buds with the sweet, tangy syrup.

To make an accurate clone of Coca-Cola at home I started with the medicinal ingredient, probably just as John did. But rather than harvesting kola nuts, we have the luxury of access to caffeine pills found in any grocery store or pharmacy. One such brand is Vivarin, but it is yellow in color with a thick coating and it tastes much too bitter. NoDoz, however, is white and less bitter, with a thinner coating. Each NoDoz tablet contains 200 milligrams of caffeine, and a 12-ounce serving of Coke has 46 milligrams in it. So if we use 8 NoDoz tablets that have been crushed to powder with a mortar and pestle (or in a bowl using the back of a spoon) we get 44 milligrams of caffeine in a 12-ounce serving, or 36 milligrams in each of the 10-ounce servings we make with this recipe.

Finding and adding the caffeine is the easy part. You'll probably have more trouble obtaining Coke's crucial flavoring ingredient: cassia oil. I was hoping to leave such a hard-to-get ingredient out of this recipe, but I found it impossible. The unique flavor of Coke absolutely requires the inclusion of this Vietnamese cinnamon oil (usually sold for aromatherapy), but only a very small amount. You'll find the cassia oil in a health food store (I used the brand Oshadhi), along with the lemon oil and orange oil. The yield of this recipe had to be cranked up to 44 10-ounce servings since these oils are so strong—just one drop of each is all you'll need. Find them in bottles that allow you to measure exactly one drop if you can. If the oils don't come in such a bottle, buy eye-droppers at a drug store. Before you leave the health food store, don't forget the citric acid.

This recipe, because of the old-fashioned technique of adding the syrup to soda water, creates a clone of Coke as it would taste coming out of a fountain machine. That Coke is usually not as fizzy as the bottled stuff. But if you add some ice to a glass of bottled Coke, and then some to this cloned version, the bubbles will settle down and you'll discover how close the two are.

Because subtle difference in flavor can affect the finished product, be sure to measure your ingredients very carefully. Use the flat top edge of a butter knife to scrape away the excess sugar and citric acid from the top of the measuring cup and teaspoon, and don't estimate on any of the liquid ingredients.

6 cups granulated sugar
2 cups (one 16-ounce bottle) light
   corn syrup
8 NoDoz tablets, crushed to
   powder
2 teaspoons citric acid
7 cups boiling water
1 tablespoon lime juice
½ teaspoon vanilla
1 drop lemon oil

1 drop orange oil
1 drop cinnamon (cassia) oil

COLOR
1 tablespoon red food coloring
1½ teaspoons yellow food
   coloring
½ teaspoon blue food coloring
18 drops green food coloring

44 cups cold soda water

1. Combine sugar, corn syrup, powdered NoDoz, and citric acid in a large pitcher or bowl. Add the boiling water, and stir until the sugar has dissolved and the solution is clear. Strain the syrup through a paper towel–lined strainer to remove the NoDoz sediment.
2. Add the lime juice, vanilla, lemon oil, orange oil, and cassia oil to the syrup and stir.
3. Add the colors to the syrup, then cover it and chill it for several hours until cold.

4. To make the soda, add ¼ cup of cold syrup to 1 cup of cold soda water. Stir gently, drop in some ice, and serve.

• MAKES 44 10-OUNCE SERVINGS.

•   •   •   •

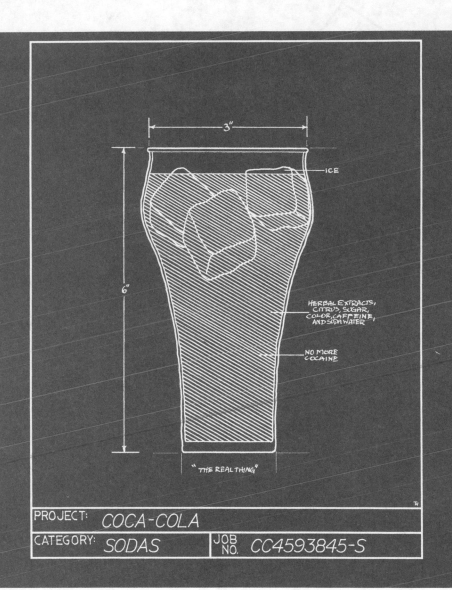

3"

ICE

6"

HERBAL EXTRACTS,
CITRUS, SUGAR,
COLOR, CAFFEINE,
AND SODA WATER

NO MORE
COCAINE

"THE REAL THING"

PROJECT:	COCA-COLA	
CATEGORY:	SODAS	JOB NO. CC4593845-S

DAIRY QUEEN
BLIZZARD

It's Dairy Queen's most successful product ever. Over 175 million Blizzards were sold in the year following the product's debut in 1985. Such a sales phenomenon was the new creation that other fast food chains invented their own versions of the soft-serve ice cream treats with mixed in chunks of cookies and candies and fruit. Today there are over a dozen varieties of the frozen treat to choose from at Dairy Queen, and I've got all of the most creative and tasty versions cloned right here.

The biggest challenge we face when making our Blizzard replicas at home is keeping the ice cream from going all soft and runny on us when the other ingredients are stirred in. To solve that problem, we'll use a special technique inspired by marble slab ice cream stores. These outfits mix your choice of chunky ingredients with your choice of ice cream on a slab of frozen stone. This method keeps the ice cream cold and firm while mixing, until it's served to a drooling you.

To incorporate this technique at home you need to put a glass or ceramic bowl in the freezer for at least 30 minutes (while you're at it you may also want to freeze the glass you're going to serve the thing in). An hour or more is even better. Then, we simply mix our ingredients in the icy bowl, while the ice cream stays frosty cold. Just be sure to use plain vanilla ice cream (not French vanilla) for these clones, if you have a choice.

BABY RUTH

1 Baby Ruth candy bar
2½ cups vanilla ice cream

¼ cup milk
3 tablespoons caramel topping

1. Before you start to make this clone, freeze a medium glass or ceramic bowl in the freezer for at least 30 minutes.
2. When the bowl is frozen, mince the Baby Ruth into small bits with a big knife.
3. Measure the ice cream into the bowl, and add the milk. Stir the ice cream and milk together until smooth and creamy. Add the candy bar pieces and caramel and stir to combine. Pour into a 20-ounce glass and serve with a long spoon.

- MAKES 1 20-OUNCE SERVING.

BANANA PUDDING

Amaze everybody with this one that tastes just like homemade banana pudding with Nilla Wafers in it.

1 ripe banana
8 Nilla Wafers

2½ cups vanilla ice cream
¼ cup milk

1. Before you start to make this clone, freeze a medium glass or ceramic bowl in the freezer for at least 30 minutes.
2. Mash the banana in a separate small bowl.
3. Crumble the Nilla Wafers into small pieces.
4. Measure the ice cream and milk into the frozen bowl. Stir with a spoon until smooth and creamy.

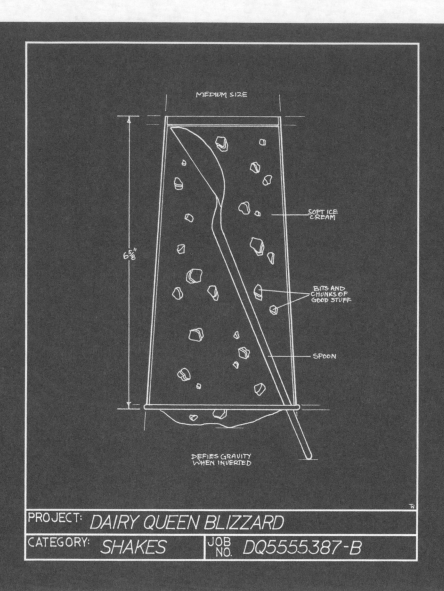

MEDIUM SIZE

$6\frac{5}{8}"$

SOFT ICE CREAM

BITS AND CHUNKS OF GOOD STUFF

SPOON

DEFIES GRAVITY WHEN INVERTED

PROJECT:	DAIRY QUEEN BLIZZARD	
CATEGORY: SHAKES	JOB NO.	DQ5555387-B

5. Add the banana and Nilla Wafers to the ice cream and stir to combine.
6. Pour into a 20-ounce glass and serve with a long spoon.

- MAKES 1 20-OUNCE SERVING.

BANANA SPLIT

Tastes like a banana split with all the toppings. Yum city.

1 ripe banana	3 tablespoons strawberry topping
2½ cups vanilla ice cream	3 tablespoons pineapple topping
¼ cup milk	2 tablespoons chocolate syrup

1. Before you start to make this clone, freeze a medium glass or ceramic bowl in the freezer for at least 30 minutes.
2. Mash the banana in a separate small bowl.
3. Measure the ice cream and milk into the frozen bowl. Stir with a spoon until smooth and creamy.
4. Add the banana, strawberry topping, pineapple topping, and chocolate syrup and stir to combine.
5. Pour into a 20-ounce glass and serve with a long spoon.

- MAKES 1 20-OUNCE SERVING.

BERRY BANANA

With strawberry ice cream topping, banana, and crumbled Vienna Fingers you can't go wrong.

1 ripe banana	¼ cup milk
2 Vienna Fingers cookies	¼ cup strawberry topping
2½ cups vanilla ice cream	

1. Before you start to make this clone, freeze a medium glass or ceramic bowl in the freezer for at least 30 minutes.
2. Mash the banana in a separate small bowl.
3. Crumble the Vienna Fingers into small pieces.
4. Measure the ice cream and milk into the frozen bowl. Stir with a spoon until smooth and creamy.
5. Add the banana, Vienna Fingers, and strawberries to the ice cream and stir to combine.
6. Pour into a 20-ounce glass and serve with a long spoon.

• MAKES 1 20-OUNCE SERVING.

CHOCOLATE CHIP

Use Magic Shell topping here, which will harden into little bits while mixing to create chocolate chips.

2½ cups vanilla ice cream　　　*3 tablespoons chocolate Magic*
¼ cup milk　　　　　　　　　　*Shell topping*

1. Before you start to make this clone, freeze a medium glass or ceramic bowl in the freezer for at least 30 minutes.
2. Measure the ice cream and milk into the frozen bowl. Stir with a spoon until smooth and creamy.
3. Add the chocolate Magic Shell and stir gently to combine.
4. Pour into a 20-ounce glass and serve with a long spoon.

• MAKES 1 20-OUNCE SERVING.

CHOCOLATE CHIP COOKIE DOUGH

The dough comes from a tube of Pillsbury cookie dough. It's simple and sinfully good.

¼ cup Pillsbury cookie dough ¼ cup milk
2½ cups vanilla ice cream ¼ cup fudge topping

1. Before you start to make this clone, freeze a medium glass or ceramic bowl in the freezer for at least 30 minutes.
2. While the bowl is freezing, separate the cookie dough into pea-sized pieces and keep the dough pieces in the refrigerator.
3. Measure the ice cream and milk into the frozen bowl. Stir with a spoon until smooth and creamy.
4. Add the cookie dough and fudge topping and stir to combine.
5. Pour into a 20-ounce glass and serve with a long spoon.

• MAKES 1 20-OUNCE SERVING.

HAWAIIAN

If you like riding a wave of tropical flavors, you'll love this blend of pineapple ice cream topping and shredded coconut. Aloha, baby.

1 ripe banana 3 tablespoons pineapple topping
2½ cups vanilla ice cream 3 tablespoons shredded coconut
¼ cup milk

1. Before you start to make this clone, freeze a medium glass or ceramic bowl in the freezer for at least 30 minutes.
2. Mash the banana in a separate small bowl.
3. Measure the ice cream and milk into the frozen bowl. Stir with a spoon until smooth and creamy.
4. Add the mashed banana, pineapple topping, and coconut and stir to combine.
5. Pour into a 20-ounce glass and serve with a long spoon.

• MAKES 1 20-OUNCE SERVING.

WHOPP'N'WILD

You can't go wrong with a blend of Whoppers and ice cream. The flavor of malted milk ball candy is accentuated with the addition of extra malted milk powder and chocolate sauce.

16 Whoppers malted milk balls
2½ cups vanilla ice cream
¼ cup milk

2 tablespoons malted milk powder
3 tablespoons chocolate sauce

1. Before you start to make this clone, freeze a medium glass or ceramic bowl in the freezer for at least 30 minutes. While you're at it, put the Whoppers in a small plastic bag and put them in the freezer too.
2. When the bowl is frozen, remove the Whoppers from the freezer and, while they are still in the bag, smash them into pieces with your fist or the handle of a knife.
3. Measure the ice cream and milk into the frozen bowl. Stir with a spoon until smooth and creamy.
4. Add the Whoppers, malted milk powder, and chocolate sauce to the ice cream and stir to combine.
5. Pour into a 20-ounce glass and serve with a long spoon.

• MAKES 1 20-OUNCE SERVING.

YUKON CRUNCHER

Just like eating s'mores, except you use a spoon and this version is cold.

2½ cups vanilla ice cream
¼ cup milk
3 tablespoons fudge topping

3 tablespoons marshmallow crème
¼ cup Rice Krispies cereal

1. Before you start to make this clone, freeze a medium glass or ceramic bowl in the freezer for at least 30 minutes.
2. Measure the ice cream and milk into the frozen bowl. Stir with a spoon until smooth and creamy.
3. Add the fudge, marshmallow crème, and Rice Krispies to the ice cream and stir to combine.
4. Pour into a 20-ounce glass and serve with a long spoon.

- Makes 1 20-ounce serving.

TIDBITS

If your Blizzard clone is not as thick as the real thing, just put the whole glass into the freezer for 5 to 10 minutes, or until it's thick.

•   •   •   •

GENERAL FOODS INTERNATIONAL COFFEES

With just a few simple ingredients you can re-create the European-style coffees that come in rectangular tins at a fraction of the cost. Since these famous instant coffee blends are created by Maxwell House, it's best to use Maxwell House instant coffee, although I've tried them all with Folgers and Taster's Choice, and the recipes still work out fine. You'll also need a coffee bean grinder to grind the instant coffee into powder. When you're finished making the mix, you can store it for as long as you like in a sealed container, until you're ready for a hot coffee drink. At that point, simply measure some of the mix into a cup with boiling water. Stir it all up and enjoy while watching shows about Europe on the Travel Channel to enhance the experience.

CAFÉ VIENNA

A creamy coffee with a hint of cinnamon.

¼ cup instant coffee
¼ cup plus 3 tablespoons
   granulated sugar

½ cup plus 1 tablespoon
   Coffee-mate creamer
⅛ teaspoon cinnamon

1. Grind the instant coffee into powder using a coffee grinder.
2. Mix all ingredients together in a small bowl. Store in a sealed container.
3. To make coffee, measure 2 tablespoons of the powdered mix into a coffee cup. Add 8 ounces (1 cup) of boiling water and stir.

- MAKES 9 SERVINGS.

FRENCH VANILLA CAFÉ

This one gets its subtle vanilla flavor from a little French Vanilla Coffee-mate creamer.

¼ cup instant coffee
¼ cup plus 3 tablespoons
   granulated sugar

½ cup Coffee-mate creamer
   (plain)
¼ cup French Vanilla Coffee-mate
   creamer

1. Grind the instant coffee into powder using a coffee grinder.
2. Mix all ingredients together in a small bowl. Store in a sealed container.
3. To make coffee, measure 2 tablespoons of the powdered mix into a coffee cup. Add 8 ounces (1 cup) of boiling water and stir.

- MAKES 10 SERVINGS.

HAZELNUT BELGIAN CAFÉ

As in the above recipe, you'll need to use flavored creamer along with the plain stuff to hit the right note.

¼ cup instant coffee
¼ cup plus 3 tablespoons
  granulated sugar
¼ cup plus 3 tablespoons Coffee-
  mate creamer (plain)

2 tablespoons Hazelnut
  Coffee-mate creamer

1. Grind the instant coffee into powder using a coffee grinder.
2. Mix all ingredients together in a small bowl. Store in a sealed container.
3. To make coffee, measure 2 tablespoons of the powdered mix into a coffee cup. Add 8 ounces (1 cup) of boiling water and stir.

• MAKES 9 SERVINGS.

SUISSE MOCHA

It takes just a couple tablespoons of cocoa to give this version its chocolate accent. When making the coffee in a cup, notice that this is the only recipe of the bunch requiring a measurement of 4 teaspoons of mix to 1 cup of boiling water.

¼ cup instant coffee
½ cup plus 2 tablespoons
  granulated sugar

½ cup plus 1 tablespoon Coffee-
  mate creamer
2 tablespoons cocoa

1. Grind the instant coffee into powder using a coffee grinder.
2. Mix all ingredients together in a small bowl. Store in a sealed container.
3. To make coffee, measure 4 teaspoons of the powdered mix into a coffee cup. Add 8 ounces (1 cup) of boiling water and stir.

• MAKES 16 SERVINGS.

VIENNESE CHOCOLATE CAFÉ

Vanilla *and* chocolate go great together in this one.

¼ cup instant coffee
¼ cup plus 3 tablespoons
　granulated sugar
½ cup Coffee-mate creamer
　(plain)

2 tablespoons French Vanilla
　Coffee-mate creamer
2 teaspoons cocoa

1. Grind the instant coffee into powder using a coffee grinder.
2. Mix all ingredients together in a small bowl. Store in a sealed container.
3. To make coffee, measure 2 tablespoons of the powdered mix into a coffee cup. Add 8 ounces (1 cup) of boiling water and stir.

• MAKES 10 SERVINGS.

•　•　•　•

HAWAIIAN PUNCH
FRUIT JUICY RED

Real Hawaiian Punch contains only 5 percent fruit juice. Even though some of the ingredients in our clone are not pure fruit juice, and we're adding additional water and sugar, this *Top Secret Recipes* version still contains a lot more tasty real fruit juice than the real thing. Plus, you can leave the food coloring out, if you like. It's only for looks, in a traditionally punchy way.

1 ½ cups water
1 cup pineapple juice
¾ cup Mauna Lai Paradise
　Passion guava/passion fruit
　blend
¼ tablespoon orange juice

¼ cup apple juice
¼ cup Kern's papaya nectar
¼ tablespoon Kern's apricot
　nectar
3 tablespoons granulated sugar
¼ teaspoon red food coloring

1. Combine all ingredients in a pitcher and stir until sugar is dissolved.

• MAKES 1 LITER.

HOT DOG
ON A STICK
MUSCLE BEACH LEMONADE

Entrepreneur Dave Barham opened the first Hot Dog on a Stick location in Santa Monica, California, near famed Muscle Beach. That was in 1946, and today the chain has blossomed into a total of more than 100 outlets located in shopping malls across America. You've probably seen the bright red, white, blue, and yellow go-go outfits and those cylindrical fez-style bucket hats on the girls behind the counter.

In giant clear plastic vats at the front of each store floats ice, fresh lemon rinds, and what is probably the world's most thirst-quenching substance—Muscle Beach Lemonade. Our clone is a simple concoction really, with only three ingredients. And with this *TSR* formula, you'll have your own version of the lemonade in the comfort of your own home at a fraction of the price.

1 cup fresh-squeezed lemon juice   7 cups water
   (about 5 lemons)   1 cup granulated sugar

1. Combine the lemon juice with the water and sugar in a 2-quart pitcher. Stir or shake vigorously until all the sugar is dissolved.
2. Slice the remaining lemon rind halves into fourths, then add the rinds to the pitcher. Add ice to the top of the pitcher and chill.
3. Serve the lemonade over ice in a 12-ounce glass and add a couple of lemon rind slices to each glass.

- Makes 2 quarts, or 8 servings.

• • • •

STRAW

ICE

$5\frac{1}{2}''$

LEMON
RIND

FRESH
LEMONADE

CROSS SECTION

PROJECT: H.D.O.S. MUSCLE BEACH LEMONADE

CATEGORY: OTHER SIPS   JOB NO. HDOS389963-MBL

JAMBA JUICE
BANANA BERRY

Jamba Juice has become America's favorite smoothie chain, with tasty fruit-filled blends served up in giant 24-ounce cups at over 325 stores. Appreciate the ease with which you are able to suck down your next Jamba Juice smoothie, since the wide straws at the chain have been through rigorous "suckability factor" testing to ensure that the good stuff gets all the way through to your gullet.

¾ cup apple juice
¾ cup Kern's strawberry nectar
⅔ cup frozen blueberries
1 sliced banana

1 scoop raspberry sherbet
1 scoop fat-free vanilla frozen
   yogurt
1 cup ice

1. Combine all ingredients in a blender and blend on high speed until all the ice is crushed and the drink is smooth.

• MAKES 1 24-OUNCE DRINK.

• • • •

JAMBA JUICE
CITRUS SQUEEZE

This smoothie is a very popular choice among the more than 16 varieties of smoothies made fresh at this smoothie chain. If your blender stalls out on you from the thickness of the drink, stop it and stir with a long spoon. That should get things going again. For the perfect clone, you want to be sure all the ice is crushed so that the drink is smooth-a-licious.

1 cup fresh orange juice
½ cup pineapple juice
⅔ cup frozen whole strawberries

1 sliced banana
2 scoops orange sherbet
1 cup ice

1. Combine all ingredients in a blender and blend on high speed until all the ice is crushed and the drink is smooth.

• MAKES 1 24-OUNCE DRINK.

• • • •

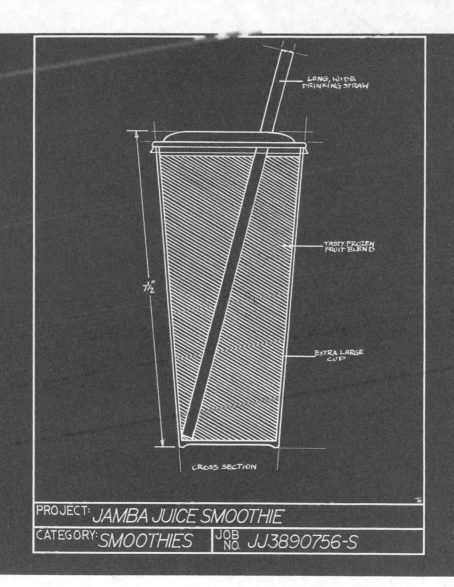

LONG, WIDE
DRINKING STRAW

TASTY FROZEN
FRUIT BLEND

EXTRA LARGE
CUP

$7\frac{1}{2}''$

CROSS SECTION

PROJECT: *JAMBA JUICE SMOOTHIE*

CATEGORY: *SMOOTHIES*   JOB NO. *JJ3890756-S*

385

JAMBA JUICE
CRANBERRY CRAZE

The menu description says that this drink includes plain nonfat yogurt (not the frozen kind), but I noticed that the server at the store I visited didn't put it in. When I asked her if she forgot the ingredient, she told me they don't include the yogurt anymore, even if the board says otherwise. Okay, right. So, while the menu might insist that this smoothie includes plain yogurt, today we make our clone without it.

1 ½ cups cranberry juice
½ cup frozen whole strawberries
¼ cup frozen blueberries

2 scoops raspberry sherbet
1 cup ice

1. Combine all ingredients in a blender and blend on high speed until all the ice is crushed and the drink is smooth.

• Makes 1 24-ounce drink.

• • • •

JAMBA JUICE
ORANGE-A-PEEL

☆   ✌   💣   ✎   ☯   ✂   ☞

Pick your juice wisely. For this smoothie Jamba Juice squeezes whole oranges with a handy orange squeezing machine in each store. So if it's the addicting taste of the real thing you're shooting for, be sure to get your orange juice freshly squeezed or squish some out yourself.

1 ½ cups fresh orange juice
⅔ cup frozen whole strawberries
1 sliced banana

2 scoops fat-free vanilla frozen
  yogurt
1 cup ice

1. Combine all ingredients in a blender and blend on high speed until all the ice is crushed and the drink is smooth.

• MAKES 1 24-OUNCE DRINK.

• • • •

JAMBA JUICE
PEACH PLEASURE

Jamba Juice got its start as "Juice Club" in San Luis Obispo, California. Early success with healthy food and juice blends led to quick growth with more stores and eventually a name change in 1995. The company claims "Jamba" means "to celebrate," just as your tastebuds do when they get a load of a smoothie like the one this recipe clones. It uses an entire can of Kern's peach nectar plus frozen peaches, banana, and some orange sherbet. Tastebuds, party on.

12 ounces Kern's peach nectar
  (1 can)
1 cup frozen peaches

½ ripe banana
2 scoops orange sherbet
1 cup ice

1. Combine all ingredients in a blender and blend on high speed until all the ice is crushed and the drink is smooth.

• MAKES 1 24-OUNCE DRINK.

• • • •

TOP SECRET RECIPES
VERSION OF
LIPTON BRISK ICED TEA

Here's a great technique for re-creating the lemony zing in a can of Brisk Iced Tea that'll make those angry little celebrity puppets in the commercials even angrier. Kool-Aid lemonade drink mix has the perfect mixture of citric acid and lemon juice solids to help us effortlessly clone this one over and over again. Puppets don't scare us.

3 Lipton tea bags (regular size)
I cup plus 2 tablespoons
   granulated sugar

½ teaspoon Kool-Aid lemonade
   unsweetened drink mix

1. Bring 2 quarts of water to a boil in a large saucepan. Add the tea bags and remove the pan from the heat. Let the tea steep for at least an hour.
2. Pour the granulated sugar and Kool-Aid drink mix into a 2-quart pitcher. Add the tea and stir so that the sugar dissolves. Add additional water if necessary to bring the tea to the 2-quart mark on the pitcher. Chill well before serving.

• MAKES 2 QUARTS.

• • • •

McDONALD'S SHAKES

Forty million customers get a dose of Mickey D's fast food every day. That also happens to be the exact same number of Americans who snore every night. Coincidence? But seriously, with all those daily McDonald's fans, you have to figure that at least a million or so go for one of the chain's three standard flavors of thick shakes: vanilla, chocolate, or strawberry (as for the special Shamrock Shake, we'll talk about that one in the next recipe). The clone recipes here are quick since each one requires just three simple ingredients and a blender to mix it all up. How McEasy is that? Throw everything in a blender and press a button—the one on the right. And if you want your shake thicker, just stash it in the freezer for a while.

CHOCOLATE SHAKE
2 cups vanilla ice cream
1 1/4 cups low-fat milk

2 tablespoons chocolate flavor
   Nesquik mix

STRAWBERRY SHAKE
2 cups vanilla ice cream
1 1/4 cups low-fat milk

3 tablespoons strawberry flavor
   Nesquik mix

VANILLA SHAKE
2 cups vanilla ice cream
1 1/4 cups low-fat milk

3 tablespoons sugar

1. Combine all ingredients for the shake flavor of your choice in a blender and mix on high speed until smooth. Stop blender, stir if necessary, and blend again to help combine the ingredients.
2. Pour into two 12-ounce cups.

- SERVES 2.

•   •   •   •

McDONALD'S SHAMROCK SHAKE

You'll find it very easy to re-create the flavors of McDonald's perennial St. Patrick's Day shake using only four ingredients. The two that make this holiday shake unique are the mint extract and green food coloring. Make sure your extract says "mint" and not "peppermint." And if you don't want shakes that are green like the real ones, you can certainly leave out the food coloring. After all, it's only for looks. Now you can sip on a Shamrock any time of the year. Blarney!

2 cups vanilla ice cream
1 ¼ cups low-fat milk

¼ teaspoon mint extract (not peppermint)
8 drops green food coloring

1. Combine all ingredients in a blender and blend on high speed until smooth. Stop blender to stir with a spoon if necessary to help blend ice cream.
2. Pour into two 12-ounce cups and serve each with a straw.

• SERVES 2.

• • • •

TOP SECRET RECIPES
VERSION OF
ORANGE JULIUS
BANANA JULIUS

It may be called Banana Julius, but there's also a little orange juice in there. Make sure your bananas are ripe for this clone so you get a nice sweet drink with the perfect thickness.

½ cup orange juice
3 tablespoons pasteurized egg
   white or egg substitute
1 teaspoon vanilla

¼ cup sugar
2 medium ripe bananas
3 cups ice

1. Combine all ingredients except bananas and ice in a blender and blend on high speed for 15 seconds or until sugar is dissolved.
2. Add bananas and ice and blend until ice is crushed. Pour into two 16-ounce glasses, add a straw and serve.

• MAKES 2 REGULAR-SIZE DRINKS.

• • • •

TOP SECRET RECIPES
VERSION OF
ORANGE JULIUS STRAWBERRY-BANANA CLASSIC SMOOTHIE

☆   ✌   💣   ✏   🎱   ✂   ☞

As the trend for fruit smoothies developed in the 1990s, the Orange Julius company didn't want to be left out. After all, Orange Julius developed what was the first smoothies on the block with the original Orange Julius blended drink back in 1926. But as thicker smoothie drinks of more complex blends became popular, Orange Julius set out to put its own twist on the fruity beverage by using a special additive called "coconut-almond compound" (and then trademarked a unique spelling of the word "smoothie" using a "Y"). In addition to a scoop of the compound that's added to the original Orange Julius drinks, servers add a scoop of this new powder to the drink. In that secret powder are some thickening agents such as powdered egg whites and flavors that include coconut and almond. So, here now is how you can clone your own version of the most popular flavor of the chain's Classic Smoothie using common coconut syrup and almond extract as part of your own secret "compound."

½ cup orange juice
3 tablespoons pasteurized egg
    white or egg substitute
1 teaspoon vanilla
¼ cup sugar
¼ cup milk

¼ cup coconut syrup (such as
    Coco Lopez)
¼ teaspoon almond extract
2 medium ripe bananas
1 10-ounce box frozen
    strawberries in syrup, thawed
3 cups ice

1. Combine all ingredients except banana, strawberries, and ice in a blender and blend on high speed for 15 seconds or until sugar is dissolved.
2. Add banana, strawberries and ice and blend until ice is crushed. Pour into two 16-ounce glasses, add a straw, and serve.

- MAKES 2 REGULAR-SIZE DRINKS.

•   •   •   •

ORANGE JULIUS, PINEAPPLE JULIUS, & STRAWBERRY JULIUS

Coffeehouses have replaced many of the old Orange Julius stands, but there's still a nostalgic group of us who long for the frothy juice drinks invented decades ago by Julius Freed. Today Orange Julius has tailored its business to meet the changing demands of customers by including several varieties of fruit drinks and updated smoothies on its menu. But it's the foamy fruit juice creation developed in the late twenties that made the company famous, and that's what I've cloned here in improved versions of the recipes found in *Top Secret Recipes* and *More Top Secret Recipes*. The flavor and consistency are better now, plus we use the blender to dissolve the sugar before adding the ice. Use pasteurized egg whites found packaged in your local supermarket or just use egg substitute, which is also made from pasteurized egg whites.

ORANGE JULIUS

1 ¼ cups orange juice
1 cup water
3 tablespoons egg white or egg substitute

1 teaspoon vanilla extract
¼ cup granulated sugar
1 ½ cups ice

1. Combine all of the ingredients except ice in a blender and blend on high speed for 15 to 20 seconds or until the sugar is dissolved. Add the ice and blend for another 10 to 15 seconds or so, until ice is mostly crushed yet still a bit coarse.

- MAKES 2 16-OUNCE DRINKS.

PINEAPPLE JULIUS

1 8-ounce can crushed pineapple
  in juice
1 cup water
3 tablespoons egg white or egg
  substitute

1 teaspoon vanilla extract
1/4 cup granulated sugar
1 1/2 cups ice

1. Combine all of the ingredients except ice in a blender and blend on high speed for 15 to 20 seconds or until the sugar is dissolved. Add the ice and blend for another 10 to 15 seconds or so, until ice is mostly crushed yet still a bit coarse.

• MAKES 2 16-OUNCE DRINKS.

STRAWBERRY JULIUS

1 cup frozen sliced strawberries,
  thawed (1 10-ounce box)
1 cup water
3 tablespoons egg white or egg
  substitute

1 teaspoon vanilla extract
1/4 cup granulated sugar
1 1/2 cups ice

1. Combine all of the ingredients except ice in a blender and blend on high speed for 15 to 20 seconds or until the sugar is dissolved. Add the ice and blend for another 10 to 15 seconds or so, until ice is mostly crushed yet still a bit coarse.

• MAKES 2 16-OUNCE DRINKS.

•   •   •   •

SNAPPLE ICED TEA

Snapple was selling juices for five years—since 1982—before the fruity line of teas was rolled out. Just five years after that, Snapple was selling more tea in the U.S. than Lipton or Nestea. Today, even though Snapple sells over 50 different bottled beverages, the iced teas are still the most successful products in the line. But not all the fruity flavors of tea were hits. Cranberry, strawberry, and orange are now extinct, so those flavors can only be enjoyed by making versions of your own at home with these simple formulas. I've also got lemon and peach flavors here, Snapple's two top-selling products, plus raspberry, another big seller.

Included here are improved versions of iced tea clones printed in the book *More Top Secret Recipes*.

CRANBERRY ICED TEA

2 quarts (8 cups) water
2 Lipton tea bags
¾ cup granulated sugar

⅓ cup plus 2 tablespoons bottled lemon juice
2 tablespoons Ocean Spray cranberry juice cocktail concentrate

DIET LEMON ICED TEA

2 quarts (8 cups) water
2 Lipton tea bags

16 1-gram packages Equal sweetener
⅓ cup bottled lemon juice

LEMON ICED TEA

2 quarts (8 cups) water
2 Lipton tea bags

¾ cup granulated sugar
⅓ cup bottled lemon juice

ORANGE ICED TEA

2 quarts (8 cups) water
2 Lipton tea bags
¾ cup granulated sugar

⅓ cup bottled lemon juice
⅛ teaspoon orange extract

PEACH ICED TEA

2 quarts (8 cups) water
2 Lipton tea bags
¾ cup granulated sugar

¼ cup plus 1 tablespoon bottled
  lemon juice
3 tablespoons Torani peach
  flavoring syrup

Alternate clone: Rather than Torani peach flavoring use one 12-ounce can Kern's peach nectar, and 3 tablespoons lemon juice instead of ¼ cup plus 1 tablespoon lemon juice.

RASPBERRY ICED TEA

2 quarts (8 cups) water
2 Lipton tea bags
¾ cup granulated sugar

¼ cup plus 1 tablespoon lemon
  juice
2 tablespoons Torani raspberry
  flavoring syrup

STRAWBERRY ICED TEA

2 quarts (8 cups) water
2 Lipton tea bags
¾ cup granulated sugar

⅓ cup lemon juice
1 tablespoon strawberry extract

1. Bring water to a rapid boil in a large saucepan.
2. Turn off heat, add tea bags, cover saucepan and let the tea steep for 1 to 2 hours.
3. Pour the sugar into a 2-quart pitcher, and then add the tea. The water will still be warm and the sugar (or sweetener if making the diet tea) should dissolve easily.
4. Add the lemon juice and fruit flavoring ingredients. Stir, cover and chill.

• MAKES 2 QUARTS.

• • • •

TOP SECRET RECIPES
VERSION OF
SONIC DRIVE-IN STRAWBERRY CHEESECAKE SHAKE

☆   ✌   💣   ✎   ☯   ✂   ☞

The cool thing about this Top Secret Recipe is that many of the ingredients come in a kit designed for making strawberry cheesecake. Find Jell-O® No Bake Strawberry Cheesecake mix near the puddings in your supermarket, and you have half of the ingredients locked up. Inside the box are three separate packets: strawberries, the cheesecake mix for flavoring, and graham cracker crumbs to sprinkle over the top of your shake as they do at the restaurant. To complete your clone, you'll just need some vanilla ice cream, a cup of milk, and a little whipped cream. The recipe below makes two regular-size shakes, but you can make another two drinks with the remaining strawberries that come in the mix. If you thaw out some frozen, sweetened strawberries (those syrupy strawberries that come in a box), you can make as many as 8 more shake clones with the remaining cheesecake mix powder and graham cracker crumbs.

1 cup milk
3 cups vanilla ice cream
1/2 cup strawberries and syrup
    (from Jell-O® No Bake
    Strawberry Cheesecake kit)
3 tablespoons cheesecake mix
    powder (from cheesecake kit)

ON TOP
canned whipped cream
2 teaspoons graham cracker
    crumbs (from cheesecake kit)

1. Combine milk, ice cream, strawberries, and cheesecake mix in a blender and mix on high speed until smooth. Pour into two 12-ounce glasses.
2. Garnish the top with a squirt of whipped cream from a can and about a teaspoon of graham cracker crumbs from the cheesecake kit. Serve each shake with a straw.

- MAKES 2 REGULAR-SIZE DRINKS.

• • • •

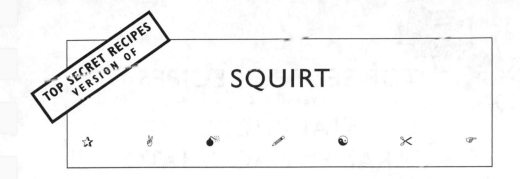

SQUIRT

Soda and citrus flavors were combined in 1938 to create a grapefruit-lemon soft drink that would later inspire Coke to make Fresca. Fresca was popular when it was introduced in the 60s since it was artificially sweetened and contained no calories. That was back when diet drinks were just catching on. Nowadays just about every soda comes in a diet version, and Fresca sales have slipped, despite a tweaking of the formula in the early 90s.

Squirt continues to hold on to a loyal cult following, with many who claim the soda is the only true cure for a hangover. To clone it, just add real bottled white grapefruit juice, along with a little Kool-Aid mix for a lemony tang, to the simple syrup recipe. Chill the syrup and soda water until cold and get ready to make a dozen cups' worth of citrus soda at home.

1 ½ cups granulated sugar   1 cup corn syrup
⅛ teaspoon Kool-Aid lemonade   1 ½ cups white grapefruit juice
   unsweetened drink mix
¼ cup boiling water   12 cups cold soda water

1. Combine sugar and Kool-Aid mix with the boiling water in a medium pitcher or bowl. Stir well. Add corn syrup and stir.
2. Add grapefruit juice and stir until sugar crystals are dissolved. Cover and chill for several hours until cold.
3. To make the soda, stir the syrup first, then add ¼ cup of cold syrup to 1 cup of cold soda water (1 to 4 ratio). Stir gently, drop in some ice, and serve.

• MAKES 12 10-OUNCE SERVINGS.

• • • •

TOP SECRET RECIPES
VERSION OF
STARBUCKS
CARAMEL MACCHIATO

☆   ✌   💣   ✏   ☯   ✂   ☞

If you've got an espresso/cappuccino machine, you're well on your way to re-creating a top-choice Starbucks coffee drink. For the caramel part, you can use any caramel sauce that you find in the grocery store near the ice-cream toppings. Pick your favorite. Just note that to make this recipe work best, you'll only need 3 tablespoons of a richer caramel sauce (like the stuff Starbucks uses), but more like 4 tablespoons of a lighter sauce (such as fat-free Smuckers). For the vanilla syrup you can use the bottled syrups, such as those made by Torani, or just whip up your own clone from scratch. By the way, if you want to make this clone super accurate, pick up bottles of the authentic vanilla syrup and caramel sauce sold in Starbucks stores.

VANILLA SYRUP

2 cups water
1 ½ cups granulated sugar
¾ teaspoon vanilla extract

½ cup fresh espresso
8 ounces milk, steamed with foam
3 to 4 tablespoons caramel sauce

1. You can use vanilla syrup from a bottle for the drink or make your own vanilla syrup following this Top Secret Recipe: Simply combine 2 cups water and 1 ½ cups sugar in a medium saucepan and bring to a boil. Reduce heat and simmer for 5 minutes, then add ¾ teaspoon vanilla extract. Remove from heat and cool. Store in a covered container.

2. To make your coffee drink, add two tablespoons of vanilla syrup to a 16-ounce glass. Add ½ cup fresh brewed espresso followed by 8 ounces of steamed milk.
3. Add 3 to 4 tablespoons caramel sauce to the drink. Stir before drinking.

* MAKES ONE 16-OUNCE DRINK (GRANDE SIZE).

• • • •

STARBUCKS
FROZEN FRAPPUCCINO

☆　　✌　　💣　　✏　　☯　　✂　　☞

It was in 1995 that Starbucks stores started selling this frozen drink, one of the company's most successful new products. The Frappuccino is blended with strong coffee, sugar, a dairy base, and ice. Each one is made to order and each one is guaranteed to give you a throbbing brain freeze if you sip too hard. The drinks come in several different varieties, the most popular of which I've cloned here for your frontal lobe–pounding, caffeine-buzzing pleasure.

Make double-strength coffee by measuring 2 tablespoons of ground coffee per cup (serving) in your coffee maker. The drink will be even more authentic if you use Starbucks beans and grind them yourself just before brewing.

COFFEE

¾ cup double-strength coffee, cold　　3 tablespoons granulated sugar
1 cup low-fat milk　　2 cups ice

1. Make double-strength coffee by brewing with twice the coffee required by your coffee maker. That should be 2 tablespoons of ground coffee per each cup of coffee. Chill before using.
2. To make drink, combine all ingredients in a blender and blend on high speed until ice is crushed and drink is smooth. Pour into two 16-ounce glasses, and serve with a straw.

- MAKES 2 "GRANDE" DRINKS.

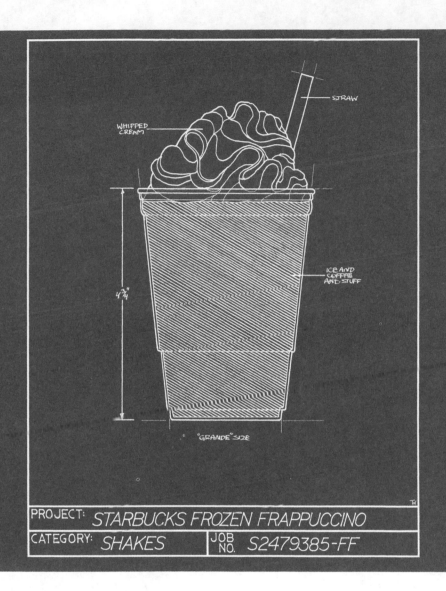

STRAW

WHIPPED
CREAM

ICE AND
COFFEE
AND STUFF

4¾"

"GRANDE" SIZE

TW

PROJECT:	STARBUCKS FROZEN FRAPPUCCINO	
CATEGORY: SHAKES	JOB NO.	S2479385-FF

CARAMEL

For this version, add 3 tablespoons of caramel topping to the original recipe and prepare as described. Top each glass with whipped cream and drizzle additional caramel over the whipped cream.

MOCHA

For this version, add 3 tablespoons Hershey's chocolate syrup to the original recipe and prepare as described. Top each glass with whipped cream, if desired.

•   •   •   •

TOP SECRET RECIPES

VERSION OF

STARBUCKS
GINGERBREAD LATTE

☆   ✌   💣   ✏   ☯   ✂   ☞

As the winter holidays come around, so too does this incredible latte from Starbucks. Into the coffee house's basic latte recipe go a few pumps of special gingerbread-flavored syrup, and we soon experience the combined sensation of munching on a ginger-bread cookie while sipping hot, milky java. Nice! To re-create the experience at home, holidays or not, all we have to do is make our own gingerbread syrup with a few common ingredients. When the syrup is done, simply brew some espresso in your espresso machine, steam some hot milk, and throw it all in cup. Top off your latte with whipped cream and a dash of nutmeg as they do at the store, and you'll fool anyone with this hot little clone. By the way, this recipe is for a single grande-size latte, but you'll have enough syrup left over for as many as seven drinks.

GINGERBREAD SYRUP

2 cups water
1 1/2 cups granulated sugar
2 1/2 teaspoons ground ginger
1/2 teaspoon ground cinnamon

1/2 teaspoon vanilla extract

1/2 cup fresh espresso
8 ounces milk, steamed (with a
    little foam)

GARNISH

whipped cream

ground nutmeg

1. Make the gingerbread syrup by combining water, sugar, ginger, cinnamon, and vanilla in a medium saucepan. Be sure the pan is not too small or the mixture could easily bubble over.

2. Bring mixture to a boil, then reduce heat and simmer syrup, uncovered, for 15 minutes. Remove the syrup from the heat when it's done and slap a lid on it.

3. Make a double shot of espresso ($\frac{1}{2}$ cup), using an espresso machine. Use the machine to steam 8 ounces of milk, or heat up the milk in the microwave if your machine does not foam and steam milk.

4. Make your latte by first adding $\frac{1}{2}$ cup espresso to a 16-ounce cup. Add $\frac{1}{4}$ cup gingerbread syrup, followed by the steamed milk. Stir.

5. Top off the drink with a dollop of whipped cream and a sprinkle of nutmeg.

- MAKES 1 16-OUNCE DRINK (GRANDE SIZE).

•　•　•　•

TOP SECRET RECIPES
VERSION OF
STARBUCKS MOCHA
COCONUT FRAPPUCCINO

☆　　　✌　　　💣　　　✏　　　☯　　　✂　　　☞

Here's one of Starbucks' newest delights that's like a cold Mounds bar in a cup with a caffeine kick thrown in for extra buzzing. Find shredded coconut in the baking aisle and toast ½ cup of it (Store the leftover coconut in the fridge.). You'll use most of the toasted coconut in the blender, but save a little for the garnish when the drinks are done.

½ cup shredded coconut
¾ cup cold double-strength coffee
1 cup low-fat milk

⅓ cup Hershey's chocolate syrup
3 tablespoons granulated sugar
2 cups ice

GARNISH
whipped cream

1. Preheat oven to 300 degrees. Spread shredded coconut on a baking sheet and toast coconut in the oven. Stir the coconut around every 10 minutes or so for even browning. After 25 to 30 minutes the shredded coconut should be light brown. Allow to cool.
2. Make double-strength coffee by brewing with twice the coffee required by your coffee maker. That should be 2 tablespoons of ground coffee per each cup of coffee. Chill before using.
3. To make the drinks, combine cold coffee, milk, ⅓ cup of the

toasted coconut, ⅓ cup chocolate syrup, and sugar in a blender. Blend for 15 to 20 seconds to dissolve sugar. Add ice and blend until ice is crushed and the drink is smooth. Pour drinks into two 16-ounce glasses. Garnish each drink with whipped cream, a drizzle of chocolate, and a pinch of some of the remaining toasted coconut. Add a straw to each one.

- MAKES 2 16-OUNCE DRINKS (GRANDE SIZE).

• • • •

YOO-HOO CHOCOLATE DRINK (IMPROVED)

Watching his wife can tomatoes inspired Natale Olivieri to create a bottled chocolate drink with a long shelf life back in the early 1920s. When New York Yankee great Yogi Berra later met Natale and tasted his drink, he was an instant fan, and went on to help raise the funds that helped make Yoo-hoo a national success.

I cloned this drink in the first book, *Top Secret Recipes*, but have since discovered an improved technique. Using a blender to mix the drink, as instructed in that version, adds too much unnecessary foam. So here now is a revised recipe that you shake to mix, that could fool even the most devoted Yoo-hoo fanatics.

¾ cup nonfat dry milk
3 tablespoons Nesquik chocolate
   drink mix

1 ½ cups cold water

Combine all ingredients in a container or jar with a lid. Shake until dry milk is dissolved. Drink immediately or chill in refrigerator.

• MAKES 1 14-OUNCE DRINK.

•   •   •   •

LITE

Introduction

I don't care who you are, or how healthy you claim to eat, or how much you boast you never divert your car in a rush through a fast-food drive-thru joint for a quickie. It's a sure bet that you have at least one favorite, sinfully delicious food that you often crave, that's high in fat and calories. I'm talking about the kind of food that gives you an ecstatic rush as you eat it, and practically gets you high from the oral gratification. I'm talking about the type of grub that washes over your tastebuds in that all-too-short belly-stuffing journey, making you close your eyes for just a moment while you chew to let out a little "mmmm." It's the euphoric palatal experience that ends much too soon. And it's the experience that's quickly followed by the post-nosh guilt, as you realize the pants are a bit more snug today, and will be a lot more snug tomorrow.

We've all been informed by the scads of nutritionists and dieticians on anti-fat crusades that if we want to stay fit, we're going to have to turn away from the greasy goodies and start looking in the direction of "low-fat alternatives." I've heard it, you've heard it; and as much as I don't want to hear it anymore, I know I will, and so will you. And the real bummer is, it's all true.

This news was even more of a bummer in the early days of the move away from foods higher in fat. Back then, smart, tasty alternatives were hard to come by. Food manufacturers were coming out with products that tasted only slightly better than potting soil. Maybe that's why when we hear the words "low-fat" or "fat-free" today, while we know it's the right thing to choose, a part of us is thinking "yech!"

But the good news is that in the last several years, fat-reduced foods have been much improved. There are many more better-tasting staple products such as mayonnaise, cheese, sour cream, and butter-flavored additives available than ever before. With these products and the skillful use of thickeners, starches, and fruit purees, it's now easier to enjoy foods that taste as though they're pumped with fat, when the nutrition facts say otherwise. The tricks we're learning to remove the fat from our meals and snacks, both in the food production plants and in the home kitchens, are quickly turning the "yechs" into "yums."

Food manufacturers are realizing that creating products that address our nutritional concerns *and* that satisfy our strongest, most insatiable cravings and are taking a quick trip down mega-profits street. Millions and millions of dollars have been spent on reduced-fat product development, and for conversion of previously higher-fat products to trendy lower-fat versions. Just look for the green packages. Not only can these healthier alternatives be found in growing numbers in supermarket aisles, but fast-food outlets and restaurant chains have also been making lower-fat choices available. It's the latest food craze, and the cost to the consumer is usually high. Ironically, many times the lower-fat or light versions of a product are more expensive or smaller in size (or both) than the higher-fat counterpart.

And as these food companies with their "healthy alternatives" are wrestling for shelf space and customers, scores of cookbook authors have jumped into the fray. Low-fat cookbooks have been some of the most popular books sold in recent years, with some scoring high on bestseller lists. Many of these books have some great ideas and delicious recipes (and some definitely don't), but not one gives us recipes for the type of food for which we really want homemade reduced-fat versions. I'm talking about the kind of food that sales figures show is the most popular food—convenience food, fast food, and junk food. America's favorite foods.

If you are discouraged to find that supermarkets are filled with record numbers of overly expensive and not-so-fresh low-fat products; or if you have wished for reduced-fat versions of your favorite brand-name foods; or if you have yearned for recipes to make at home that taste good rather than tasting low-fat, then I'm hoping to make your day.

This section will show you how to make low-fat and fat-free food at home that will taste just like these reduced-fat products you find in restaurants and supermarkets.

When creating these clone recipes I've made every attempt to keep fat gram numbers the same as the real item. This was not always easy. In fact, it was rarely easy, and next to the boxes, cans, and bottles of ingredients on the kitchen counter could always be found a well-stained calculator, ready to spew running fat totals.

You can now re-create your favorite low-fat and fat-free foods with everyday ingredients. This gives you the opportunity to enjoy a product that may not be available where you live, and, in most cases, you will find that creating the product at home from scratch saves a significant amount of money versus buying the real thing. Plus, fresh food is always better than the packaged stuff, which may contain preservatives.

Special Author's Note

The nutritional facts (fat and calories) included with each of the clone recipes were compiled with the help of manufacturers' labels, and fat gram and a calorie-content reference material. Care was taken to make very accurate calculations, but these numbers can vary slightly from brand to brand for certain ingredients. In these cases, I used the numbers from the most popular brands available.

Most of the fat and calorie information for the manufacturers' original products comes from that company's printed nutritional information materials produced by corporate offices. Any nutrition information that was not available was calculated based on full-fat versions of the low-fat clone recipe. When these are estimated figures, I have indicated so.

As with my other recipes, none of these has been created with the cooperation of the manufacturers. No manufacturers have endorsed this work, but I thank each and every one of them for creating the great food that has become so popular as to warrant its inclusion here.

Please know that I did not swipe, heist, or bribe, or otherwise obtain any formulas through coercion or illegal means. However, I do admit to occasionally kidnapping samples of the restaurant food in doggie bags (after paying for them, of course), and transporting it to my hardly secret laboratory for further examination and experimentation.

While the product dissections may have appeared cruel, I assure you that no foodstuffs were harmed in the creation of this book.

So Let's Get Cooking!

Now, if you're ready to munch out on some fat-saving clones, get out some ingredients and measuring spoons and tie on that apron. Or, better yet, start being really, really nice to the person you intend to persuade to do all of the cooking for you.

Whoever decides to give these recipes a try will find the recipes easy to follow, even for the novice chef. So dive right in, and get ready to enjoy lower-fat clones that are so good you don't even miss the fat.

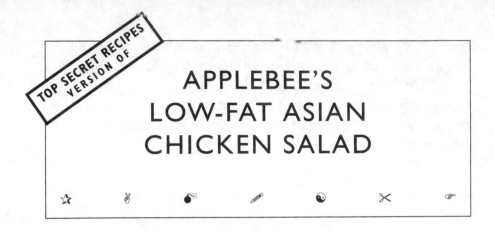

APPLEBEE'S LOW-FAT ASIAN CHICKEN SALAD

My new diet plan is called the Chopsticks Diet. It requires that you use only chopsticks to eat everything: spaghetti, peas, hamburgers, cookies, ice cream, salads—whatever. As the food slips off the chopsticks, the pounds slip off of you. It's especially effective if you've never used chopsticks before. For those who can use them well, you've got to switch to the other hand.

As the seasons change, so does the menu at this popular, casual, restaurant chain. You'll find this item in the "Low-Fat and Fabulous" column of the menu during the summer months where it's been a favorite since 1997. As with any salad, the waistline violator is the traditionally fat-filled dressing that is drizzled in gobs over the top of very healthy greens (a tablespoon of dressing usually contains around ten to twelve grams of fat). So if we can just figure out a cool way to make the dressing fat-free, we're well on our way to making a huge salad—four of them to be exact—with only twelve grams of fat on each plate. Most of those grams come from the chicken breast, and the crunchy chow mein noodles pick up the rest.

Just be sure to plan ahead when you make this one. The chicken should marinate for a few hours if you want it to taste like the original. Hope you're hungry.

1 cup teriyaki marinade   4 skinless chicken breast fillets

FAT-FREE ASIAN DRESSING
2 cups water   1 teaspoon salt
1/2 cup granulated sugar   1/4 teaspoon garlic powder
3 tablespoons dry pectin   1/4 teaspoon ground black
1 tablespoon white vinegar   pepper
1/2 teaspoon soy sauce   1/4 teaspoon paprika

8 cups chopped romaine   2 cups shredded carrots
   lettuce   1 cup chopped green onion
8 cups chopped iceberg   1 1/3 cups crispy chow mein
   lettuce   noodles
3 cups shredded red cabbage
3 cups shredded green cabbage

1. Combine teriyaki marinade and chicken breasts in a medium bowl or resealable plastic bag. Marinate chicken for 3 to 4 hours.
2. Prepare the dressing by combining all of the ingredients in a small saucepan over medium heat. Bring mixture to a rolling boil while stirring often with a whisk, then remove the pan from the heat to cool. When the dressing has cooled, pour it into a covered container and chill.
3. When chicken breasts have marinated, preheat barbecue grill to high heat. Grill chicken for 3 to 4 minutes per side or until done.
4. Combine the romaine and iceberg lettuce, red and green cabbage, and 1 cup of shredded carrots in a large bowl with the dressing. Toss well.
5. Divide the tossed greens among four plates. Sprinkle 1/4 cup of green onions over each salad, followed by 1/3 cup of crispy chow mein noodles.
6. When the chicken breasts are done, slice each one, width-

wise, into bite-size pieces. Sprinkle the sliced chicken breasts over each salad.

7. Place a ¼-cup pile of shredded carrots in the center of each salad.

- SERVES 4 AS AN ENTRÉE.

Nutrition Facts

SERVING SIZE—1 SALAD	FAT (PER SERVING)—12 G
TOTAL SERVINGS—4	CALORIES (PER SERVING)—575

• • • •

APPLEBEE'S
LOW-FAT & FABULOUS
BROWNIE SUNDAE

☆　　✌　　💣　　✏　　☯　　✂　　☞

The Applebee's chain is now the world's largest casual dining restaurant, with over one thousand units in seven countries and forty-eight states. In less than four years, the chain has doubled in size. That's great if you're a restaurant chain, but put enough fat-filled desserts in your belly, and you'll double in size, too.

That's why we're happy to see items like this one on the menu. It tastes like a decadent, guilty pleasure, but it actually contains only four grams of fat per serving. This is possible because the brownie "pie" is made in a special way using a combination of low-fat and fat-free chocolates, some egg whites, and just a bit of shortening. Grab yourself some fat-free frozen yogurt, and share this one with eight hungry friends.

LOW-FAT BROWNIE

2 egg whites	1 teaspoon vanilla
¾ cup granulated sugar	1 ½ cups all-purpose flour
2 tablespoons shortening	¼ cup cocoa
½ cup Hershey's chocolate syrup	¾ teaspoon salt
½ cup fudge topping	¼ teaspoon baking soda
¼ cup warm water	2 teaspoons chopped walnuts

9 scoops fat-free vanilla frozen yogurt

chocolate syrup, heated

1. Preheat oven to 350°F.
2. Make the brownie cake by whipping the egg whites in a large

bowl (not plastic) with an electric mixer until they become thick.

3. Add the sugar to the egg whites and continue beating until the mixture forms soft peaks.
4. To the egg white and sugar mixture, add the shortening, chocolate syrup, fudge, water, and vanilla.
5. In a separate bowl, combine the flour, cocoa, salt, and baking soda.
6. While beating the wet mixture, slowly add the dry mixture and mix until smooth.
7. Lightly grease a 9-inch pie pan with shortening. Pour the brownie batter into the pan and sprinkle the chopped walnuts over the top. Bake for 35 minutes or until a toothpick poked into the center comes out clean.
8. When the brownie pie has cooled a bit, slice it into 9 equal pie-shaped portions.
9. Arrange a slice of the low-fat brownie pie on a plate next to a scoop of vanilla frozen yogurt.
10. Drizzle the warmed chocolate sauce over the top of the brownie and frozen yogurt, and serve.

• MAKES 9 DESSERTS.

Nutrition Facts

SERVING SIZE—1 DESSERT   FAT (PER SERVING)—4 G
TOTAL SERVINGS—9   CALORIES (PER SERVING)—424

• • • •

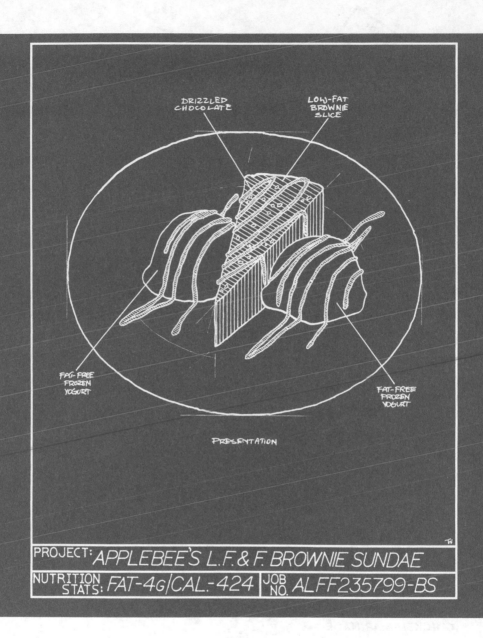

DRIZZLED CHOCOLATE

LOW-FAT BROWNIE SLICE

FAT-FREE FROZEN YOGURT

FAT-FREE FROZEN YOGURT

PRESENTATION

PROJECT: *APPLEBEE'S L.F. & F. BROWNIE SUNDAE*

NUTRITION STATS: *FAT-4g/CAL.-424*

JOB NO. *ALFF235799-BS*

APPLEBEE'S LOW-FAT BLACKENED CHICKEN SALAD

The big secret to keeping a tasty salad low in fat is to develop a dressing that's low in fat, or even better, fat-free. This recipe clones one of Applebee's most popular low-fat dishes from its "Low-Fat and Fabulous" selections. It's one dish that customers have raved about, because it's so delicious it just doesn't seem possible it could contain only 7 grams of fat. The burst of flavor from the marinated and blackened chicken helps to hide the lack of fat. And the dressing, which is made so incredibly light by using a fat-free mayonnaise base, is indescribably delicious.

DRESSING

¼ cup fat-free mayonnaise
¼ cup Grey Poupon Dijon
　　mustard
1 tablespoon prepared mustard

¼ cup honey
1 tablespoon white vinegar
⅛ teaspoon paprika

CHICKEN MARINADE

1 cup water
3 tablespoons lime juice
2 tablespoons soy sauce

½ tablespoon Worcestershire
　　sauce

2 chicken breast fillets

CAJUN SPICE BLEND

½ tablespoon salt
1 teaspoon sugar
1 teaspoon paprika
1 teaspoon onion powder

1 teaspoon black pepper
½ teaspoon garlic powder
½ teaspoon cayenne pepper
½ teaspoon white pepper

½ tablespoon butter

SALAD

8 cups chopped iceberg lettuce
½ cup shredded red cabbage
½ cup shredded carrot
½ cup shredded fat-free
   mozzarella cheese

½ cup shredded fat-free cheddar
   cheese
1 hard-boiled egg white, diced
1 large tomato, diced

1. Make the dressing by first combining the mayonnaise with the mustards in a small bowl. Whisk thoroughly until the ingredients are well combined. Mix in the honey, then the vinegar and paprika. Store the dressing in a covered container in the refrigerator until the salads are ready.

2. Combine the water, lime juice, soy sauce, and Worcestershire in a medium bowl, and stir. Add the chicken fillets to the marinade, cover the bowl, and keep it in the refrigerator for several hours. Marinate the chicken overnight, if you've got the time.

3. When the chicken is well marinated, preheat a frying pan or skillet (an iron skillet, if you've got it) over medium/high heat. Also, preheat your barbecue grill to medium/high heat.

4. Combine the spices for the Cajun spice blend in a small bowl. Sprinkle a teaspoon of the spice blend over one side of each chicken fillet. Cover the entire top surface of the chicken with an even coating of the spice blend.

5. Melt the butter in the hot pan, then sauté the chicken fillets for 2 to 3 minutes on the side with the spices. While the first

side cooks, sprinkle another teaspoon of spice over the top of each chicken breast, coating that side as you did the other. Flip the chicken over, and sauté for another 2 to 3 minutes. The surface of the chicken should end up with a charred-looking black coating.

6. Finish the chicken off on your barbecue grill. Grill each breast on both sides for 2 to 3 minutes, or until done.

7. While the chicken is cooking, prepare the salads by splitting the lettuce into two large bowls. Toss in the red cabbage and carrots. Mix the cheeses together, then top the salad with the cheese blend and hard-boiled egg white. Sprinkle half of the diced tomato over each salad.

8. Slice the chicken breasts crosswise to ½-inch-thick pieces. Spread the chicken over the top of the salads and serve immediately with dressing on the side.

- SERVES 2 AS AN ENTRÉE.

Nutrition Facts

SERVING SIZE—1 SALAD   FAT (PER SERVING)—7G

TOTAL SERVINGS—2   CALORIES (PER SERVING)—420

• • • •

ARBY'S LIGHT MENU
ROAST CHICKEN DELUXE

Here's an awesome kitchen clone for a selection off of Arby's 3-item "Light Menu." As other fast food chains were zigging by creating giant gooey burgers with fat grams in the 40-plus range, this 3,100-outlet roast beef sandwich chain opted to zag, offering a selection of scrumptious sandwiches with only 6 to 10 grams of fat each.

The secret to re-creating the special Arby's taste in the Roast Chicken Deluxe is in the marinade. Let your chicken soak in it for several hours, or even overnight, if you've got the patience. It also helps if you have a meat slicer to get that paper-thin, deli-style cut to the chicken. If you don't have a slicer, just do what I do. It's called the "poor man's meat slicer"—a very sharp knife and a steady hand.

CHICKEN MARINADE

2 tablespoons water	1/4 teaspoon paprika
1 tablespoon vegetable oil	1/8 teaspoon onion powder
2 teaspoons ketchup	1/8 teaspoon coarse black pepper
1/2 teaspoon sugar	1/8 teaspoon savory
1/2 teaspoon salt	dash garlic powder

2 chicken breast fillets	2 tablespoons light mayonnaise
butter-flavored spray or spread	1 medium tomato, sliced
4 whole wheat hamburger buns	1 cup shredded lettuce

1. First make the marinade for the chicken breasts. In a small bowl, combine all of the ingredients for the marinade and stir well. Add the chicken breasts to the bowl and cover. Marinate the chicken for several hours. Overnight is even better.
2. When you are ready to make the sandwiches, preheat the oven to 400 degrees. Prepare to roast the chicken breasts by removing them from the marinade and placing them in a foil-lined baking pan. Bake for 20 to 25 minutes or until the chicken is fully cooked. When the chicken is cool enough to handle, slice each breast very thinly with a sharp knife. If you have a meat slicer, that works even better.
3. Preheat a frying pan or griddle to medium heat. Apply butter-flavored spread or spray to the faces of the top and bottom wheat buns. Grill the bun faces lightly on the hot cooking surface until light brown.
4. Build each sandwich by first placing one-quarter of the sliced chicken on the bottom bun.
5. Spread mayonnaise on the face of the top bun.
6. Invert the top bun. On the bun, stack a tomato slice or two, then ¼ cup of lettuce on top of that.
7. Slap the top portion of the sandwich onto the bottom and serve while the chicken is still warm. Repeat the process to make the remaining sandwiches.

- MAKES 4 SANDWICHES.

Nutrition Facts

SERVING SIZE—1 SANDWICH   FAT (PER SERVING)—6.5G
TOTAL SERVINGS—4   CALORIES (PER SERVING)—201

• • • •

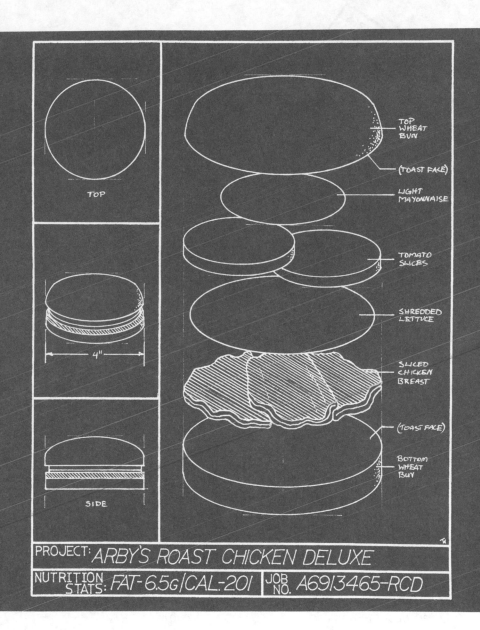

TOP

SIDE

4"

TOP
WHEAT
BUN

(TOAST FACE)

LIGHT
MAYONNAISE

TOMATO
SLICES

SHREDDED
LETTUCE

SLICED
CHICKEN
BREAST

(TOAST FACE)

BOTTOM
WHEAT
BUN

PROJECT: *ARBY'S ROAST CHICKEN DELUXE*

NUTRITION STATS: *FAT- 6.5G/CAL.-201*   JOB NO. *A6913465-RCD*

429

CALIFORNIA PIZZA KITCHEN DAKOTA SMASHED PEA & BARLEY SOUP

☆   ✌   💣   ✏   ☯   ✂   ☞

Got one of those cool hand blenders? You know, the kind of gadget that used to be pitched on those annoying yet compelling late-night infomercials? It comes in handy for this recipe, which requires the split peas to be smashed into a smooth consistency, just like the original. If you don't have a hand mixer, a standard blender works just fine. This soup is very tasty and very low in fat. And the barley gives it a special chunky consistency and added flavor that aren't found in most pea soups. If you want to go even lower in fat, use fat-free chicken broth instead of the regular stuff, then run in place with a can in each hand to burn some extra calories.

2 cups split peas
6 cups water
2 14½-ounce cans chicken broth
   (4 cups)
⅓ cup minced onion
1 large clove garlic, minced
2 teaspoons lemon juice
1 teaspoon salt
1 teaspoon granulated sugar

¼ teaspoon dried parsley
⅛ teaspoon white pepper
dash dried thyme
½ cup barley
6 cups water
2 medium carrots, diced (about
   1 cup)
½ stalk celery (¼ cup)

GARNISH
chopped green onion

1. Rinse and drain the split peas, then add them to a large pot with 6 cups of water, chicken broth, onion, garlic, lemon juice, salt, sugar, parsley, pepper, and thyme. Bring to a boil, then reduce heat and simmer for 75 to 90 minutes or until the peas are soft and the soup is thick.
2. While the peas are cooking, combine the barley with 6 cups of water, carrots, and celery in a saucepan. Bring to a boil, then reduce heat and also simmer for 75 to 90 minutes or until the barley is soft and most of the water has been absorbed.
3. When the split pea mixture has become a thick soup, use a handheld blender to puree the peas until the mixture is smooth. You may also use a standard blender or food processor for this step, pureeing the soup in batches. Alternately, if you like, you may skip this step, keeping the soup rather chunky. It's still good, just not as smooth as the real thing.
4. Drain the barley mixture in a sieve or colander and add it to the split pea mixture. Continue to simmer for about 15 minutes, stirring occasionally. Turn off the heat, cover the soup, and let it sit for 15 minutes before serving.

- MAKES 8 CUPS.

Nutrition Facts

SERVING SIZE—2 CUPS	FAT (PER SERVING)—3 G
TOTAL SERVINGS—4	CALORIES (PER SERVING)—450

• • • •

CALIFORNIA PIZZA KITCHEN VEGETARIAN PIZZA

Who needs to cook with animal parts when you can make a pizza taste like this? It's grilled veggies and mozzarella cheese stacked on a great clone for the chain's tasty honey-wheat dough. With regular mozzarella cheese, the total fat for three slices comes in at around nineteen grams, which is still much less than you'd get from, say, the pepperoni-topped variety (tipping the scales at about fifteen grams *per slice*). Just remember to prepare your dough a day before you plan to make the pizza. This way you'll get the best consistency in the final product. And one heck of a better clone.

HONEY-WHEAT DOUGH

⅓ cup plus 1 tablespoon warm
    water (105 to 115 degrees F)
1 tablespoon honey
¾ teaspoon yeast

⅔ cup bread flour
⅓ cup whole wheat flour
½ teaspoon salt
½ tablespoon olive oil

SAUCE

1 teaspoon olive oil
1 tablespoon minced white onion
1 clove garlic, minced
1 tomato, chopped
1 15-ounce can tomato sauce
2 teaspoons granulated sugar

¼ teaspoon dried oregano
¼ teaspoon dried basil
¼ teaspoon salt
⅛ teaspoon dried thyme
dash ground black pepper
1 ½ tablespoons soy sauce

1 tablespoon olive oil
1/8 teaspoon cayenne pepper
1/8 teaspoon garlic powder
1/8 teaspoon cumin
1/2 eggplant, sliced lengthwise
   1/4-inch thick
1 cup shredded mozzarella
   cheese
3/4 cup mushrooms, sliced thin
   (2 to 3 mushrooms)

1/3 medium onion, sliced into thin
   rings (about 2/3 cup)
1/3 cup reconstituted sun-dried
   tomatoes,* sliced into strips
1 1/2 cups steamed broccoli florets
   (bite-size)
1 teaspoon minced fresh oregano

1. Prepare the pizza dough by combining the water with the honey and yeast in a small bowl or measuring cup. Stir until the yeast is dissolved, then let the mixture sit for 5 minutes until the surface turns foamy. (If it doesn't foam, either the yeast was too old or the water was too hot. Try again.) Sift the flours and salt together in a medium bowl. Make a depression in the flour and pour the olive oil and yeast mixture into it. Use a fork or spoon to stir the liquid, gradually drawing in more flour as you stir, until all the ingredients are combined At this point you will have to use your hands to blend the dough until it is smooth and to form it into a ball. Knead the dough with the heels of your hands on a lightly floured surface for 10 minutes or until the texture of the dough is smooth and elastic. Form the dough back into a ball, coat it lightly with oil, and place it into a clean bowl covered with plastic wrap. Keep the dough in a warm place for about 2 hours to allow the dough to double in size. Punch the dough down and put it back into the covered bowl and back into the refrigerator overnight. Take the dough from the refrigerator 1 to 2 hours before you plan to build the pizza so that the dough can warm up to room temperature.

2. When you are ready to make the pizza, preheat oven to 500 degrees. Use a pizza stone if you have one.

*Heat a couple cups of water to boiling in the microwave. Add 6 to 8 sun-dried tomato slices to the water and let them sit for about 1/2 hour. Remove and drain the slices on paper towels until you need them.

3. Prepare the sauce by first heating the olive oil over medium heat in a medium saucepan. Sauté the onion and garlic for 1 minute in the oil. Add the tomato and sauté for an additional minute before adding the remaining sauce ingredients to the pan. Bring the sauce to a boil, then reduce heat and simmer for 20 to 30 minutes, or until thicker. Cover the sauce until it is needed.
4. Preheat barbecue grill to high temperature.
5. Combine the soy sauce with 1 tablespoon olive oil, cayenne pepper, garlic powder, and cumin in a small bowl.
6. Brush the entire surface of the eggplant with the soy sauce mixture. Grill the eggplant slices for 2 to 3 minutes per side, then remove the slices from the heat and set them aside until they are needed.
7. On a lightly floured surface, form the pizza dough into a circle that is approximately 10 inches across.
8. Spread about ½ cup of the sauce evenly over the surface of the dough.
9. Arrange the grilled eggplant on the pizza, then sprinkle the cheese evenly over the top of the eggplant.
10. Next sprinkle the mushrooms onto the pizza, followed by the onion slices.
11. Sprinkle the sun-dried tomato slices on the pizza, followed by the broccoli florets.
12. Bake the pizza for 10 to 12 minutes or until the crust is light brown and the cheese begins to bubble. Pop any bubbles in the crust that may form as the pizza bakes.
13. Remove the pizza from the oven and sprinkle the fresh oregano over the top. Use a pizza wheel to slice the pizza into 6 pieces and serve.

- MAKES 1 10-INCH PIZZA.

Nutrition Facts

SERVING SIZE—3 SLICES   FAT (PER SERVING)—19 G
TOTAL SERVINGS—2   CALORIES (PER SERVING)—632

• • • •

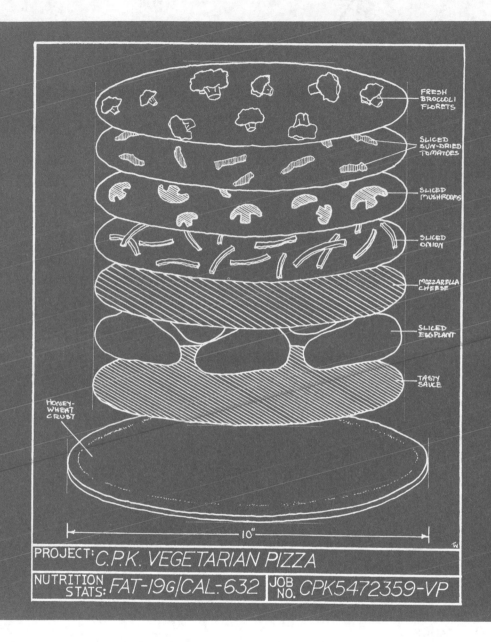

FRESH
BROCCOLI
FLORETS

SLICED
SUN-DRIED
TOMATOES

SLICED
MUSHROOMS

SLICED
ONION

MOZZARELLA
CHEESE

SLICED
EGGPLANT

TASTY
SAUCE

HONEY-
WHEAT
CRUST

|←————— 10" —————→|

PROJECT: *C.P.K. VEGETARIAN PIZZA*

NUTRITION STATS:	*FAT-19g/CAL.-632*	JOB NO.	*CPK5472359-VP*

CHILI'S GUILTLESS GRILL GUILTLESS PASTA PRIMAVERA

According to one Chili's spokesperson, "The Guiltless Grill selections are extremely popular. Guiltless Grill was a smash from the start." And to ensure that customers keep coming back to these lighter selections on the menu, Chili's often rotates items and introduces new ones. The Guiltless Pasta Primavera is one of the new kids on the block among the Guiltless Grill selections. This clone recipe of the recent favorite dish makes two huge dinner-size portions, just like the restaurant serves. The recipe should even be enough for three, perhaps four—if there's a big dessert coming.

CHICKEN MARINADE

1 cup water
1/4 cup pineapple juice
1 tablespoon soy sauce
1/2 teaspoon salt

1/4 teaspoon liquid smoke
1/4 teaspoon onion powder
dash garlic powder

2 chicken breast fillets

SAUCE

2 15-ounce cans tomato sauce
1 1/2 cups water
1/2 cup diced onion
2 cloves garlic, minced

1 tomato, diced
1 tablespoon dried parsley
1 tablespoon brown sugar
2 teaspoons lemon juice

2 teaspoons red wine vinegar
1 teaspoon dried basil
1 teaspoon dried oregano
½ teaspoon salt
¼ teaspoon pepper

1 1-pound package penne pasta
4 quarts water
1 summer squash, sliced

1 zucchini, sliced
1 slice red onion, halved and
   separated
¼ red bell pepper, seeded and
   sliced
¼ green bell pepper, seeded and
   sliced
salt
pepper

1. Prepare the chicken marinade by combining the marinade in-gredients in a medium bowl. Add the chicken breast fillets to the marinade, cover, and refrigerate for 24 hours. If you're in a hurry, you can get by with a minimum of four hours' marinating time, although the flavors will not be as intense.

2. When the chicken is marinated, prepare the sauce by combining all of the ingredients in a large saucepan over high heat. Bring the sauce to a boil, then reduce the heat to low and simmer for 1 to 1½ hours or until the diced tomato is soft, the onions are translucent, and the sauce thickens.

3. About 20 minutes before the sauce is done, prepare the penne pasta by bringing 4 quarts of water to a boil. Dump the penne into the water, stir, and cook for 11 to 15 minutes or until it is *al dente*, or tender but not soft. Drain.

4. As the pasta cooks, grill the chicken fillets on a preheated barbecue or indoor grill set to a high temperature for 4 to 7 minutes per side or until done.

5. As the pasta and chicken cook, steam the vegetables in a steam basket over boiling water or in a steamer, for 8 to 10 minutes or until tender. Salt and pepper the vegetables to taste.

6. Build the dish by arranging half of the pasta on a plate. Distribute half of the vegetables over the pasta and spoon the marinara sauce over the top. Slice a chicken fillet into bite-size pieces and arrange over the top of the pasta. Repeat for the second serving.

- MAKES 2 LARGE DINNER-SIZE PORTIONS.

Nutrition Facts

SERVING SIZE—
    I DINNER-SIZE PORTION
TOTAL SERVINGS—2

FAT (PER SERVING)—15G
CALORIES (PER SERVING)—1200

•   •   •   •

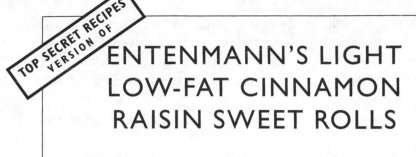

ENTENMANN'S LIGHT LOW-FAT CINNAMON RAISIN SWEET ROLLS

Entenmann's was one of the first on the block to throw irresistible, low-fat versions of its delicious baked goods in front of us at the supermarket. The company's specialty is its low-fat sweet cinnamon rolls that taste as good as any of the full-fat varieties produced by other established brands.

ROLLS

2 teaspoons yeast
½ cup warm water
¼ cup granulated sugar
1⅔ cups bread flour

½ teaspoon baking powder
¼ teaspoon salt
2 tablespoons shortening, melted
3 tablespoons egg substitute

FILLING

¼ cup fat-free butter-flavored
    spread
⅓ cup light brown sugar

2 tablespoons Wondra flour
2 teaspoons cinnamon
¼ cup raisins

ICING

½ cup powdered sugar
2 tablespoons fat-free cream
    cheese

couple drops vanilla extract
dash salt

1. Dissolve the yeast in the warm water. When the yeast is dissolved, add the sugar and stir until it is dissolved as well. In about 5 minutes, foam will form on the surface. (If foam does not form, your yeast may be too old or the water may be too hot. Try again.)
2. In a large bowl, mix together the flour, baking powder, and salt.
3. Melt the shortening in the microwave, set on high, for about 1 minute. Add the melted shortening, egg substitute, and yeast mixture to the flour, and stir by hand until all ingredients are combined. Use your hands to knead the dough for about 5 minutes, then form it into a ball and put it into a covered bowl in a warm spot for 1 to 1½ hours or until it doubles in size.
4. Roll dough out onto a floured surface so that it is a rectangle measuring 12 inches wide and 18 inches long.
5. Use a spatula to spread the butter-flavored spread evenly over the surface of the dough. Combine the brown sugar, Wondra flour, and cinnamon in a small bowl. Spread this mixture evenly over the surface of the dough. Sprinkle the raisins evenly over the filling.
6. Starting from the top edge, roll the dough down until it forms a long roll. Cut off the ends, then slice the dough into 12 even slices and arrange them, cut side down, in an 9 x 13-inch greased baking pan or dish. Cover the pan with plastic wrap and let the rolls rise again for another 1 to 1½ hours in a warm place.
7. Preheat oven to 400 degrees.
8. Remove the plastic from the pan and bake the rolls for 18 to 22 minutes or until brown.
9. As rolls bake, combine the icing ingredients in a medium bowl with an electric mixer. Mix on high speed for about 1 minute.
10. When rolls are cool, spread icing over the top of each one. Cover the baking dish, and store the rolls at room temperature until you are ready to serve them.

- MAKES 12 ROLLS.

Nutrition Facts

SERVING SIZE—1 ROLL	FAT (PER SERVING)—2 G
TOTAL SERVINGS—12	CALORIES (PER SERVING)—160

• • • •

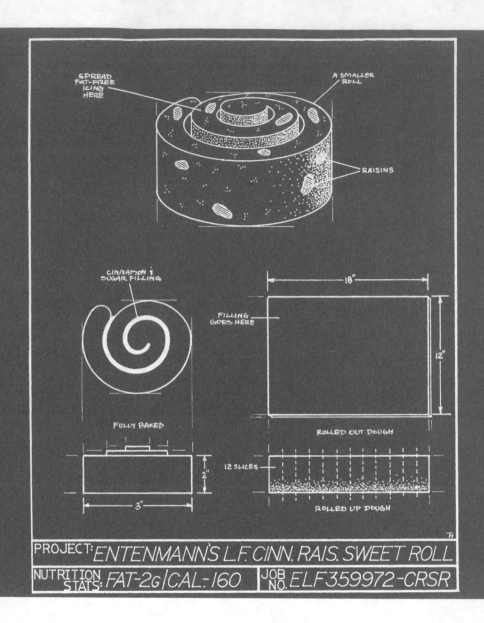

SPREAD
FAT-FREE
ICING
HERE

A SMALLER
ROLL

RAISINS

CINNAMON &
SUGAR FILLING

FILLING
GOES HERE

18"

12"

FULLY BAKED

ROLLED OUT DOUGH

12 SLICES

2"

3"

ROLLED UP DOUGH

PROJECT: ENTENMANN'S L.F. CINN. RAIS. SWEET ROLL

NUTRITION STATS: FAT-2G/CAL.-160

JOB NO. ELF359972-CRSR

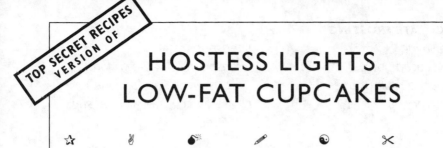

HOSTESS LIGHTS LOW-FAT CUPCAKES

☆   ✄   💣   ✎   ◉   ✂   ☞

The Twinkie company, otherwise known as Hostess, was one of the first to introduce reduced-fat baked goods to the masses. In 1990 the company took its most popular products and created lower-fat versions under the "Hostess Lights" label. Among the company's well-known low-fat offerings is this popular cupcake, with its trademark seven loops of white icing on the top of frosted, crème-filled cake. Here's a way you can re-create these popular cupcakes at home, with applesauce in the cake to help replace the fat, and filling made with marshmallow crème.

CAKE

1 cup sugar
1/3 cup unsweetened applesauce
1/4 cup egg substitute
1 teaspoon vanilla
1 1/4 cups cake flour
    (unsifted)

1/2 cup cocoa
1 teaspoon baking soda
1/2 teaspoon salt
1/2 cup buttermilk
1/2 cup whole milk

FILLING

1 7-ounce jar marshmallow crème
1/3 cup shortening
2 tablespoons powdered sugar

1/4 teaspoon salt
1 teaspoon water
1/4 teaspoon vanilla

CHOCOLATE FROSTING

1 cup sugar	1 teaspoon vanilla
1/3 cup cocoa powder	1 teaspoon dark brown food
1/4 teaspoon salt (rounded)	paste coloring (optional)
1/3 cup very hot water	1 1/4 to 1 1/2 cups powdered sugar, sifted

WHITE FROSTING

1/3 cup powdered sugar, sifted	1 teaspoon meringue powder
1 teaspoon fat-free milk	(optional)

1. Preheat the oven to 350 degrees.
2. To make the cake, beat together the sugar, applesauce, egg substitute, and vanilla in a large bowl for one minute.
3. In a separate medium bowl combine the cake flour, cocoa, baking soda, and salt and use a wire whisk to break up any lumps of cocoa.
4. Add the dry ingredients to the previous wet ingredients and mix together. Add the buttermilk and whole milk, then beat the mixture until smooth.
5. Spoon the batter into a 12-cup muffin tin, sprayed lightly with nonstick spray. Bake for 20 to 24 minutes or until a toothpick inserted into the center of the cake comes out clean. Turn the cupcakes out onto a cooling rack.
6. As the cupcakes cool, prepare the filling by combining 1/4 teaspoon salt with 1 teaspoon water in a small bowl or cup. Microwave for 10 to 20 seconds on high, then stir until the salt is dissolved.
7. Beat the marshmallow crème with the shortening in a medium bowl with an electric mixer until smooth and fluffy. Add the powdered sugar, water, and vanilla and beat well.
8. When the cakes have cooled, use a toothpick to poke a hole in the top of each cupcake. Swirl the toothpick around inside the cake to make room for the filling. Fill each cupcake with about 2 teaspoons of the filling.

9. For the chocolate frosting, measure 1 cup of sugar and 1/3 cup of cocoa powder into a deep 1 1/2- to 2-quart Pyrex bowl. Add a rounded 1/4 teaspoon of salt and mix the ingredients together.
10. Add the 1/3 cup of very hot water and the vanilla to the mixture and stir until all ingredients are well combined.
11. Loosely cover the bowl with plastic wrap and microwave at 50 percent power for 2 minutes. Stir carefully to continue dissolving the sugar crystals. Then replace the plastic wrap tightly over the bowl. Microwave on high in 30-second increments (to avoid boiling over) for 2 minutes. The mixture should begin to bubble, but watch it carefully so that it doesn't boil over. Remove the mixture from the microwave, poke holes in the plastic wrap so that steam will escape, and let the mixture stand for 15 minutes.
12. Carefully uncover the bowl (the contents will be very hot). Add 1 teaspoon dark brown food paste coloring to the hot syrup. (This is an optional step that creates dark frosting like the original.)
13. Stir in the sifted powdered sugar, 1/2 cup at a time. Mix thoroughly after each addition. You may need to add a few drops of water to the frosting to make it easier to spread. Spread about 2 teaspoons of frosting on each cupcake. You may want to moisten your knife to help the frosting spread on smoothly.
14. Make the white frosting for the design on the top of the cupcakes by mixing 1/3 cup sifted powdered sugar with 1 teaspoon nonfat milk. Add 1 teaspoon of meringue powder to the mixture, if you like, to make the frosting more opaque, like the original. Use a pastry bag with a #3 tip and make small loops down the middle of the top of each frosted cupcake.

• MAKES 12 CUPCAKES.

TIDBITS

You can create small pastry bags for the filling and the white frosting decoration by cutting the corner off of small plastic storage bags. First add the filling or frosting to the bag, then just clip the tip of a corner with scissors. Also, the cupcakes are best if eaten within a couple days of filling.

Nutrition Facts

SERVING SIZE— 1 CUPCAKE FAT (PER SERVING)—1.5G
TOTAL SERVINGS—12 CALORIES (PER SERVING)—220

• • • •

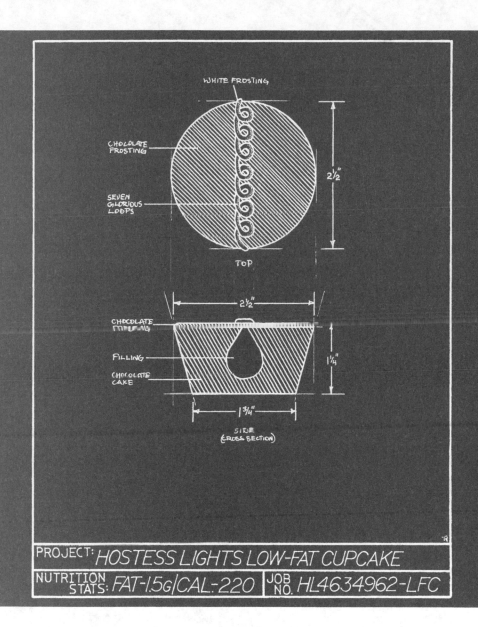

WHITE FROSTING

CHOCOLATE
FROSTING

SEVEN
GLORIOUS
LOOPS

2½"

TOP

2½"

CHOCOLATE
FILLING

FILLING

CHOCOLATE
CAKE

1¼"

1¾"

SIDE
(CROSS SECTION)

PROJECT: *HOSTESS LIGHTS LOW-FAT CUPCAKE*

NUTRITION
STATS: *FAT-1.5g/CAL-220*   JOB
NO. *HL4634962-LFC*

447

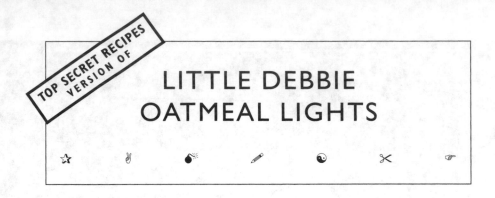

LITTLE DEBBIE OATMEAL LIGHTS

These soft, creme-filled cookies are one of the most drooled-over goodies in the popular line of Little Debbie snacks. Good thing they're wrapped in plastic. The secret to cloning the light version of these mouthwatering sandwich cookies is in re-creating the soft, chewy consistency of the oatmeal cookies. To duplicate the texture, the cookies are slightly underbaked. For the filling, we just use marshmallow creme straight out of the jar. I found that this is the best way to get the taste and texture of the original's fat-free filling. Just be sure to eat these within a day or two of filling them, since the filling will begin to slowly creep from between the cookies. Also, keep these sandwich cookies wrapped in plastic or sealed in an airtight container so that they'll stay moist and chewy.

COOKIES

3½ tablespoons softened margarine
¾ cup dark brown sugar
¼ cup granulated sugar
1 tablespoon molasses
1 teaspoon vanilla

½ cup egg substitute
1½ cups all-purpose flour
1¼ cups 1-minute Quaker Oats
¾ teaspoon salt
½ teaspoon baking soda
¼ teaspoon cinnamon

1 7-ounce jar marshmallow creme

1. Preheat oven to 350°F.
2. In a large bowl, cream together margarine, sugars, molasses, vanilla, and egg substitute with an electric mixer.
3. In a separate bowl, combine the flour, oats, salt, baking soda, and cinnamon.
4. Combine the dry ingredients with the wet ingredients and mix by hand.
5. Drop the dough by tablespoonfuls onto a well-greased baking sheet. The dough will be very tacky, so you may wish to moisten your fingers so that the dough does not stick. With moistened fingers, press down on the dough and form it into circles about ⅛ inch thick. The circles should be about 2 inches in diameter before baking. Bake for 6 to 8 minutes or until a couple of the cookies start to darken around the edges. They will still be very tender in the center until cool. Be careful not to overcook. When cooled, the cookies should be about ¼ inch thick and very soft and chewy.
6. When the cookies have completely cooled, assemble each creme pie by spreading about 1½ tablespoons of marshmallow creme over the flat side of a cookie and press another cookie on top, making a sandwich. Repeat for the remaining cookies and filling.

- MAKES 20 SANDWICH COOKIES.

Nutrition Facts

SERVING SIZE—1 SANDWICH COOKIE

TOTAL SERVINGS—20

FAT (PER SERVING)—2.5 G

CALORIES (PER SERVING)—146

• • • •

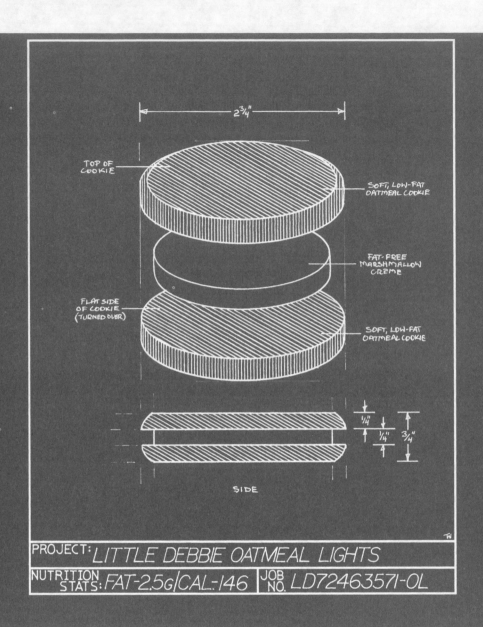

2¾"

TOP OF
COOKIE

SOFT, LOW-FAT
OATMEAL COOKIE

FAT-FREE
MARSHMALLOW
CREME

FLAT SIDE
OF COOKIE
(TURNED OVER)

SOFT, LOW-FAT
OATMEAL COOKIE

¼"
¼"
¾"

SIDE

PROJECT: *LITTLE DEBBIE OATMEAL LIGHTS*

NUTRITION STATS: *FAT-2.5g/CAL.-146* JOB NO. *LD72463571-OL*

NABISCO
HONEY MAID GRAHAMS

☆   ✌   💣   ✐   👁   ✂   ☞

The beginning of the graham cracker goes back to the early 1800s when Sylvester Graham thought his new invention was the secret to a lifetime of perfect health, even sexual prowess—certainly extraordinary claims for a cracker. But this came from the man thought to be quite a whacko in his time, since he had earlier claimed that eating ketchup could ruin your brain. So, while his crispy whole wheat creation was not the cure for every known ailment, the sweet crackers still became quite a fad, first in New England around the 1830s and then spreading across the country. Today, graham crackers remain popular as a low-fat, snack-time munchable, and they're the main ingredient in s'mores.

You don't need to use graham flour for this recipe, since it's similar to the whole wheat flour you find in your local supermarket. Just pick your favorite variety among these three clones of Nabisco's most popular crackers, and be sure to roll out the dough paper thin.

Honey (Original)

⅓ cup shortening
¾ cup plus 1 tablespoon
    granulated sugar
3 tablespoons honey, warmed
1½ teaspoons vanilla
1¾ cups whole wheat flour

1¼ cups all-purpose flour
1¼ teaspoons salt
1 teaspoon baking powder
½ teaspoon baking soda
½ cup plus 2 tablespoons water

1. Preheat oven to 300°F.
2. Combine shortening with sugar, honey (warmed for 20 to 30 seconds in the microwave), and vanilla in a large bowl. Blend with an electric mixer until smooth.
3. Combine flours, salt, baking powder, and baking soda in another large bowl, and then add the dry mixture to the wet ingredients and blend well with an electric mixer.
4. Slowly add the water to the mixture while beating. You may have to mix by hand until the mixture forms a large ball of dough.
5. Divide the dough in thirds and roll $\frac{1}{3}$ out in the shape of a rectangle that is at least $\frac{1}{16}$ inch thick on wax paper. This dough should be paper thin! It will double when cooked to the desired $\frac{1}{8}$-inch thickness. Use a knife to trim the dough so that it has straight edges in the shape of a rectangle slightly smaller than the size of the baking sheet you are using.
6. Grease the baking sheet with a light coating of shortening. Turn the dough over onto the baking sheet, and carefully peel away the wax paper.
7. Use a knife to score the dough in 5 x 2$\frac{3}{8}$-inch rectangles. Use a toothpick to poke holes that are $\frac{1}{4}$ inch apart across the entire surface of the dough.
8. Bake for 22 to 24 minutes or until the dough begins to turn light brown around the edges. Be sure to turn the baking sheet around about halfway through the cooking time.
9. Cool the graham cracker sheets before breaking them apart along the scored lines. Repeat the process with the remaining dough.

- MAKES 44 CRACKERS.

Cinnamon

$\frac{1}{3}$ cup shortening
$\frac{3}{4}$ cup plus 1 tablespoon
   granulated sugar
2 tablespoons honey, warmed
1 tablespoon molasses
1$\frac{1}{2}$ teaspoons vanilla

1$\frac{3}{4}$ cups whole wheat flour
1$\frac{1}{4}$ cups all-purpose flour
1$\frac{1}{4}$ teaspoons salt
1 teaspoon baking powder
$\frac{1}{2}$ teaspoon baking soda
$\frac{1}{2}$ cup plus 2 tablespoons water

TOPPING

1 ½ teaspoons cinnamon   *2 tablespoons sugar*

1. Preheat oven to 300°F.
2. Combine shortening with sugar, honey (warmed for 20 to 30 seconds in the microwave), molasses, and vanilla in a large bowl. Blend with an electric mixer until smooth.
3. Combine flours, salt, baking powder, and baking soda in another large bowl, and then add the dry mixture to the wet ingredients and blend well with an electric mixer.
4. Slowly add the water to the mixture while beating. You may have to mix by hand until the mixture forms a large ball of dough.
5. Divide the dough in thirds and roll ⅓ out in the shape of a rectangle that is at least ¹⁄₁₆ inch thick on wax paper. This dough should be paper thin! It will double when cooked to the desired ⅛-inch thickness. Use a knife to trim the dough so that it has straight edges in the shape of a rectangle slightly smaller than the size of the baking sheet you are using.
6. Grease the baking sheet with a light coating of shortening. Turn the dough over onto the baking sheet, and carefully peel away the wax paper.
7. Use a knife to score the dough in 5 x 2⅜-inch rectangles. Use a toothpick to poke holes that are ¼ inch apart across the entire surface of the dough.
8. Sprinkle a light coating of the cinnamon/sugar over the top surface of the dough. Shake the baking sheet around gently to evenly distribute the cinnamon/sugar topping.
9. Bake for 22 to 24 minutes or until the dough begins to turn light brown around the edges. Be sure to turn the baking sheet around about halfway through the cooking time.
10. Cool the graham cracker sheets before breaking them apart along the scored lines. Repeat the process with the remaining dough.

- MAKES 44 CRACKERS.

Chocolate

⅓ cup shortening
¾ cup plus 1 tablespoon
    granulated sugar
3 tablespoons honey, warmed
1 tablespoon chocolate syrup
1 ½ teaspoons vanilla
1 ½ cups whole wheat flour
1 ¼ cups all-purpose flour

⅓ cup cocoa
1 ¼ teaspoons salt
1 teaspoon baking powder
½ teaspoon baking soda
¼ cup water
¼ cup fat-free milk
2 tablespoons whole milk

TOPPING
2 tablespoons granulated sugar

1. Preheat oven to 300°F.
2. Combine shortening with sugar, honey (warmed for 20 to 30 seconds in the microwave), chocolate syrup, and vanilla in a large bowl. Blend with an electric mixer until smooth.
3. Combine flours, cocoa, salt, baking powder, and baking soda in another large bowl, and then add the dry mixture to the wet ingredients and blend well with an electric mixer.
4. Slowly add the water and milk to the mixture while beating. You may have to mix by hand until the mixture forms a large ball of dough.
5. Divide the dough in thirds and roll ⅓ out in the shape of a rectangle that is at least 1/16 inch thick on wax paper. This dough should be paper thin! It will double in thickness when cooked to the desired ⅛-inch thickness. Use a knife to trim the dough so that it has straight edges in the shape of a rectangle slightly smaller than the size of the baking sheet you are using.
6. Grease the baking sheet with a light coating of shortening. Turn the dough over onto the baking sheet and carefully peel away the wax paper.

7. Use a knife to score the dough in 5 x 2⅜-inch rectangles. Use a toothpick to poke holes that are ¼ inch apart across the entire surface of the dough.
8. Sprinkle a light coating of granulated sugar over the top surface of the dough. Gently shake the baking sheet around to help evenly distribute the sugar.
9. Bake for 22 to 24 minutes or until the dough begins to turn light brown around the edges. Be sure to turn the baking sheet around about halfway through the cooking time.
10. Cool the graham cracker sheets before breaking them apart along the scored lines. Repeat the process with the remaining dough.

- MAKES 44 CRACKERS.

Nutrition Facts

SERVING SIZE—2 CRACKERS	FAT (PER SERVING)—3 G
TOTAL SERVINGS—22	CALORIES (PER SERVING)—120

• • • •

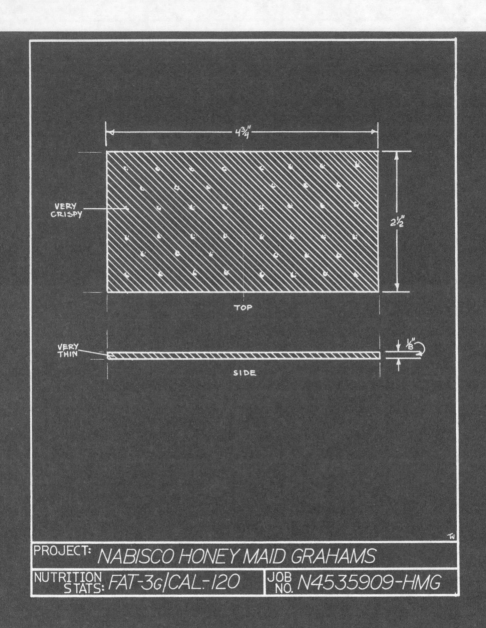

VERY
CRISPY

4¾"

2½"

TOP

VERY
THIN

⅛"

SIDE

PROJECT: *NABISCO HONEY MAID GRAHAMS*

NUTRITION STATS: *FAT-3g/CAL.-120*   **JOB NO.** *N4535909-HMG*

NABISCO
OLD FASHION GINGER
SNAPS

☆　　　✌　　　💣　　　✏　　　☯　　　✂　　　☞

According to legend, if you place a ginger snap in the palm of your hand and press down on the middle, and it breaks into three pieces, good luck will follow. Though you'll wish a broom would follow, since you just got crumbs all over your clean floor.

I cup packed dark brown sugar
¾ cup granulated sugar
6 tablespoons shortening
¼ cup molasses
¼ cup egg substitute
½ teaspoon vanilla
2½ cups all-purpose flour

2 teaspoons baking soda
2 teaspoons ground ginger
I teaspoon salt
I teaspoon ground cinnamon
½ teaspoon ground cloves
¼ cup water

1. Preheat oven to 300°F.
2. Cream together the sugars, shortening, molasses, egg substitute, and vanilla in a large bowl. Beat with an electric mixer until smooth.
3. In another large bowl, combine the flour, baking soda, ginger, salt, cinnamon, and cloves.
4. Pour the dry mixture into the wet mixture and beat while adding the water. Continue to mix until ingredients are incorporated.
5. Measure I rounded teaspoon of dough at a time. Roll the dough into a sphere between the palms of your hands, then press the dough onto a lightly greased cookie sheet. Flatten

to about ¼ inch thick, and leave at least ½ inch between the cookies since they will spread out a bit when baking. Use flour or water on your fingers if the dough sticks.

6. Bake cookies for 12 to 14 minutes or until edges begin to turn light brown. Cookies should be crispy, not soft, when cool.

- MAKES 120 COOKIES.

Nutrition Facts

SERVING SIZE—4 COOKIES   FAT (PER SERVING)—2.5 G

TOTAL SERVINGS—30   CALORIES (PER SERVING)—110

• • • •

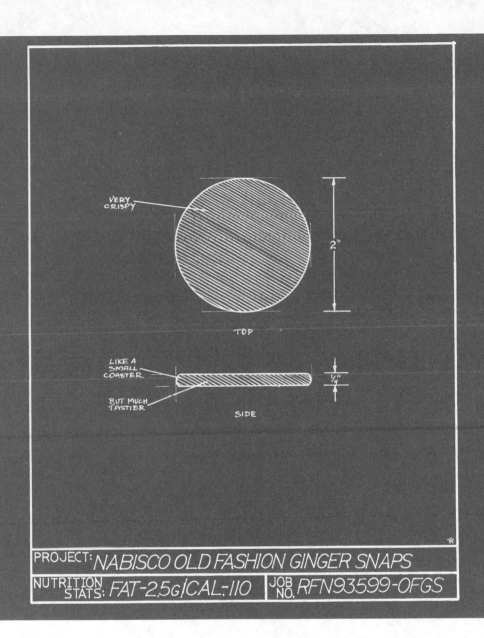

VERY
CRISPY

2"

TOP

LIKE A
SMALL
COASTER

BUT MUCH
TASTIER

SIDE

¼"

PROJECT: *NABISCO OLD FASHION GINGER SNAPS*

NUTRITION STATS: *FAT-2.5g/CAL.-110*   **JOB NO.** *RFN93599-0FGS*

NABISCO REDUCED-FAT OREO COOKIES

☆　✌　💣　✐　☯　✂　☞

I've been researching the King of All Cookies for years now, and I've still not found anyone who is sure where the name *Oreo* came from. One of the most interesting and obscure explanations I've heard is that the two *o*'s from the word *chocolate* were placed on both sides of *re* from the word *creme*. This way the name seems to mimic the construction of the famed sandwich cookie.

That may not be true, but I do know this for sure: Nabisco introduced a reduced-fat version of its popular cookie in 1994. With only half the fat, it manages to taste just as good as the original version invented way back in 1912. We cut back on the fat for our clone here by re-creating the creme filling without any of the shortening you'd find in the original full-fat version. We do this with a special technique developed in the secret underground Top Secret Recipes test kitchen that allows you to create a delicious, fat-free filling in your microwave. If you want the cookies as dark as the original, include the optional brown paste food coloring in your recipe.

COOKIES

1 18¼-ounce package reduced-fat devil's food cake mix (Betty Crocker Sweet Rewards is best)
¼ cup shortening, melted
½ cup all-purpose flour, measured then sifted

¼ cup egg substitute
3 tablespoons brown paste food coloring (2 1-ounce containers)*
3 tablespoons water

*This addition of brown paste food coloring is an optional step to help re-create the color of the original cookie. If you do not use the paste food coloring, be sure to change the amount of water added to the

FILLING

1 cup granulated sugar	dash salt
1/4 cup hot water	1 1/3 cups powdered sugar
1/2 teaspoon vanilla (clear is best)*	

1. Combine the cookie ingredients in a large bowl. Add the water a bit at a time until the dough forms. (You may need as much as 1/4 cup of water to create a dough ball that is pliable and easy to roll but not sticky.) Cover and chill for 2 hours.
2. Preheat oven to 350°F.
3. On a floured surface, roll out a portion of the dough to just under 1/16 inch thick. To cut, use a cutter or lid from a spice container with a 1 1/2-inch diameter (Schilling brand is good). Arrange the cut dough on a cookie sheet that is sprayed with a light coating of nonstick spray. Bake for 10 minutes. Remove the chocolate wafers from the oven and cool completely.
4. As the wafers bake, make the filling by combining the granulated sugar, hot water, vanilla, and salt in a medium bowl. Stir mixture for about 30 seconds to begin dissolving the sugar.
5. Cover bowl with plastic wrap and microwave on 50% power for 2 minutes. Remove the bowl from the microwave. Stir very gently to help dissolve the sugar crystals around the sides and bottom of the bowl. Cover bowl again and microwave at full power for 2 more minutes. Remove the bowl from the microwave, and poke holes in the plastic wrap to let the steam escape. Let the mixture cool for 15 minutes. Do not let the mixture stand for longer than this or sugar crystals may begin to form.
6. After mixture has cooled for 15 minutes, stir it very gently once again to dissolve any additional crystals that may have

wafer cookies from 3 tablespoons to 1/3 cup. The food coloring gives the cookies the dark brown, almost black color. The coloring can be found with cake decorating supplies at art supply and craft stores.

*This clear vanilla can also be found with cake decorating supplies in craft stores. The clear vanilla will give you a much whiter filling like the original, although the brown vanilla works fine for taste, if that's all you've got on hand.

formed, then add the 1 1/3 cups of powdered sugar. Stir gently to incorporate the sugar, until mixture is smooth. Cover mixture again until it can be handled.

7. When the cookies have cooled, roll a small portion (rounded 1/4 teaspoon) of the filling into a ball (just over 1/4 inch in diameter), and press it between two of the cookies. Repeat with the remaining cookies.

- MAKES 54 SANDWICH COOKIES.

TIDBITS

If the dough for the wafers seems too sticky, you can work in as much as 1/4 cup of additional flour as you pat out and roll the dough. Use just enough flour to make the dough workable but not tough.

Nutrition Facts

SERVING SIZE—3 COOKIES FAT (PER SERVING)—3.5 G
TOTAL SERVINGS—18   CALORIES (PER SERVING)—150

• • • •

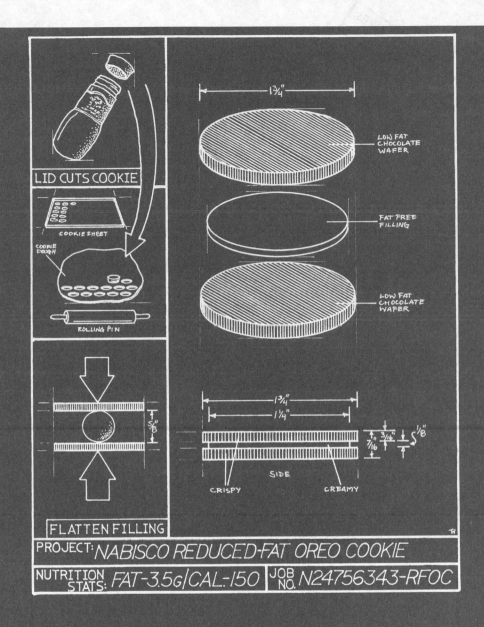

LID CUTS COOKIE

COOKIE SHEET

COOKIE DOUGH

ROLLING PIN

FLATTEN FILLING

5/8"

LOW FAT CHOCOLATE WAFER

FAT FREE FILLING

LOW FAT CHOCOLATE WAFER

1¾"

1¾"
1¼"

7/16" 3/16 1/8"

SIDE

CRISPY   CREAMY

PROJECT: NABISCO REDUCED-FAT OREO COOKIE

NUTRITION STATS: FAT-3.5g/CAL.-150

JOB NO. N24756343-RFOC

NABISCO
SNACKWELL'S
APPLE RAISIN SNACK BARS

☆　　✌　　💣　　✎　　☯　　✂　　☞

Nabisco unveiled a line of reduced-fat products in 1992 with the introduction of SnackWell's Devil's Food cookie cakes. The product was an instant hit with demand quickly outstripping the supply, leaving store shelves empty. The company poked fun at the situation with a series of humorous TV spots, showing the dweebish "Cookie Man" hounded by pushy shoppers trying to get their hands on his cookies. The successful product launch was followed up with the introduction of dozens of new SnackWell's products through the years, including Apple Raisin Snack Bars. Our clone uses a secret combination of unsweetened applesauce along with molasses and apple juice to keep the cake moist and tasty.

2 egg whites
1 cup plus 5 tablespoons
    granulated sugar
2 tablespoons brown sugar
1 tablespoon molasses
1 tablespoon dark corn syrup
½ cup unsweetened applesauce
¼ cup apple juice concentrate

3 tablespoons shortening
½ teaspoon vanilla
1½ cups all-purpose flour
¾ teaspoon salt
½ teaspoon cinnamon
¼ teaspoon baking soda
½ cup raisins

1. Preheat oven to 350°F.
2. In a large bowl, whip the egg whites with an electric mixer until they become thick. Do not use a plastic bowl for this.
3. Add the granulated sugar to the egg whites and continue to beat until the mixture forms soft peaks.

4. Add the brown sugar, molasses, dark corn syrup, applesauce, apple juice concentrate, shortening, and vanilla to the mixture while beating.
5. In a separate bowl, combine the remaining ingredients, except raisins.
6. While beating the wet mixture, slowly add the dry mixture.
7. Add the raisins, and combine by hand.
8. Lightly grease a 9 x 14-inch pan with a light coating of non-stick cooking spray. Be sure to coat the sides as well as the bottom of the pan. Dump about 3 tablespoons of sugar into the pan, then tilt and shake it so that a light layer of sugar coats the entire bottom of the pan and about halfway up the sides. Pour out the excess sugar.
9. Pour the batter into the pan and spread it evenly around the inside. Sprinkle a light coating of sugar—about 2 tablespoons—over the entire top surface of the batter. Gently shake the pan from side to side to evenly distribute the sugar over the batter. Bake for 25 to 28 minutes or until the cake begins to pull away from the sides of the pan.
10. Remove the cake from the oven and turn it out onto a cooling rack. When the cake has cooled, place it onto a sheet of wax paper on a cutting board and slice across the cake 6 times, creating 7 even slices. Next cut the cake lengthwise twice, into thirds, creating a total of 21 snack bars. When the bars have completely cooled, store them in a resealable plastic bag or an airtight container.

- MAKES 21 BARS.

Nutrition Facts

SERVING SIZE—1 BAR   TOTAL FAT (PER SERVING)—1.7 G
SERVINGS—21   CALORIES (PER SERVING)—120

• • • •

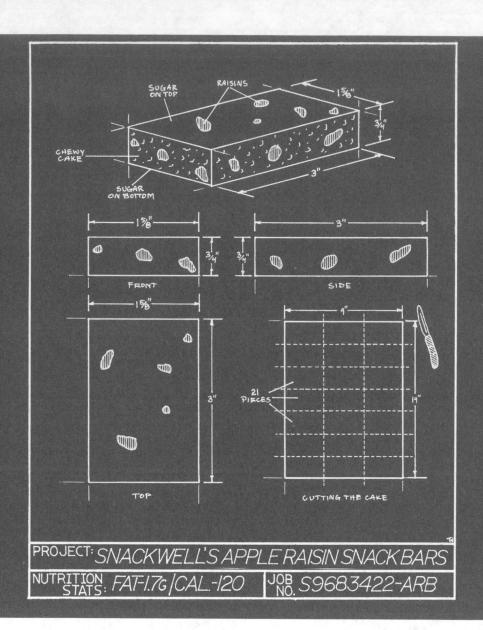

SUGAR ON TOP

RAISINS

1⅝"

¾"

CHEWY CAKE

3"

SUGAR ON BOTTOM

1⅝"

¾"

FRONT

3"

¾"

SIDE

1⅝"

3"

TOP

9"

21 PIECES

14"

CUTTING THE CAKE

PROJECT: *SNACKWELL'S APPLE RAISIN SNACK BARS*

NUTRITION STATS: *FAT-1.7G /CAL.-120*

JOB NO. *S9683422-ARB*

NABISCO SNACKWELL'S BANANA SNACK BARS

In 1996, Nabisco built up its growing line of SnackWell's baked products with the introduction of low-fat snack bars in several varieties, including fudge brownie, golden cake, apple raisin (see previous recipe), and the chewy banana variety cloned here.

The secret to keeping the fat grams down in this recipe is the use of egg whites, molasses, and just a little shortening. But it's the banana puree that really slips in there to replace most of the fat while giving the cake real banana flavor and helping to keep it very moist.

2 egg whites
1 cup plus 5 tablespoons
   granulated sugar
2 tablespoons brown sugar
2 tablespoons molasses
1 1/2 cups banana puree*
3 tablespoons shortening

1/4 cup whole milk
1/2 teaspoon vanilla butter nut
   extract
1 1/2 cups all-purpose flour
1/2 teaspoon salt
1/4 teaspoon baking soda

1. Preheat oven to 350°F.
2. In a large bowl, whip the egg whites with an electric mixer until they become thick. Do not use a plastic bowl for this.
3. Add the sugar to the egg whites and continue to beat until the mixture forms soft peaks.

*Puree whole bananas (approximately 3) in a food processor or blender until smooth and creamy.

4. Add the brown sugar, molasses, banana puree, shortening, milk, and vanilla butter nut flavoring to the mixture, beating after each addition.
5. In a separate bowl, combine the remaining ingredients.
6. While beating the wet mixture, slowly add the bowl of dry ingredients.
7. Lightly grease a 9 x 14-inch pan with a light coating of non-stick cooking spray. Be sure to coat the sides as well as the bottom of the pan. Dump about 3 tablespoons of sugar into the pan, then tilt and shake it so that a light layer of sugar coats the entire bottom of the pan and about halfway up the sides. Pour out the excess sugar.
8. Pour the batter into the pan and spread it evenly around the inside of the pan. Sprinkle a light coating of sugar—about 2 tablespoons—over the entire top surface of the batter. Gently shake the pan from side to side to evenly distribute the sugar over the batter. Bake for 25 to 28 minutes or until the cake begins to pull away from the sides of the pan.
9. Remove the cake from the oven and turn it out onto a cooling rack. When cake has cooled, place it onto a sheet of wax paper on a cutting board and slice across the cake 6 times, creating 7 even slices. Next cut the cake lengthwise twice, into thirds, creating a total of 21 snack bars. When the bars have completely cooled, store them in a resealable plastic bag or an airtight container.

- MAKES 21 BARS.

Nutrition Facts

SERVING SIZE—1 BAR

SERVINGS—21

TOTAL FAT (PER SERVING)—1.8 G

CALORIES (PER SERVING)—118

• • • •

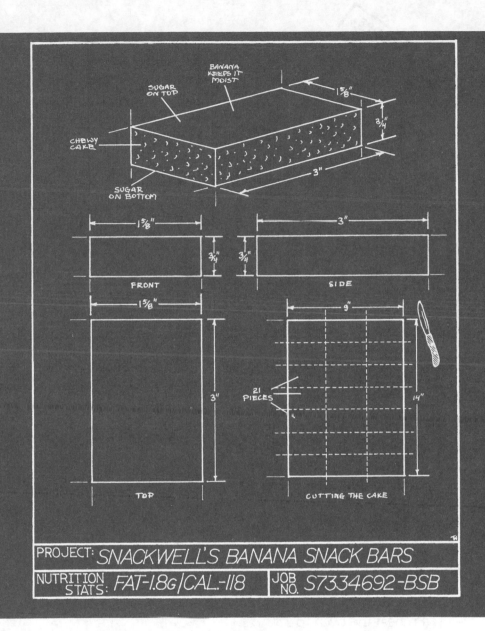

SUGAR ON TOP

BANANA KEEPS IT MOIST

CHEWY CAKE

SUGAR ON BOTTOM

1⅝"

¾"

3"

FRONT

1⅝"

¾"

SIDE

3"

¾"

TOP

1⅝"

3"

CUTTING THE CAKE

9"

14"

21 PIECES

PROJECT: SNACKWELL'S BANANA SNACK BARS

NUTRITION STATS: FAT-1.8g/CAL.-118

JOB NO. S7334692-BSB

NABISCO SNACKWELL'S FUDGE BROWNIE BARS

☆ ✌ 💣 ✏ ☯ ✂ ☞

One of the favorite SnackWell's creations are the very low-fat snack bars that now come in several varieties, including apple raisin, banana, golden cake, and this one, which tastes like a brownie. But, while a single brownie might contain around 6 to 10 grams of fat, this snack bar weighs in with just a fraction of that—at only 2 grams of fat per serving.

The secret to keeping the fat to a minimum in this recipe is the use of egg whites, corn syrup, and chocolate syrup. These fat-free ingredients help to replace much of the fat that would be found in a traditional recipe, while keeping the finished product moist and chewy, and filled with flavor.

2 egg whites
1 cup plus 5 tablespoons sugar
2 tablespoons corn syrup
2 tablespoons shortening
½ cup Hershey's chocolate syrup
½ cup fudge topping
¼ cup warm water

1 teaspoon vanilla
1½ cups all-purpose flour
¼ cup cocoa
¾ teaspoon salt
¼ teaspoon baking soda
nonstick cooking spray

1. Preheat the oven to 350°F.
2. In a large bowl, whip the egg whites with an electric mixer until they become thick. Do not use a plastic bowl for this.
3. Add 1 cup of sugar to the egg whites and continue to beat until the mixture forms soft peaks.
4. To the egg white and sugar mixture, add the corn syrup, shortening, chocolate syrup, fudge, water, and vanilla.

5. In a separate bowl, combine the flour, cocoa, salt, and baking soda.
6. While beating the wet mixture, slowly add the dry mixture.
7. Lightly grease a 9 x 13-inch pan with a light coating of nonstick cooking spray. Be sure to coat the sides as well as the bottom of the pan. Dump about 3 tablespoons of the remaining sugar into the pan, then tilt and shake the pan so that a light layer of sugar coats the entire bottom of the pan and about halfway up the sides. Pour out the excess sugar.
8. Pour the batter into the pan, spreading it evenly around the inside. Sprinkle a light coating of sugar—about two tablespoons—over the entire top surface of the batter. Gently shake the pan from side to side to evenly distribute the sugar over the batter. Bake for 25 to 28 minutes or until the cake begins to pull away from the sides of the pan.
9. Remove the cake from the oven and turn it out onto a cooling rack. When the cake has cooled, place it onto a sheet of wax paper on a cutting board and slice across the cake 6 times, creating 7 even sections. Next cut the cake lengthwise twice, into thirds, creating a total of 21 snack bars. When the bars have completely cooled, store them in a resealable plastic bag or an airtight container.

- MAKES 21 SNACK BARS.

Nutrition Facts

SERVING SIZE—1 BAR   TOTAL FAT (PER SERVING)—2G
SERVINGS—21   CALORIES (PER SERVING)—144

• • • •

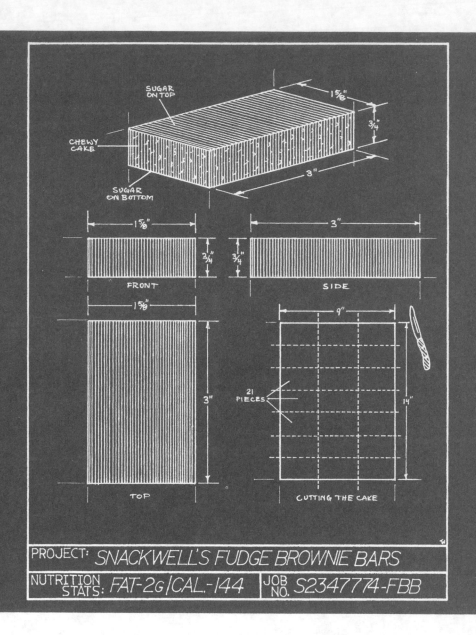

SUGAR
ON TOP

CHEWY
CAKE

SUGAR
ON BOTTOM

1⅝"

¾"

3"

1⅝"

¾"

FRONT

3"

¾"

SIDE

1⅝"

3"

TOP

9"

21
PIECES

14"

CUTTING THE CAKE

PROJECT: *SNACKWELL'S FUDGE BROWNIE BARS*

NUTRITION
STATS: *FAT-2g/CAL.-144*

JOB
NO. *S2347774-FBB*

472

PLANTERS
FAT-FREE FIDDLE FADDLE

☆   ✌   💣   ✎   ☯   ✂   ☞

For many years now, the monocled Mr. Peanut has been Planters' nutty pitchman. The character was created in 1916 by a Virginia schoolboy, Anthony Gentile, who won $5 in a contest for drawing a "little peanut person." A commercial artist later added the top hat, cane, and monocle to make Mr. Peanut the stuffy socialite that he is today. But the character has not always been in the limelight. Planters' adman Bill McDonough says, "Though Mr. Peanut has always been identified with the brand, over the years he has been dialed up or down to different degrees." In 1999, the company dialed up the polite-and-proper legume to capitalize on nostalgia for the older folks and the young buyers' craving for retro chic.

Even though we think of Planters as the "nut company," you won't find a single nut, with or without monocle, in the fat-free version of Planters' popular Fiddle Faddle. All you need to whip together this clone is a good low-fat microwave popcorn and a few other common ingredients. This recipe requires your microwave to help coat the popcorn with a thin, crunchy coating of the tasty candy mixture.

1 teaspoon vegetable oil	½ teaspoon salt
½ cup light corn syrup	¼ teaspoon vanilla extract
¾ cup light brown sugar	1 bag 94% fat-free microwave
¼ cup water	popcorn

1. Combine the oil, corn syrup, brown sugar, water, and salt in a small saucepan over medium heat. Stir while bringing mixture

to a boil, then use a candy thermometer to bring mixture to 300 degrees (also known as the hard crack stage to candy makers).

2. When the candy reaches about 275°F, start cooking the popcorn by following the directions on the package. You want to time it so that the popcorn is done at approximately the same time as the candy. This way, the popcorn will be hot when you pour the candy over it.

3. When the candy has reached the right temperature, add the vanilla, then remove it from the heat. Pour the hot popcorn into a large plastic or glass bowl and quickly pour the candy over the top. Stir the popcorn so that the candy coats all of the pieces. To better help the candy coat the popcorn, place the bowl into the microwave and zap it for about 30 seconds on high. Stir the popcorn, and then, if necessary, microwave it for another 30 seconds. Stir it once more. By this time, the popcorn should be very well coated with a thin layer of the candy.

4. Quickly pour the popcorn out onto wax paper and spread it around to cool it.

5. When candy is cool, break it into bite-size pieces. Store it in a sealed container.

- MAKES 12 CUPS.

Nutrition Facts

SERVING SIZE—1 CUP

TOTAL SERVINGS—12

FAT (PER SERVING)—0 G

CALORIES (PER SERVING)—114

• • • •

SWISS MISS
FAT-FREE CHOCOLATE
FUDGE PUDDING

☆　　　✌　　　💣　　　✏　　　👁　　　✂　　　☞

Hunt-Wesson first introduced a light variety of Swiss Miss Puddings in 1990, but three years later changed the formula to fat-free. This chocolaty clone of the rich pudding you find in the refrigerated section of the supermarket will satisfy your chocolate craving without contributing any of those nasty fat grams. You'll notice that the sweetened condensed milk helps to replace fat, and the cornstarch jumps in to keep the pudding thick and creamy. Add two types of chocolate and you've got an irresistible snack that tastes just like the real deal.

2½ cups fat-free milk
2 tablespoons unsweetened cocoa
　powder
3 tablespoons cornstarch
½ cup sweetened condensed
　skim milk

3 tablespoons Hershey's chocolate
　syrup
dash salt
½ teaspoon vanilla extract

1. In a saucepan, combine the fat-free milk with the cocoa powder and cornstarch and whisk thoroughly until the powders are dissolved.
2. Add the condensed milk, chocolate syrup, and salt to the saucepan. Set the pan over medium/low heat. Heat the mixture, stirring constantly, until it comes to a boil and then thickens. This will take about 6 minutes.

3. Remove the pan from the heat and let it sit, covered, for 5 minutes. Then add the vanilla.
4. Transfer the pudding to serving cups, cover each with plastic wrap, and chill for at least 2 to 3 hours before serving.

• SERVES 4.

TIDBITS

Cover the pudding tightly when chilling and eat it within a few days or it may begin to thin.

Nutrition Facts

SERVING SIZE—¾ CUP	FAT (PER SERVING)—0G
TOTAL SERVINGS—4	CALORIES (PER SERVING)—170

• • • •

SWISS MISS FAT-FREE TAPIOCA PUDDING

When the first instant hot cocoa mix was developed in the fifties, it was available only to the airlines in individual portions for passengers and was called Brown Swiss. This mix was so popular that the company packaged it for sale in the grocery stores and changed the name to Swiss Miss. In the seventies, the first Swiss Miss Puddings were introduced and quickly became the leader of dairy case puddings. When the fat-free versions of the puddings were introduced some 23 years later, they, too, would become a popular favorite.

No sugar needs to be added to this recipe that re-creates one of the best-tasting brands of fat-free pudding on the market. The condensed milk is enough to sweeten the pudding; plus it provides a creamy consistency, which, along with the cornstarch, helps to replace the fat found in the full-fat version of this tasty tapioca treat. It's a simple recipe to make and you won't even "miss" the fat.

2 tablespoons cornstarch
2½ cups fat-free milk
½ cup sweetened condensed
   skim milk

dash salt
2½ tablespoons instant tapioca
½ teaspoon vanilla extract

1. Combine the cornstarch with the fat-free milk in a medium saucepan and whisk thoroughly to dissolve the cornstarch.
2. Add the condensed milk, salt, and tapioca to the pan. Stir until smooth and then set the pan aside for 5 minutes.

3. After 5 minutes, bring the mixture to a boil over medium/low heat, stirring constantly until it thickens, then cover and remove from the heat. Let the pudding sit, covered, for 20 minutes.
4. Stir in the vanilla, then transfer the pudding to serving cups. Cover the cups with plastic wrap and let them chill for at least 2 to 3 hours before serving.

- SERVES 4.

TIDBITS

Cover the pudding tightly when chilling and eat it within a few days or it may begin to thin.

Nutrition Facts

SERVING SIZE—¾ CUP　　FAT (PER SERVING)—0G
TOTAL SERVINGS—4　　　CALORIES (PER SERVING)—140

• • • •

T.G.I. FRIDAY'S
FAT-FREE CHEESECAKE

☆ ✌ 💣 ✎ ☯ ✂ ☞

For the last couple of years T.G.I. Friday's has been serving a delicious cheesecake drizzled with strawberry sauce. The cheesecake tastes like a decadent, fat-filled dessert; it's creamy and delicious. But the shocker comes when you realize that there is not one gram of fat in a single serving. Many recipes for fat-free cheesecakes produce a cheesecake with an unusual taste or one that is very hard on top. This clone recipe will solve those problems and produce a dessert that tastes like the popular cheesecake you can order at one of America's most successful restaurant chains.

You'll need a 2½-inch springform pan for this recipe, and be sure to let the cream cheese come to room temperature (keep It covered) before you use it. Serve this one to your friends and watch the surprise when you tell them it's 100 percent fat-free.

5 8-ounce pkgs. fat-free
    Philadelphia cream cheese
1 ¼ cups sugar
⅔ cup fat-free sour cream

2 ½ tablespoons flour
2 teaspoons vanilla
½ cup egg substitute

CRUST
1 tablespoon ground pecans
3 tablespoons graham cracker
    crumbs

1 ½ teaspoons sugar
nonstick cooking spray

STRAWBERRY SAUCE

8 ounces frozen strawberries   2 tablespoons water
⅓ cup sugar

1. Bring the cream cheese to room temperature. Preheat the oven to 325°F.
2. Using an electric mixer, whip the cream cheese in a large bowl until smooth. Add the sugar, sour cream, flour, and vanilla and beat until well incorporated.
3. Add the egg substitute and mix only until combined. Do not overmix once the egg substitute is added.
4. To make the crust, measure the pecans after grinding them up in a food processor or blender, then return them to the processor. Add the graham cracker crumbs and 1½ teaspoons of sugar to the pecans and pulse for about 15 seconds to form a fine meal. Spray the inside of a 9½-inch springform pan with a light coating of cooking spray. Wipe off any excess spray around the top rim of the pan. The spray should only coat the bottom and up about two inches on the sides. Anything sprayed above that can be wiped off. Dump the crumbs into the pan and swirl the pan so that the bottom and sides are coated with the crumbs. Lightly tap out any excess.
5. Pour the cream cheese mixture into the springform pan, being careful not to disturb the crumbs when pouring. Gently spread the cheese mixture close to the edge, but don't touch the sides or you may disturb the crumbs.
6. Bake the cheesecake for 50 to 60 minutes or until the top of the cheesecake is firm. The center may not entirely set until the cheesecake cools. Cover and cool for 2 hours at room temperature, and then refrigerate.
7. As the cheesecake cools, prepare the strawberry sauce by combining the strawberries, sugar, and water in a microwave-safe bowl. Cover, and microwave on 50 percent power for 2 minutes. If the strawberries are still frozen, you may have to heat the mixture for as long as 4 to 5 minutes. Stir to dissolve

the sugar, then let stand for 10 to 15 minutes. Pour the mixture into the blender or food processor and puree until smooth. Strain and chill.

8. Cut the cheesecake into 12 slices. Serve each slice with about 1 tablespoon of the strawberry sauce poured over the top.

- SERVES 12.

Nutrition Facts

SERVING SIZE— 1 SLICE   FAT (PER SERVING)—0G
TOTAL SERVINGS—12   CALORIES (PER SERVING)—223

• • • •

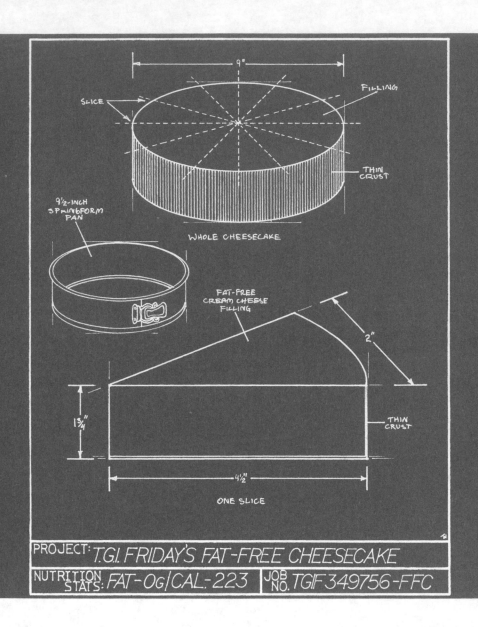

9"

SLICE

FILLING

THIN
CRUST

WHOLE CHEESECAKE

9½-INCH
SPRINGFORM
PAN

FAT-FREE
CREAM CHEESE
FILLING

2"

1¾"

THIN
CRUST

4½"

ONE SLICE

PROJECT: *T.G.I. FRIDAY'S FAT-FREE CHEESECAKE*

NUTRITION STATS: *FAT-0g/CAL.-223*   JOB NO. *TGIF349756-FFC*

TRADEMARKS

A&W, 7UP, Squirt, and Hawaiian Punch are registered trademarks of Dr Pepper/Seven Up, Inc.

Almond Roca and Brown and Haley are registered trademarks of Brown and Haley, Inc.

Applebee's, Low Fat & Fabulous, and Tijuana 'Philly' Steak Sandwich are registered trademarks of Applebee's International, Inc.

Arby's is a registered trademark of Arby's Inc.

AriZona is a registered trademark of AriZona Beverage Co.

Auntie Anne's is a registered trademark of Auntie Anne's, Inc.

Baskin-Robbins is a registered trademark of Baskin-Robbins, Inc.

Bennigan's and Cookie Mountain Sundae are registered trademarks of Metromedia Co.

Big Boy is a registered trademark of Elias Brothers Restaurants, Inc.

Big Mac, Egg McMuffin, Filet-O-Fish, and McDonald's Breakfast Burrito are registered trademarks of McDonald's Corporation.

Bisquick is a registered trademark of General Mills Inc.

Blizzard, Orange Julius, Pineapple, Strawberry Julius, Dairy Queen and Smoothie are registered trademarks of American Dairy Queen Corp.

Boston Market, are registered trademarks of McDonald's Corporation

Burger King and Whopper are registered trademarks of Burger King Corp.

Butterscotch Krimpets, Peanut Butter Kandy Kakes, and Tastykake are registered trademarks of Tasty Baking Company.

California Pizza Kitchen is a registered trademark of California Pizza Kitchen, Inc.

Carl's Jr. and Charbroiled Santa Fe Chicken Sandwich are registered trademarks of Carl Karcher Enterprises, Inc.

Carl's Jr., Sante Fe Chicken, Western Bacon Cheeseburger, Six Dollar Burger are registered trademarks of Carl Karcher Enterprises.

Carnegie Deli is a registered trademark of Carnegie Delicatessen and Restaurant.

The Cheesecake Factory is a registered trademark of The Cheesecake Factory, Inc.

Chevys is a registered trademark of Chevys, Inc.

Lone Star Steakhouse & Saloon and Amarillo Cheese Fries are registered trademarks of Lone Star Steakhouse & Saloon, Inc.

Long John Silver's is a registered trademark of Jerrico, Inc.

M&M/Mars, Snickers, and Munch are registered trademarks of Mars, Inc.

Maid-Rite is a registered trademark of Maid-Rite Inc.

Marie Callender's is a registered trademark of Marie Callender's Pie Shops, Inc.

Mounds, Almond Joy, and Peter Paul are registered trademarks of Cadbury U.S.A., Inc.

Nabisco, Nutter Butter, Oreo, Double Stuff, Big Stuff, SnackWell's, Fudge Brownie Bars, HoneyMaid Grahams, Apple Raisin Snack Bars, Banana Snack Bars, and General Foods International Coffees are registered trademarks of Nabisco, Inc.

Nestlé, and 100 Grand Bar are registered trademarks of Nestlé USA, Inc.

Old Bay is a registered trademark of McCormick & Co. Inc.

The Olive Garden is a registered trademark of Darden Restaurants, Inc.

Outback Steakhouse and Bloomin' Onion, are registered trademarks of Outback Steakhouse, Inc.

Pal's and Sauceburger are registered trademarks of Pal's Sudden Service.

Panda Express is a registered trademark of Panda Management Company, Inc.

Peanut Butter Dream Bar and Mrs. Fields are registered trademarks of Mrs. Fields, Inc.

Pizza Hut and Stuffed Crust Pizza are trademarks of Pizza Hut, Inc.

Planters and Fiddle Faddle are registered trademarks of Planters, Inc.

Popeye's Famous Fried Chicken is a registered trademark of AFC Enterprises, Inc.

Ragu is a registered trademark of Unilever Bestfoods.

Reese's, Hershey, and York are registered trademarks of Hershey Foods Corporation.

Ruby Tuesday and Strawberry Tallcake are registered trademarks of Morrison Restaurants, Inc.

Ruth's Chris Steak House is a registered trademark of Ruth's Chris Steak House, Inc.

Sara Lee is a registered trademark of Sara Lee Corporation.

7-Eleven and Slurpee are registered trademarks of Southland Corporation.

Shoney's is a registered trademark of Shoney's, Inc.

Skyline is a registered trademark of Skyline Chili Inc.

Snapple is a registered trademark of Quaker Oats Company.

Sonic Drive-In is a registered trademark of Sonic Corp.

Starbucks and Frappuccino are registered trademarks of Starbucks Corporation.

Subway is a registered trademark of Doctor's Associates Inc.

Swiss Miss is a registered trademark of Hunt-Wesson Foods, Inc.

T.G.I. Friday's and Jack Daniel's Grill are registered trademarks of T.G.I. Friday's, Inc.

Tony Roma's A Place for Ribs, Carolina Honeys, and Red Hots are registered trademarks of NPC International, Inc.

Twinkie and Hostess are registered trademarks of Continental Baking Company.
Wendy's, Frosty, and Garden Sensations are registered trademarks of Wendy's International.
White Castle is a registered trademark of White Castle System, Inc.
Yoo-hoo is a registered trademark of Yoo-hoo Chocolate Beverage Corporation.

Index